The Last Call

DAVID WAMBAUGH

authorHOUSE®

AuthorHouse™
1663 Liberty Drive
Bloomington, IN 47403
www.authorhouse.com
Phone: 1-800-839-8640

Published by AuthorHouse   08/31/2012

ISBN: 978-1-4772-6274-0 (sc)
ISBN: 978-1-4772-62733 (hc)
ISBN: 978-1-4772-6272-6 (e)

Library of Congress Control Number: 2012915834

For my Mom.
Without her, I would not have been here to write this book.

And of course, for my bear cub, Jake.

"If I fall down 100 times, and if I fail 100 times trying to get back up, and I give up, do you think I'm ever going to get up? No! But If I fail, and I try again, and again, and again, and I simply can't seem to get back up, it's not the end. It matters how you're going to finish. Are you going to finish strong? If so, then you will find the strength to get back up."

--Nic Vujicic

Contents

Preface ix

Chapter One 1

Chapter Two 15

Chapter Three 25

Chapter Four 36

Chapter Five 49

Chapter Six 63

Chapter Seven 81

Chapter Eight 95

Chapter Nine 111

Chapter Ten 121

Chapter Eleven 132

Chapter Twelve 145

Chapter Thirteen 166

Chapter Fourteen 177

Chapter Fifteen 193

Chapter Sixteen 214

Chapter Seventeen 220

Afterword 229

Preface

This memoir chronicles my 30-year journey from riches to rags and back again. My alcoholic spark was ignited when I was only five years old with my very first taste of beer, which they say is an acquired taste, but I acquired the taste right then and there. The end result was a lifetime of harrowing experiences, some funny in an edgy way, some sad, but mostly tragic. Every ridiculous or insane story or event on these pages is true. A few of the names have been changed to protect the privacy of those that had the misfortune to be involved with me during those years, but the stories are real.

It's not uncommon for children of celebrities to have problems, sometimes with addiction, sometimes with the law, and sometimes both. But I feel my memoir is unique in that my father is bestselling author, Joseph Wambaugh, an ex-LAPD cop who has written more than twenty books, both fiction and nonfiction. What could be worse than a famous cop having a son who is bent on self-destruction? You will laugh at me, laugh with me, hate me, be disgusted by me, maybe pity me, but ultimately, I think you may like me.

On June 20th, 2007 a guardian angel entered my heart and has remained with me ever since. He doesn't have a name or a face, but he has a voice. His voice gave my son a dad, my parents a son, and me a wonderful life that I had never imagined possible. At the end of the day, my story is proof that miracles do happen, and the Power of God is awesome. Just ask my parole officer!

I give thanks to my parents who suffered through so many years of me making their lives miserable, and being a menace to them and to society. They encouraged me to tell my story, to get it on paper, feeling it would be a great therapeutic exercise, and that's how this book came about. I give special thanks to my mother who helped me, working diligently, editing it with me for more than three years. My very private father is supportive and encouraging, but his position is that it is *my* life, *my* story and *my* book and would like to see me enjoy this accomplishment as my very own.

Chapter One

"I thought you weren't going to bullshit people anymore."

"Jesus, gimme a break."

"What about the man who just called you? He poured his heart out to you and you told him that if you were able to do it, so could his son. That's bullshit! Without me, you'd be long-gone dead by now."

"What was I *supposed* to say to the guy? Should I have said, 'Well, sir, one day a voice that I cannot identify came into my head and my heart and changed my life forever? The guy would think I'm *crazy* if I told him that."

"Well, you <u>are</u> crazy!"

"So what do you want me to do?"

"I want you to call that man back and tell him the truth about your life as it was, what happened, and what it's like now. Tell him you were once just like his son."

"Okay, I'll tell him, but he'll probably think I'm psychotic like most people that hear voices."

"I want you to tell him about the only hope remaining for his son."

I suddenly realized that I'd been so fast-forward on the road to redemption for the past few years that I hadn't had the time or the desire to verbally relive my miserable life.

I was staring out of my window, watching the surfers on the morning glass, and I was overcome with gratitude. There were no *bars* on my

1

windows! I'd been behind bars of one kind of another for much of my lifetime.

I'm not a writer like my father. I don't have his talent, education or even his DNA. I entered the world on July 15th 1964, at Harbor General Hospital in Los Angeles, the biological child of alcoholics or drug addicts like almost all of the others that ended up in the care of L.A. County. I was born into the "hard to adopt" group at the L.A. County Adoption Agency and was shuffled around in foster homes until I was six months old. I would have been an easy-to-adopt child if not for my worrisome heart murmur. I was blond, blue eyed, and very cute. Someone told my future parents that it was possible that my heart murmur would heal itself if I got into a secure and loving home, and they were right. However my new parents *weren't* told that my bouts of anger would cure themselves on their own, no matter how secure and loving the home might be. My forehead was constantly bruised during that first year from me banging it on the floor when anything pissed me off. And everything pissed me off.

In my new family, I had a brother named Mark who was two years and two days older. Mark was adopted when he was a mere seven days old, and also was most likely the product of a pair of addicts. He was Latino, with dark hair, dark eyes, dark complexion, a slender happy-go-lucky little ball of fire who was already well established in the Wambaugh family. In contrast, I had pale skin, blue eyes, blond hair, was a little on the chubby side and had a permanent scowl on my face. My new parents had no idea what they'd signed up for. We came with factory-installed problems that could never have been anticipated. My parents probably had hopes and dreams that someday I would be headed to Penn State, not the state pen.

My parents had wanted to adopt another baby, but one that would "fit in" with Mark so he wouldn't feel "different," hence, a county adoption worker told them that I was half-Mexican, probably just to appease them. Sure. I always figured I was about as Mexican as Mickey Rooney, but I went along with it.

My dad was a Los Angeles police officer and my mom was happy to stay home with her boys. My parents were both driven and highly disciplined people. My dad went to school at night, and acquired both a bachelor's and a master's degree in English from Cal State, L.A.. His goal at that time was to become an English teacher after retirement from the LAPD. In addition to being a cop, student and father, he moonlighted, selling cheap suits out of the trunk of his car to fellow cops for their court appearances. His inventory was provided by an Arab who wholesaled suits in the garment district of Los Angeles.

My mom, who was artistically inclined, had a little art studio in the basement of our home. Eventually, she opened a retail art supply shop called "Dee's Art Shack" where she could work on her paintings, and display some them along with the works of other local artists. On some weekends, she would load up my brother and me, along with her paintings, and off to the outdoor bazaars we would go where she would display some of her art for sale. She managed to sell enough of them to buy new canvases and paints, and to be involved with her art association group. For a while, she even taught painting classes in our garage on Saturday mornings. We were of modest means, but my parents were always struggling to earn a few extra bucks, hoping to climb up the economic ladder. My earliest memories were that our family was very close and my parents were nurturing and attentive.

My brother and I attended a Catholic school near our home, which was in the rural area of Walnut, about an hour outside of Los Angeles. I remember getting my ears tugged and knuckles smacked by the Cuban nuns who had to run from Castro, so maybe they took it out on us. I began having behavioral problems at a very young age, and those early beginnings were probably indicative of a not so promising future.

I was a mean spirited little kid who took my anger out on Mark, and over the years sent him to the emergency room a couple of times. One assault left him with an injury that sent him to the hospital where he was in traction for a month. I was five years old when we were playing tag in a large tree and I intentionally pushed him off the branch he was climbing.

He crashed to the ground and shattered his elbow, which never properly healed and was disfigured forever. Mark didn't realize that I'd pushed him, and my parents never knew.

While my brother was in the hospital, my parents took turns at his bedside, morning, noon and night. During that time I stayed with my paternal grandparents, Nana and Pappap. Nana loved her daily routine of soap operas and Budweisers, so every afternoon she would park herself in the recliner and enjoy her soaps and suds.

Nana was large women, so it was a real effort for her to get out of her La-Z- Boy, make the trip to the fridge, grab a Bud, and get back to her seat by the end of the commercial break. Therefore, she assigned me the job. My first job. Maybe the only job I ever had that I didn't get fired from. Her favorite Bob's Big Boy glass held eight ounces, and a standard beer is twelve, so by the end of each day I abandoned all my GI Joes for my new friends, Mr. Anheuser and Mr. Busch. I was five years old when the spark was ignited.

———

At our home in Walnut, we had a corral containing an old horse, a stubborn pony, three dogs, and a goat named Charlie who thought he was a dog. In fact, when my dad jogged on the country roads, the dogs followed, and Charlie trotted right along with them. We had Happy, Dolly and Cleo, all big dogs that my parents had adopted from the pound. Happy, the young male, and Dolly, attacked two of our neighbor's sheep and my parents had to pay them for the dead animals. We had to find Happy a new home, away from that kind of temptation.

Charlie, our goat, got so horny after he grew up that he started dry-humping Mark and me, and then when he started doing the same thing to my mom, we all complained. Dad thought Charlie was just behaving like a friendly dog, but when he finally tried to dry-hump Dad, he decided we had to find old Charlie a new home.

Mark, Dad and I, had some interesting misadventures. Once when we were pretty young, my dad came up with a bright idea for an outing. He wanted the three of us to ride his beat up old bicycle over thirty miles from our home in Walnut to my grandparent's house in Fontana. The plan was for my mom to meet us there, have dinner, then drive us all back in the car. It was an old three-speed bike that was totally rusted out, had only one seat, and the tires were frayed. With Dad taking the seat, there were only two other places left for Mark and me. One was the crossbar, which was my brother's seat, and the other place was in the basket attached to the handlebars, which is where I sat. Of course, for our ultimate comfort, Dad padded the crossbar and the basket with towels, and off we went on a smoggy summer day.

He pedaled his heart out and we made it over half way, but eventually he stopped at a McDonald's and called my mom to pick us up since he was close to a heat stroke. When she arrived, she really didn't need to say much because her eyes did the talking. The look she gave my dad before driving us to Nana's house said, "You idiot, what were you thinking?"

A more pleasant memory of a ride we had with the old man was when he was a uniformed sergeant doing crowd control in downtown Los Angeles for Chinese New Year, and my brother and I rode with him along the parade route on a three-wheel police motorcycle, gaping at all the colorful dragons. And just for fun that day, he took us into the station and snapped black and white mug shots of each of us with "Los Angeles Police Department" and booking numbers printed on them. Little did he know that it would wind up to be the first of many to come.

In 1971, the first of my Dad's many books was published. It immediately landed on the New York Times bestseller list where it stayed for nearly a year. He'd taken creative writing classes at night, and had hopes of one day getting a short story published. He'd been met with continued rejection from all the popular magazines until eventually, he got a personal letter from *The Atlantic Monthly* saying that his short story wasn't the type of material they were interested in for their magazine, but if he should write a novel with that same flavor, they would be interested in seeing it. It didn't take him long to turn that short story into a novel, and *The New Centurions* was born. My dad became known as the father of the modern police novel, and his early books all became movies or TV shows starring actors like George C. Scott, William Holden and Lee Remick. His anthology

TV series, *Police Story*, guest starred people like William Shatner, Angie Dickinson, and young Sylvester Stallone.

After his second novel, *The Blue Knight*, was published, our family moved from a middle-class lifestyle to a mansion in San Marino, a pricey residential suburb of Los Angeles. My brother was nine and I was seven, still little boys, so we didn't quite understand what was happening, but it must've been totally surreal for my parents. They became rich and famous almost overnight! But even so, my dad remained a cop for nearly three more years, making the commute to the cop shop every day.

Right away, my mom was inundated with new responsibilities. She typed, and retyped, while doing minor editing of my dad's books, which was a big job before word processing and computers. She also managed their growing wealth and position, ran a big home, and looked after three high maintenance guys: my brother, my dad, and me.

My mom remodeled our new home, creating beauty and comfort. Some of the amenities on the property included a tennis court, pool and spa, and a state-of-the-art gym and sauna. Our new life was amazing. We were privileged and indulged. My brother and I took tennis lessons, golf lessons, guitar lessons, dance lessons, all sorts of lessons. Needless to say, my mom, brother, and I were pretty busy in those early days.

My dad had become a celebrity. He was famous, and was treated like he was famous. While he was still on the department working as a detective, he also made time for appearances on *The Tonight Show, Good Morning America, Today,* and just about every national chat show. It was a drastic change from horses, horny goats and rusty bikes. Finally, the fame and fortune became too much, and my dad had to resign from the LAPD after fourteen years.

Over the next several years we did a lot of traveling, and we went first class all the way. When we were in London my parents would go antique shopping, and my brother and I would be driven around the city in a Rolls Royce limo, doing whatever we fancied while my parents shopped. We went on numerous ocean cruises all over the world. We traveled to Egypt and rode camels in front of the Great Pyramids. We visited incredible places like Turkey, Greece, Russia when it was still a communist country, Sweden, Italy, France, Caribbean Islands, Hawaii, and the Mexican Riviera.

When we were in Tahiti, we stayed in bungalows that were built on stilts over the water. At night, we could turn on the floodlights that shined into the water directly beneath the bungalow, and within a few minutes, manta rays with just under twenty-foot wing spans would come up, and do graceful back-flips.

After settling into our new home in San Marino, I was off to elementary school where I was entering second grade, halfway through the school year. We'd come from a Catholic school that had a dress code, but now we had the freedom to wear whatever we desired. There was no way my brother and I were going to show up in the hillbilly clothes we had from our past life, so my mom took us on a shopping spree prior to starting at our new school.

I was very careful in choosing a wardrobe that would most likely allow me acceptance with the other seven-year-olds. I got a bunch of Hang Ten shirts and matching pants in an array of colors: purple, green, yellow, red, in assorted patterns. In the early seventies, the wild choices were vast, and I thought my new Keds were to die for. I honestly believed I was going to be the sharpest kid on campus, and I was ready to make a grand entrance. Mom even gave me her signature haircut, which I wasn't too keen on, but that was just part of the deal.

On the morning I was being introduced to my second grade class, I almost bolted when the whole room erupted in laughter. As I scanned the room, I could see that everything about me was totally different from my new classmates. Compared to them, I looked like a goddamned rodeo clown. There I was, wearing purple pants, matching purple shirt, and Keds with zebra stripes on them. I felt really sick, and the other kids were in hysterics. I was devastated but I managed to laugh with them, and assured my new classmates that I would have a new wardrobe immediately. The only thing I couldn't change was my haircut.

My new classmates wore brand names like Polo, La Coste, Levi's 501 authentic straight leg, Sperry Topsiders, Stan Smith Tennis Shoes, and dry-clean only Khaki pants, so after that first day, my mom took us to Bullocks Wilshire in Pasadena, which was the right place to go. When I showed up to school the next day, I definitely looked like I belonged, however, I didn't *feel* like I belonged.

No matter what kind of clothes my brother wore, he never looked like he fit in, being dark skinned, overweight by then, with thick eyeglasses and a bush of dark hair. San Marino was almost lily white, so most of the Mexicans seen around town were either maids or gardeners. There were no blacks, and at that time, very few Asians, so basically, my brother was a minority kid in our new world. Maybe I was too, but you couldn't tell it by looking at me.

Right away I was a hit with the rich kids of San Marino. I was the class cut-up. They found me funny, and of course I loved being center-stage. I became one of the most popular boys in my class, and it was amazing how quickly it happened. Instantly, I had three or four sleepover invitations every weekend. I declined invitations all the time, which is ironic because later in life, I wouldn't be invited anywhere.

Although I'm sure I appeared settled and confident in front of my classmates, I had constant anxiety and feelings of inferiority around them, with no idea why. I felt unattractive inside and out, and couldn't find any peace. I lived with an unidentifiable fear, and couldn't escape it. I guess I had the makings of an alcoholic, an egomaniac with an inferiority complex. In my neighborhood I was the alpha male and leader of the boys. The only person who challenged my self-appointed position was my brother Mark. When he and I fought, it was big neighborhood news. Kids would miss dinner in order to see us scrap. We had knockdown fights that seemed to last forever. He was much taller, stronger, and a lot heavier, but I would always give him a run for his money.

Our last fight took place a few years later at our house in Newport Beach, and that time I kicked his ass, but in the process we knocked my parents' most treasured painting off the wall. Luckily it wasn't damaged, because we never would've been able to explain that one away. After the dust settled, we put the house back together, re-hung the painting, hugged each other, and said, "Peace!" We agreed that we should call a truce and stop assaulting each other. It was too painful for both of us.

We established ourselves in the San Marino Catholic Church where my dad, brother and I attended Mass each Sunday. Mark and I hated going to church, but my dad made us see it through until we were confirmed Catholics. He liked to go to Mass early in the morning, but Mark and I liked to sleep in, so we convinced him to trust us to get to church on our own. We were about nine and eleven at the time, and I think it was the first time he ever trusted us to do *anything* on our word. Well, we didn't pass the first test. He let us to ride our bikes to church, put the offering money that he had given us in the collection basket, and then come back home. We had other notions.

Mark and I would ride our bikes to Carl's Jr., spend the offering money on Superstar Combos, and enjoy ourselves until church was about to get out. At the appropriate time we'd go back to the church, get the parish bulletin, and my friend who happened to be the altar boy at the ten o'clock Mass would fill us in on the topic of the sermon. I think we became suspect after a few sketchy explanations of the sermon and some basic inconsistencies in our stories, so eventually my dad tracked us down at the Carl's Jr. and he was really pissed. Needless to say, he didn't let us ride our bikes to church after that.

We had a lot of fun in the early years. In 1973, my parents bought a condo in Rancho Mirage, at the time when most areas outside Palm Springs proper were still undeveloped. We went to our desert home almost every weekend, and my brother and I usually each brought a friend. We played golf, tennis, swam, and drove around in our golf cart, tearing up the fairways and always looking for little spankers to flirt with. We also drank my parent's booze whenever we got the chance.

My dad, my brother and I played a lot of golf together. I was always trying to hustle my dad for money, or something else of value, so one time I bet him that if I shot a certain score, he would have to buy me a little motorcycle to ride out in the desert. And if I didn't shoot the score we agreed upon he didn't have to buy it. Since the proposed score was something ridiculously low, a number that should've been next to impossible for me to shoot, he agreed to the bet. When the round was over and we pulled our golf cart into the garage, I ran into the house and told my mom that I had only missed winning a new motorcycle by one stroke. I explained the whole deal to her and with a look of shock, she said, "You're kidding me! Your dad made that bet with you? A *motorcycle?*"

Just as she said that, my dad and brother walked through the door, and I said, "Dad, isn't it true that I almost won a motorcycle? That I only missed by one stroke? It's true, right, Dad?"

He shrugged and grinned sheepishly. My mom gave him a look of disgust, shook her head and walked out of the kitchen.

The most memorable round of golf in The Wambaugh Hall of Golf, was the one we always referred to as "The Round," which took place on a spectacular winter day. It was the kind of desert day that made you realize why rich people from all over the world came to enjoy the breathtaking beauty and world-class golf courses spread throughout the Coachella Valley. On the day of the infamous round, I wasn't able to talk my dad into any crazy bets, or anything my mom would disapprove of, so it was just a kickback day of golf. I still liked to play just for the sake of playing, but a bet on the side always made it more fun and exciting. And I loved to watch my dad sweat.

However, by the time that day was over, I swore I would *never* play golf with him again. His game was always suffering, so he'd buy any and every new club that came along. He must've gone through a dozen putters in the first three years we played, and God only knows how many full sets of clubs he'd bought and given away. I had to give him credit because he definitely put forth a substantial mental, emotional and financial investment to master the game.

It just didn't work out for him, that's all. He and his putter never came together. He's the only person I've ever seen, who could four-putt from six feet away, and I've seen him hit a tee shot that dribbled right back between his legs. Now, *that* would be almost impossible to duplicate.

That morning while my brother and I were on the range hitting balls, my Dad walked out of the pro shop with a huge grin. In his hand, he had the newest, biggest, hottest driver on the market, one of the first graphite drivers made. He said he was going to take a thirty-minute lesson before we teed off so he could test that baby out. He'd taken a lesson the day before and seemed to be striking the ball well, so I thought he might have a good day. A good day for him was breaking a hundred.

After his lesson was over, he walked over to me and my brother while we were practicing our putting, and said, "Hey you guys, I was hitting drives like rockets, ppshhh, pssshhh, ppssssshhh, one after another! I was crushing it, boys! You guys ready to tee it up?"

He bragged that he'd only had a couple of bad drives out of a whole bucket of balls. Then he walked up to the first tee box with a confidence he'd never shown before. He teed up his ball, and let her rip. He drove the ball straight down the middle. It was one his best drives ever. He closed out the front nine with a forty-seven, the best nine holes of his life.

He was playing really well with that new driver, and his putter was working okay. He was hitting the ball straight, time after time. On that course, you need to hit it straight because there were water hazards all over the place. And God bless him, he didn't lose a single ball on the front nine, which was unprecedented. If he maintained, he would shatter his best score ever by several strokes. For once, he had sort of a peaceful look.

Everything was great until the sixteenth hole, the most difficult on the course. It always freaked him out. As he approached the tee box, I could see that his peaceful look had disappeared and he was a little twitchy, like a gopher looking out for predators. The only predators around there were two huge swans that would attack if provoked, or sometimes, unprovoked.

He teed up his ball, surveyed the fairway, and was ready to crush his drive just like he had been doing all day. On that hole, the only thing you needed to do in order to keep the ball in play was to get the ball in the air, going fairly straight for only sixty or seventy yards. There was a small inlet of water directly in front of the tee box that you'd have to clear, but that was all. Then the fairway was wide open. It was actually the bunkers and the approach shot over the water to the green that was the killer shot.

I had a feeling there was going to be a problem as soon as he took his backswing. He took the club back so far he nearly fell down, and then on his follow through, he hit the ground so hard I thought he may have broken his wrist. He made a divot the size of a lunch box, and I don't know if it was the club or the divot that made contact with the ball, but it dribbled forward right into the drink.

He didn't say a word, but motioned for me to throw him another ball, which I did. Mark and I kept silent. The second one wasn't much better. He swung too hard again, and the result was not good. His ball didn't have any trajectory, so it skipped like a rock across the water, then sank.

"Goddamnit, Dave, what did I do?" he yelled.

"You looked up, Dad," I said.

"Jesus Christ!" he muttered. "Throw me another ball."

I said, "Dad, why don't you just drop a ball on the other side of the water?"

He snapped, "Just throw me another goddamn ball!"

I shrugged and tossed him another ball from the golf cart while my brother began chuckling very quietly. I'm afraid the third tee shot wasn't much better than the first two. I already knew where the next tee shot was going, and it wasn't going to be good. I wanted to tell him to calm down, to regroup, but it was too late.

He lined up, took one wild practice swing, and then gingerly stepped up to the ball. This drive took off like a rocket. Unfortunately, this rocket went straight up, and straight down, right into the lake again.

He yelled, "Jesus Christ, David! Did you see it?"

I so badly wanted to tell him that I lost it in the sun, but I said, "Yeah, Dad. It's in the water."

He looked toward the water. "Where?"

"Right there," I said, pointing to a ripple about fifty feet to the left of him.

He looked at me, then at his new driver, then at the lake, then back at me, and said, "Did anybody else see me do that?"

"No, I don't think so. Just us," I said.

"You sure?"

"Yeah, I'm pretty sure it was just us."

"Throw me another ball," he growled.

"Dad..."

"David, just throw me a freaking ball!"

Again I shrugged, didn't say a word, and tossed my old man another ball. After that, I sat back and shook my head, dreading what was going to happen.

This time he didn't even take a practice swing. He simply teed it up and swung for the fences. It didn't help his chances by keeping his face tilted to the right until after he made contact. Well, actually, he *didn't* make contact. When he swung, the breeze from his driver blew the ball off the tee.

He spun like a top and launched his driver into outer space. After he realized what he'd done, he said, "Oh shit! Where did it go?"

"It's right there, next to your tee," I said, pointing to the ball.

He looked down and saw his ball and said, "No, I mean my goddamn club!"

I said, "Dad, it's gone. It's in the middle of the lake. Maybe you can ask one of the groundskeepers to get it for you."

His eyes were spinning, and he said, "No! I don't want anyone finding out about this!"

My brother was shaking his head in disbelief and trying to maintain a somber expression when I said, "Well then, that really sucks, 'cause that was an expensive drive!"

I was thinking, Oh my God, the guys in the pro shop were going to ask him how he played with the pricey new driver. I just figured he would *quit* this country club and join another one so he wouldn't have to face those people again. That would not have been beyond him, by any means.

He focused on the spot in the lake where his club had sunk and suddenly shifted his eyes directly at me. He said very calmly, "Dave, go get my club. I need you to do that for me, son."

I almost shit. I screamed, "Hell no! That's bullshit! Make Mark go get it!"

Mark shook his head slowly, saying, "Don't even trip, dude, I ain't getting that club. No, no, no!"

My dad drilled me with his eyes and said, "Dave, I'm sorry, but this is not a democracy. Take off your pants, and go get my club. I'm serious."

I said, "Well, I'm serious too! I ain't going in that nasty lake with those big violent goddamn birds!"

"Dave, don't swear like that," he said. Take your clothes off and go get my club."

It wasn't written in the rules, regulations, and it wasn't part of golf etiquette, but my dad made up a special rule for the Wambaugh boys that stated it was permissible to sometimes swear on the golf course, because my dad knew it was impossible to play the game without doing so. I knew I could swear on land, and figured the same rule applied now that I was going to be in the water.

After mouthing every profanity I could think of, I took off my shirt and pants, and started wading in, screaming at my dad every inch of the way. I couldn't believe he'd subject me to those hostile swans, and the duck shit was ankle deep. After I waded through the muck, the water got deeper, so I had to swim the rest of the way. When I got to where I thought the club was, I had to submerge myself all the way under to look for it. When I finally found the club, and started swimming back, the angry swans followed. They chased me all the way out of the water, doing mock attacks, making honking noises, and basically scaring the shit out of me. Mark was laughing his ass off, and my dad was trying his best not to laugh. When we got back to the clubhouse, I spent twenty minutes in the locker room washing off all the muck and duck shit.

It was a traumatic event for me then, but my dad and I have laughed about it many times over the years. I even wrote a short story for a school assignment in sixth grade, and got an A on it. My dad finally gave up on the game of golf, figuring he'd just better stick to writing books.

Chapter Two

I loved those first few years in San Marino. In fact, they were the best years of my life. I had adapted incredibly well to my new surroundings. My life was perfect. I did very well at being a spoiled rich kid. Things were going beautifully until my parents dropped a bombshell that fractured my world.

I was nine years old when I was informed that we were going to adopt a little girl, a nearly-six-year-old Mexican-American girl named Jeannette who was expected to arrive soon. I tried not to show it, but I was devastated. I'd been the prince of this household thus far, Prince David, but I knew in my heart and soul that my reign was coming to an end with the arrival of my new sister.

My mom created a storybook bedroom for her, and the day Jeannette arrived, I checked out emotionally. I knew I couldn't compete with her because she was too cute, and the novelty of her would probably last for a while, so my new objective was to make her life as a Wambaugh as miserable as I could. I was upset, and was hoping she would want to go back to her foster home.

She'd been in a foster home with three other children for two years after being taken from her biological mother who was a junkie. She was addicted to heroin at birth, and had to be detoxed as an infant, just like any other junkie. Her chances for a reasonably happy and productive life were not good, no matter how nurturing and rich her adoptive family might be. Regardless of her history, I wasn't very sympathetic to any of it, and I honestly wouldn't have been disappointed at all if there had been a return policy.

At some point when I was very young, my parents had informed me that the L.A. County adoption people said that I was half-Mexican and that didn't sit well with me at all. I didn't want to be half-Mexican or half anything else for that matter. I wanted to be all white like my classmates, and the thought of being Latino made me cringe. I used to think that someone had made a mistake in my case about the Mexican part, and had switched the nametags at the hospital or something of the sort. I couldn't nurture that vibe at all. As I got older I figured that L.A. County just told my parents what they wanted to hear because of the heart murmur making me hard-to-adopt: "You want one to go with the one you've already got? Take this little blond, blue-eyed half-breed with a heart murmur."

So, little Jeannette was set to take over my throne, and she did just that, but I made sure she paid a price. When we dined at fancy restaurants we were treated like celebrities, and Jeannette was referred to as "the little princess" by the waiters and maitre d's alike. Once she came along, I was barely noticed by anyone, and that pissed me off to no end. I'd take it out on her when the opportunity presented itself, either by giving her a few good pinches under the table or some spitballs in her hair when we got home. Mark liked being invisible, so he didn't need or want any extra attention. Although my new sister had dethroned me, her novelty at school was short lived, so I didn't have to field any unwanted questions about whether or not I too had been adopted. That was a good thing.

About the time Mark entered high school he began experimenting with pot, was having behavioral problems, and was being seen by a psychiatrist on a regular basis. My parents worked very hard during that time trying to get him the help he needed, but his issues continued. He began staying out after curfew, and avoided our parents as often as he could.

One time my mom went into his room when he wasn't there and found a goose-necked lamp turned on inside his closet, which was dangerously close to a newspaper down on the carpet where he was drying out his weed.

If she hadn't seen the bright light from under the closed door, I'm sure it would've started a fire.

Actually, there was a time when Mark *did* cause a fire. He'd nodded off while smoking in bed and the mattress caught on fire. When the smoke alarm went off, my parents ran into his room and threw the mattress off the balcony onto the driveway below. Luckily, there were large French doors in Mark's room that led to a balcony, or it could've been a real disaster.

Mark had standing appointments twice a week with his shrink, and twice a month my parents and I would go in for family sessions. The doctor said he needed to know Mark's family in order to get the full picture. Many years later, my parents told me that the psychiatrist had informed them that he felt *I* was definitely more emotionally unstable than Mark, and that there could be real trouble ahead with me. They just couldn't believe that about their golden boy.

They could see how I was thriving in school, was heavily involved in sports, had lots of friends and seemed to be happy, so they didn't believe the shrink could possibly be right. Mark was their problem child. While they were distracted by my brother's drug use and emotional needs, our live-in housekeeper supervised me to some degree, but I was able to sneak drinks at will, and she was never even suspicious.

There were three elementary schools in San Marino, one middle school, and one high school. When I entered middle school, it was a real challenge because I'd been quite popular at my grammar school, but now it was a melting pot of the three elementary schools, so I knew I had my work cut out for me. I campaigned hard, and halfway through the sixth grade I became probably the most popular kid in my class. At least that was my perception, and everything in my life was wonderful again. I didn't even concern myself about my little sister anymore. I'd torture her every now and then, but for the most part, I dismissed her as if she didn't exist.

I was a good athlete, still getting decent grades, and had found my first love. She had come from one of the other grammar schools across town, and was beautiful, definitely one of the most sought-after girls in our class. She dumped me after a few weeks because I became jealous and possessive. I must've had severe abandonment issues from my early life in foster homes because I sabotaged every crush I had as a kid, and even as an adult, for that matter. I took hostages, not girlfriends, and invariably ruined every relationship I had.

Regardless, I briefly hooked up with some of the hotties in my class, was a big hit with all the boys, and was Mister Popularity. I had a bunch of new friends, and there were parties every weekend, many at my own house. Our parties were still cake and ice cream for the most part, however, there were a few of us that would steal booze from our parents and that would give me the courage to hit on the girls. Those were incredible times, being Mister Popularity, and I also met Ziggy, my new best friend, on the first day of school.

I'll never forget that day I met Ziggy. It was at the beginning of sixth grade, and as fate would have it we wound up in the same P.E. class. He showed up wearing a putrid orange and yellow Hawaiian shirt, and what looked like some hand-me-down jeans, but the most noticeable thing about Ziggy was that he had the most piercing blue eyes I'd ever seen. Although I had no experience with the mentally ill, other than myself, but I could definitely see *mucho loco* in those aquamarine eyes.

After some calisthenics to warm up, the girls went to play foursquare, and the boys went to the basketball court to choose teams for a game of hoops. Ziggy and I were among the shorter guys, so we were the last to be chosen. I was second to last and Ziggy was the last. By the end of that week it was clear that we were probably the best two athletes in our class, at least in the top five. For the P.E. final at the end of the year we had to be able to run a mile in a certain amount of time in order to pass the class, and my new best friend and I wound up being two of the three people in the entire sixth grade class who ran sub six-minute miles.

P.E. was the only class that we shared because Ziggy was in all special ed classes which were made up of kids with learning disabilities, the mentally challenged, and the handicapped. So there we were: two retards whose friendship would last a lifetime. One mentally retarded, and one emotionally retarded, drawn to each other because of what we shared: behavioral problems.

———

Things were smooth sailing for a while, until my parents dropped another bombshell that would change the course of my life again. My brother was screwed up on drugs, and his behavior was getting out of control. Also, my dad was having problems getting his creative juices flowing there in San Marino, so they came to the conclusion that it would be a good time to buy a home in Newport Beach, and move the crew down to Orange County.

Halfway through my seventh grade year, we moved to Linda Isle, an exclusive gated island in Newport Beach. My parents bought a beautiful house with its own dock on the main turning basin in Newport Harbor, big enough for a large yacht plus a couple of smaller boats. The house had been featured in Architectural Digest shortly after it was built a few years earlier.

We could stand on our dock, look directly across the channel, and see John Wayne's house. When the Newport Harbor commercial tour boats passed by our house, the tour guide would say, "And that's where author and movie maker, Joseph Wambaugh, lives." And, of course, they would point out John Wayne's crib and mention some of his successes. One of our neighbors was the inventor and owner of Armor All. Another was a billionaire who owned the Seattle Mariners, and another was the boss at Tri-Star Pictures.

I was both terrified and angry that I had to start all over in a strange environment, and had a real bad feeling from the very moment I stepped foot in our new house that things were going to be much different in Newport Beach. I knew in my heart that I wasn't going to fit in, no matter what I did or how I dressed. I figured the kids of Newport had already established their own circle of friends, and judging by their attitudes, they weren't about to let an outsider like me into their cliques. Halfway through seventh grade was way too late to make any friends. That's what I thought, and I was right. I constantly complained to my parents, and told them over and over just how mad I was about moving us there.

I made him feel incredibly guilty for making me move away from my life, my friends, and my identity, so he wound up buying some pretty stellar boating craft with hopes it would help us adjust life on the bay.

After a day of boat shopping, I had a seventeen-foot Montauk Boston Whaler with a 90 Merc on the back. I named it *Muskrat*, from the Captain and Tenile song, *Muskrat Love*. And Mark, being more of a laidback stoner type, opted for a fourteen-foot sailboat that he named *Tiburon*, meaning *Shark* in Spanish. It was a perfect boat for a loner like Mark. He would get baked and listen to the *Grateful Dead* while he tacked and jibed all over the harbor.

The salesman who sold us the two boats convinced my dad that he may as well buy a sailing yacht while he was at it, because he said everyone who's anyone in Newport has a yacht of some kind in their slip, whether they used it or not. So that day my dad walked out of that place the proud owner of a Santana 39 footer. Of course he didn't even know how to sail the little fourteen-footer, let alone *Venganza*, which was the name he'd given her, meaning "revenge." As in, "Sailing well is the best revenge." He was into literary quotes and shit like that.

The young salesman loved to sail, and figured he could save money by not having to pay rent, so he offered to live on the boat, teach us how to sail, and take us out anytime we wanted to go. Was he a good salesman or what? So, we had a live-aboard captain to maintain and skipper the boat when, and if, we ever decided to use it. My parents would occasionally take houseguests out for cocktail cruises, and motor around the bay in the evenings, but we only went on one *real* sailing trip. Our one adventure was a popular race from Newport Beach to Ensenada, Mexico. There was no wind, and it was considered the slowest Ensenada race ever, but we had a great time anyway.

It was pretty easy for me to get away with drinking during this period of time because my parents were so incredibly busy they didn't have time to smell my breath every thirty minutes, and even if they hadn't been that busy, what parent would imagine that their seven, nine, or even thirteen year old would be secretly drinking? By the time I was thirteen, I was a chronic alcoholic. I became very sneaky in every aspect of getting, drinking, and concealing it.

Addicts often exhibit sociopathic characteristics. At least *I* did. If you look up the definition of *sociopath*, you would be alarmed at the similarities between the addict and the sociopath. An addict in its grip will steal your dope, and then help you look for it. If there *is* a practicing addict in your life, you should lock the doors, and hide your wives and daughters.

Life would teach me there were many drugs of choice and degrees of addiction, but alcoholics of my type are the real heartbreakers. We'll give you glimmers of hope with our words, only to devastate you again with our extreme selfishness and weakness for our drug. I think we use alcohol and drugs for the same reason everyone does: to feel good. Normal people resume their everyday lives after a few drinks, without the need to capture the feeling again and again. Addicts fail to drink like ladies and gentlemen, yet they always try one more time to find a way to be social drinkers. One definition of insanity is to do the same thing over and over, expecting different results.

———

Prior to starting at my new school, I anticipated having the wrong wardrobe again, so before I showed up at my first class, I was prepared. I'd met a kid who lived on Linda Isle who told me very specifically where to go for the right clothes. It was a store in Fashion Island called *At Ease*. Their stuff didn't look very "at ease" to me. Talk about preppy. They had every kind of saddle oxfords you could imagine.

I started school in Newport on the first day of the second semester of my seventh grade year, and it was a total bust from the beginning. I could feel the negative vibes, and as a whole, the kids seemed mean spirited and snobby. There were two types: the preppies, and the surf rats. The surf rats seemed a much more laidback group, but that's probably because they were stoned half the time. None of the surfer crew even gave me the time of day, since my clothes made it very clear that I was definitely not one of them. But the feeling I got from the surf rats was much more warm and fuzzy than the cold shoulder I got from the preppies who wore faggot pants and clown shoes like the ones I'd just bought.

I made it through the first half of the first day without incident, but the tranquility lasted only until the period just after lunch. While our P.E. teacher was taking attendance, he mispronounced my name, and when I corrected him, it was all eyes on me. The last thing I wanted was attention directed toward me. Everyone turned around and stared for a few seconds, and then turned back around, except for a big fat kid with headgear and a mouth full of braces. He looked like a bulldog with a muzzle guard. He glared right at me, and wouldn't look away. I had a bad feeling that all this staring meant I was going to have to deal with the meatball at some point. I could tell he was a bully and wasn't going to let me slide.

Within a couple of days, he started flicking boogers on me, just like I used to do to my sister. He would pinch me, just like I used to do to my sister. He flicked spitballs on me, just like I used to do to my sister. He also gave me Ernies, which I also gave to my sister on a regular basis. That's a quick flick to the side of someone's head with your ring finger, and if done correctly, hurts like hell.

After school I would go home and go up in my room and cry, longing for my friends back in San Marino. There I was, with privileges and opportunities that most people only fantasize about, and yet I felt like I was lost at sea with no land in sight. I was always involved in drama of some kind or another. I had little peace in my life and the bully made it far more miserable.

Because he was the biggest guy in our class, no one had ever stood up to him. I became the target of his bullshit day after day, and endured it until I just couldn't take it any longer. He finally crossed the line that brought out the other David. He didn't know that I fought my brother on a regular basis, and my brother was twice his size. In fact I liked to fight, but I didn't want all the trauma that would take place afterward. If I kicked his ass, then the next tough guy would want to fight me, and on and on until I lost. I knew the deal.

On the bully's day of reckoning, we were all standing around getting ready to play volleyball when he walked up behind me and flicked me on the ear so hard it felt like a bumblebee had stung me. That was it! When the fight was over, he looked almost like Rocky Balboa after he got thumped by Apollo Creed. I beat the living shit out of the fat boy.

When the school called my mom to pick me up, the principal suggested that it might be a good idea for me to enroll in the Catholic School across the street. He was respectful, but really encouraged us to make that move. The following day, I transferred to the Catholic School, where I actually wound up doing pretty well. I made a couple of friends right away, and was confirmed by the bishop of Orange County.

Mark was still out of control and his addiction was progressing rapidly, so our move to Newport Beach with the idea of helping him with his issues proved to be a losing effort. My parents were miserable and so was he. And of course, I was miserable too.

We were in Newport Beach for less than a year when my dad made an announcement that was music to my ears. He said we were moving back to San Marino, but we would also be keeping the Newport house as a weekend and summer escape. That was the best news ever. Within days, we packed our belongings and I was headed back to my old stomping grounds.

My parents bought an incredible five-acre estate located in the most exclusive part of San Marino. Our property backed up to the famous Huntington Library and Gardens, and our adjoining neighbors were Mr. and Mrs. Winchell, as in Donuts. At that crib we had two full time gardeners as well as a live-in couple that cooked and cleaned, and drove me to school. We had everything but a bartender, but my brother Mark filled that position when our parents weren't at home.

My parents did a total restoration and remodel on our new digs, even relocating the swimming pool, adding a spa, and building a tennis court. They transformed the huge basement into a wine cellar that was larger than the average one-bedroom apartment, and the living room was the size of a small chapel. There was a quaint little guesthouse, an award winning rose garden, and toward the back part of the property there was a waterfall that cascaded down into a Koi pond. They had created their Shangri-La.

I had the whole summer to become reacquainted with my old crew, so I was stoked. But strangely enough, most of my friends were unavailable during that summer. I guess, before we'd moved back, they'd made plans that didn't include me. There was even an occasion when I discovered there had been a party and I wasn't invited. I was devastated but wanted to believe that it had just been an oversight. After all, I had been the most popular guy around when I'd left. But things had changed, and I soon realized I wasn't number one anymore, or even number two or three, for that matter.

However, my old friend, Ziggy, was right there for me, waiting with open arms. He became my very best friend in the world, and then ironically, some years later, became my *only* friend in the world.

At thirteen, I had my first scrape with the law. We were boozing it up outside the ice cream parlor that we frequented on weekends, and I decided to chop down the tree that had recently been planted directly in front of the store. I walked inside the store, reached around the counter and took an ice cream cutting knife. Then I went outside and started hacking at the trunk, doing considerable damage. When the cops arrived, I was the only one sweating profusely from my effort, so it was open and shut. They took me home to my parents, and didn't file charges, but I had to make restitution for the tree. My parents were not happy.

That fall of 1978, I entered my freshman year of high school. My brother was a total screw-up by then, and my parents didn't know how to deal with him. They tried everything, and yet he seemed to be getting worse by the day. At one point he was secretly selling pounds of weed out of our house and actually didn't see anything wrong with it.

When my dad finally busted him, Mark became so violent they had to call the police for assistance. During that time, alcohol and drug rehabs weren't on every corner as they are now, so Mark was admitted into the mental ward of a nearby hospital to treat his addiction. After a couple of weeks in the locked ward, a few of his friends broke him out and dropped him at his girlfriend's house. He and his gal decided to hide out on her old man's boat that was docked in Newport Harbor, but after my parents reported him missing from the hospital, the U.S. Coast Guard located them and arrangements were made for Mark to be transported by ambulance back to the hospital.

After being released from the hospital's drug abuse program, it seemed the best arrangement was for Mark to go to a boarding school. He was more than happy with the idea, and after considering several schools in Southern California, they settled on Dunn, a college prep school in Los Olivos, which was about a two and a half hour drive north. Mark knew a couple of San Marino boys there, so that was an extra bonus for him.

Chapter Three

My dad had just produced his first motion picture from his most famous non-fiction book, *The Onion Field*. His first book, *The New Centurions* had been made into a major motion picture, and *The Blue Knight* had been a big TV mini-series, so we met quite a few A-list actors, and rubbed elbows with the rich and famous. We visited the home of a mogul in Holmby Hills, across the street from Henry Mancini and down the road from Hugh Hefner. His wife, who had been a professional photographer, shot a family photo of us that speaks volumes. My mom and dad, brother and sister, are all smiling huge, and I'm scowling like a ten-year-old cage fighter.

Out of all the movie actors I'd met, James Woods was the funniest and most garrulous. He truly believed he was *hot*. Years after he starred in *The Onion Field*, I saw Woods on another set where he was the leading man. I was there because I was an extra in the film, and my job description was to surf while they shot a beach scene. My parents and I went into his trailer to say hello, and as we did, he actually took off his shirt and started flexing as he looked into the mirror. Was he really seeing the same dude I was seeing? I'm positive that his beautiful co-star, Sean Young, had more muscle mass.

———

My mom was the glue that held everything together in our family, at least as well as circumstances would permit. After my brother was off to boarding school, it really sucked because the focus had shifted to yours truly.

The first time I was caught drinking at home, I was fourteen. Mark was home for a long weekend, and I was in his bedroom with some of his friends. We were drinking bottles of wine they had stolen from my parents' wine cellar. God only knows how valuable those bottles of wine may have been. My parents came home unexpectedly, and when we saw them drive through the gated entrance, everyone scattered like cockroaches. We had a long driveway, and the guys had a little time to scatter, so I decided to escape down the trellis next to the balcony outside Mark's bedroom, but I slipped and fell into the bushes below and got stuck like a cork in a bottle. My parents busted me and I was grounded until further notice, which was for about three weeks.

From that point on, it seemed as though I was always in trouble. Soon after my mom had uncorked me from the bushes, I pulled another shenanigan that would cost me a whole month of restriction. A friend was spending the night at my house, and we got news that all the little hotties from our class were having a slumber party at the home of one of the girls. My friend and I wanted to show up like big dogs, so we waited until my house was quiet, disarmed the house alarm, and silently pushed my housekeeper's car out of the garage and hauled ass. I recklessly drove all over town at dangerously high speeds with a car packed full of terrified girls who were all of fourteen years old.

On our way home, my luck ran out. I was drunk of course, and could barely see over the steering wheel, and my depth perception was off. After going around a corner at a high speed, I lost control, went up and over a tall curb, popped one of the front tires, and buckled the front fender. But somehow the car limped home, and I pushed it back into the garage without getting busted--at least not yet.

First thing the next morning my dad's voice came over the intercom, saying, "David, get down here immediately, and tell your friend to go home!"

I knew my dad was going to be extra pissed because it was the maid's car I'd messed up. He was going to flip out and tell me how hard she had to work for her material things, and that I was a spoiled, rotten kid that doesn't do shit. He was going to tell me about how difficult her life had been, and that she had family in Guatemala to help support, blah, blah, blah. I could already hear it. I was in deep shit.

I walked into the kitchen, and the glare of the sun that came through the window was blinding, making me realize how hung-over I was. It was hard for me to focus on my dad or the housekeeper, but it was obvious that she'd been crying, and being the spoiled and selfish bastard I was, my only thought was that I needed some aspirin and just wanted to go back to bed.

My dad glared at me and said, "David, what did you do to Helena's car?"

"Nothing," I said.

"Did you steal Helena's car? Yes or no?"

"I crashed it. I didn't mean to. I'm sorry."

"So you *did* steal her car. Jesus Christ! Don't you realize that's a felony? Goddamnit, don't you know how hard she had to work for that car? She sends her paychecks to her family in Guatemala. You wouldn't understand anything about helping your family or anyone else for that matter, would you?" He looked at Helena and then back at me, and said, "Go to your room and stay there! Get out of my sight!"

I went up to my room and just laid on my bed waiting, agonizing about the outcome of this episode. I didn't hear anything for hours upon hours. It was torture. When the verdict came down, my sentence was as follows: I was to be grounded for one month, beginning the day after I got off my current restriction which had eight days left to go. Secondly, I could not attend my first formal dance that was coming up the following week. And last but not least, I'd been planning to go on trip to Vail with a friend a few weeks later to snow ski. Bye, bye Vail.

At that point I was never off restriction and my sentences always ran consecutively, so I had no chance at freedom. Even at school, I was in the detention hall on a daily basis--at least that's where I was *supposed* to be.

During my ninth and tenth grade years, Ziggy and I were always up to no good, but not much worse than when we'd met in sixth grade. The first time we got in trouble back then was when we were throwing oranges at cars from his parents' balcony. When we ran out of oranges, I threw a pair of scissors, breaking the windshield of a passing car. While the man was trying to beat down the front door of Ziggy's house, his sister opened it. She fingered us, telling the man that although she couldn't prove we were the culprits she would've bet anything that we were guilty. The man decided not to call the police since he didn't have proof that it was us, but his sister did rat us out to Ziggy's parents who were sorry the man didn't press charges.

Ziggy and I were synonymous. Wherever he was, I was, and vice versa. Although he was in special needs classes, he was much smarter than anyone ever gave him credit for, because when we were in tenth grade, he made a brilliant discovery. Ziggy's dad would check the odometer on his car every time he left town, so Ziggy came up with a solution that would allow us to joyride as we pleased when they'd be gone from home for a couple of days. He figured out that if he drove the car in reverse, the odometer wouldn't record the mileage.

When he made that discovery, he called me with the breaking news, saying, "Wambuh, we could drive this bitch in reverse all day long!"

I said, "God is good, homie!"

The idiot savant picked me up that night--in reverse. As I was standing on the balcony outside my bedroom, Ziggy wheeled around the corner, brake lights first. On his own, without a navigator, he drove his dad's car from his house to mine in reverse, and it was well over two miles of winding roads. It was the most hilarious thing I'd ever seen in my life! I made up elaborate stories so I could get out of the house and ride with Ziggy. I'd tell my parents that I had to rehearse a scene with my drama partner from school, but I didn't tell them that Ziggy just happened to be my drama partner.

There was a liquor store in Pasadena that sold to minors, owned by an old Asian man who pretended he didn't speak English. We pretended we didn't speak English either, so we never had a problem getting booze. Unfortunately, this particular liquor store closed very early in the evening, so sometimes we had to make the longer journey to the 'hood where they would sell booze to anyone over ten. It was a full ghetto in an area referred to as *Afrodena*, a predominantly black neighborhood in Pasadena, so you can imagine the looks we got. Two white boys rolling through the 'hood in an old station wagon--backwards! We would drive around aimlessly, chugging Mickey's Big Mouths, stopping by our girlfriends' houses and making complete assholes of ourselves. Those joyrides came to an abrupt end when a family friend told Ziggy's dad that he saw us swerving down the main drag in town--in reverse.

If it wasn't one thing it was another with me. Nothing surprised my mom anymore. One Christmas day, a friend of mine who lived down the street came over to show me his Christmas gift. He showed up at my pad riding a radical Supercross motorcycle, made for racing. It was similar to the one I'd almost won off my old man in the golf game a few years before, but much bigger and faster. I begged him to let me try it, so he reluctantly allowed me to test it out, but only in the driveway. He showed me how to work the clutch and throttle in sync, and finally I got it. I was having so much fun on the driveway, I decided to go off road.

We had a huge expanse of beautifully manicured lawn throughout our whole property, and much of it was special dichondra grass. I was having a blast, doing big donuts on the dichondra, churning it up like a rototiller and watching my friend laugh hysterically. I could see him in my peripheral vision, and suddenly noticed a dramatic change in his expression. I put the brakes on to see what the hell was wrong with him. He gestured toward the front door of my house, and when I looked up I saw my mom standing in the doorway shaking her head in disbelief. She told my friend to go home, and informed me that this caper would cost me another two weeks of restriction.

I think she was beyond mad, because she just looked at me with a confused look on her face and said, "David, look at the damage you did to our property. What's *wrong* with you? What were you thinking?"

Actually, I didn't *give* any thought as to right or wrong. The truth was, I had no idea what I was thinking except I was having fun and my friend was laughing his ass off. I just shrugged and said, "I don't know."

Starting my ninth grade year, I was drinking every day and barely scraping by in school. I was able to avoid academic confrontation because I was funny and I charmed teachers as well as students. I would also keep a safe physical distance from everyone so nobody would smell the booze on my breath. I mastered the art of cheating on tests, so I somehow managed to stumble through school. I had someone in every class who would share homework or let me cheat off their tests when I needed to, which was more often than not. The only class I ever got a legitimate "A" in was in advanced drama. I guess it figures because my whole life had been an act.

I was never busted for drinking at school even though I drank in the morning before school, I drank at snack break, at lunch, and during woodshop. I was a fourteen-year-old alky.

There was one thing that I did like though, and that was playing football. I loved getting the pads on and putting the hurt on people. I was actually pretty good, and was one of the hardest hitters on my football team. I probably would've been the starting running back if I hadn't been drunk every day, but the bottom line was I didn't start because I was always fucked up. I was the kickoff return guy, and I was very good at that. All I had to do was catch the ball when it was kicked to me and then try to run it back for a touchdown, which I did in our season opener. It was the opening kickoff of my first varsity game. The bad news was that a guy on my team clipped somebody, so it got called back. That was my *Almost Claim to Fame*.

By the time I was fifteen my problems were continuing to mount. My parents had no experience with addiction or mental illness before Mark and I came along, therefore had no point of reference as to how to deal with people like us. My dad knew how to arrest drunks and dopers but not how to guide them into a recovery mode. By then Mark had come home without finishing his senior year. When the low grade notices came in the mail for me, I would intercept them, and Mark would forge my mom's signature, acknowledging that she was aware of my poor grades. When I ditched school, which was a fair amount, he would write me an excuse. He could forge both of my parents' signatures like a pro, therefore, I utilized his talents on a regular basis.

During those years my parents had engagements of some kind or another several times each week, but we always had a live-in housekeeper that would do her best to keep tabs on us and report anything she found unacceptable. They entertained at home fairly often too, hosting beautiful dinner parties for their friends. I was always a happy cat when my parents entertained, because when the guests left the living room where they'd had their pre-dinner cocktails, Mark and I would swill all the drinks that had anything left in them.

I loved the feeling of relief that alcohol brought me. As soon as that warm feeling coursed through my veins, I *did* fit in. They say that alcohol is an acquired taste, and they are right. I just so happened to acquire it within seconds after my first slug.

When Mark came home from boarding school he was capable of causing major havoc too. A few times when my parents were out of town, Mark would throw *ragers* at our house, major keg parties, and charge everyone ten bucks at the gate. The partygoers loved our pad, and how could they not? They had over five acres to do whatever they wanted to do. Sex, drugs, and rock 'n roll! The day following the rager, Mark and his friends would restore the property to its original condition, and our parents were none the wiser.

They made enough money from the parties to keep their drug habits going until the next bash. Eventually, one of the ragers went sideways, with damage to the property, and plenty of party paraphernalia left behind that the gardener pointed out to my parents. That ended *those* business opportunities for Mark and his pals.

When Mark was seventeen-and-a-half, after failing to finish his senior year of high school, he wanted to move out of our house and get his own apartment. My parents weren't willing to allow that since they would be responsible for him until he became eighteen in July, so Mark, being very headstrong, actually filed a petition for emancipation. Seeing how serious he was about it, my parents went along and assisted him. That gave Mark his freedom, and also gave my parents the reassurance that they could legally cut him loose a few months early, and wouldn't be held accountable for any trouble that might come his way. Mark got a job, and with part of the money from his trust fund, he bought a condo in Pasadena. He loved his condo and seemed happy and content, so I guess it was the right thing for him to do.

———

By the time my junior year began, my anti-social behavior and drinking were escalating even more. Of course, my parents never realized just how much I drank, so they must have thought there was a good possibility that I was a psychopath, and they weren't too far off. As I grew older, bipolar episodes were hitting me, so my need for relief became more and more demanding. I had disassociated myself from the popular kids, and Ziggy and I were unwelcome, or at least uninvited, to most of the parties. It certainly didn't help when he peed on a girl who'd passed out at a homecoming party, and several people saw him do it. The poor girl he urinated on wound up in therapy after that incident. We both already had bad reputations, but his definitely became worse than mine following that scene.

While my old pals were taking college entrance exams and making plans for their future, I spent my time looking for my next drink. I had checked out of normal life in every way. I didn't even know what SAT stood for, let alone did I ever take it. Halfway through my junior year I did something that would take my life on another dramatic turn for the worse. There were several of us on the varsity football team who drank before our games. One of the seniors on the team would have a couple of kegs of beer at his house, and we'd all congregate there at lunchtime. We'd get hammered and then go to the Sizzler for dinner before our Friday night games. One time after drinking for a couple of hours at the keg party some of us piled into my friend's car and bee-lined it to a guy's house where we could score some black beauties.

We were driving down the main drag in town, and happened to see the cross-country team running along the grassy median in their Richard Simmons silky shorts. I saw a guy on the team who I heard had talked some shit about me, and true or not true, I decided to smash him. As we approached them, I jumped out of the car, sprinted across the street and blindsided the guy. When he was down, I beat him relentlessly, for no reason other than I was blitzed and angry. I was angry at myself for a multitude of reasons, but I took it out on that innocent boy.

Later that evening when the detectives showed up at my house I knew I was in deep trouble. Very soon after that, my parents transferred me to the public high school in South Pasadena, a neighboring town, which just so happened to be our archrivals. We'd recently played against them, and I had had a pretty good game that night. I think they hated San Marino kids because San Marino was a much more affluent town. They thought San Marino boys were a bunch of spoiled sissies, which was mostly true, and they also thought all the San Marino chicks were a bunch of stuck up bitches, which was also probably true.

On my first day at South Pasadena High, I was assaulted by a few of the football players who recognized me. One of the guys grabbed my backpack from behind and threw me to the ground. I focused on him and did as much damage as I could, but they wound up giving me a pretty good beating. I wasn't about to face that crap every day, so I simply quit going to school. I would ditch, steal some booze and go to the park. I would play the same song over and over again, and I would cry. The song was *Gold Dust Woman*, by Stevie Nicks. I was so empty, confused and sad, a tortured soul living in darkness, with no hope for sunlight. And I was angry at my parents and blamed them for causing my problems by taking me out of San Marino High.

My lack of impulse control made it impossible to have any consistency or stability in my life. After the school contacted my parents and told them that I'd been truant for weeks, my parents pulled up stakes and moved the family back to Newport, this time to try to save *me*. All the while, I was breaking their hearts and making them crazy. They tried hard, but nothing they did ever worked.

———

I believe Jeannette never felt as though she belonged in our family, or anywhere else for that matter. When she started the ninth grade, she was so unhappy and insecure at San Marino High, she sometimes would refuse to go into a classroom. She wouldn't leave the campus, but would just sit outside on the curb and wait for the class to end. After my parents consulted with the school counselor, they decided to look into boarding schools for her. They visited several schools, some in California and one in Arizona. When Jeannette saw Fenster School in Tucson, she was anxious to make the change. It was a college prep boarding school with a rustic, ranch-like atmosphere, and had a broad ethnic mix. She immediately felt at ease and at home, and stayed there through graduation, just coming home on school breaks.

Jeannette seemed to resent our parents for having adopted her, taking her from a foster home in a very modest neighborhood, and into a life that fairy tales are made of. She was given opportunities that very few people in this world are afforded. I wondered how my mom felt about the ill feelings that Jeannette harbored for her. My mom was all integrity, and that's not just what she possessed, but who she was. She could've adopted a newborn, but instead, took a little Mexican-American girl who'd been born addicted to heroin, was almost six years old, with her chances of being placed for adoption diminishing by the day. My parents had adopted three rejects who each presented them with nothing but trouble, and still, they kept trying. They naively thought they could trump nature with nurture.

———

With my brother living on his own, and my sister away at boarding school, my parents' eyes were on me. Back in Newport, I Immediately hooked up with the bad boys of Corona Del Mar High. Screw-ups have some kind of gravitational pull that brings them together, and we somehow find each other. I never even *attempted* to make friends with any of the clean-cut popular crowd. The guys I chose as friends came directly from the seaweed, and they were delinquents, just like me.

At least four days a week, the bad boys and I would steal from beer trucks on our lunch break. When they'd stop at a 7-11 or liquor store to make a delivery, we'd watch them stack their dollies with cases of beer and as soon the driver would go into the store, a couple of us would hop out of the car, throw open the rolling doors and each pinch a case of brew. After we committed our theft, we would drive to a place we called *Castaways* and drink for the rest of the day. Depending on the situation, it wasn't uncommon for us to make two beer runs in the same day.

Once, during a long drinking session at the Castaways it started to rain, so we decided we needed to find a place that had a roof overhead. I came up with the idea that we should break into the Linda Isle clubhouse and do our drinking there. When all was said and done, we totally vandalized the place, puking, pissing, and smashing beer bottles everywhere. We could've gotten into serious trouble with the law, but amazingly, the homeowners of Linda Isle didn't press charges. My parents were outraged, and to top it off, everyone on the island knew I'd been the ringleader.

Chapter Four

My second major fiasco in Newport Beach was on a summer night when my parents had guests over for the evening, and they'd planned to take them out to dinner. The couple brought their twelve-year-old son with them, and they figured he'd have a much better time hanging out with me for the evening instead of going to a restaurant with them, so my dad gave me money to take him out for pizza and to play games at the Fun Zone arcade just across the bay. I'd just turned seventeen so the kid's parents probably figured I'd watch over him.

The kid and I hopped in my boat, I hit the running lights, and we zipped over to Lido Peninsula. His father was a well-known Los Angeles radio talk show host, and his late grandfather was the famous movie star, Alan Ladd. They lived a privileged life in Beverly Hills. I felt like bitch slapping the kid from the very beginning, and I couldn't imagine why my parents would give me the job of babysitting the little dork.

After we got to the peninsula and I fed him a few slices of pizza, I broke it down to him. I said, "Here's the deal. We're gonna play games at the arcade *after* we swill a few brews over at the pier. But first, we're gonna stand around the corner from that liquor store over there until some old geezer comes by, and then we're gonna ask him to buy us a couple six-packs."

I could see the fear growing in the kid's eyes as I spoke, so before he said anything, I pointed to another location across the street and said, "Go wait over there. I'll do it myself."

A few minutes after dark I got an old queer to buy me a couple of six packs, so I motioned for the kid to follow me, and we were off to the beach for a party. I don't think he had ever had a sip of alcohol in his life, at least that's what his mom said later that night. We got to the fire pits next to the pier where it was usually safe to drink, but not *this* time! I was on my third or fourth brew, and the kid had barely gotten his tongue wet when it happened--and it happened quickly.

They came at us from different directions with their spotlights on us, commanding us to stay right where we were. I took a look at the kid and knew in my heart he wasn't going to bail with me, so I stared at him dead in the eye, and said slowly and deliberately, "Listen to me, we have to get the hell outta here! We'll get in very serious trouble if we don't run, so don't be a pussy!"

He was frozen, and at that moment I knew I was screwed. I hit the afterburners and bolted. I lost the cops by running through alleys and corridors known only to the local delinquents. My boat was docked at the Fun Zone, so when I thought the coast was clear I slinked into the Whaler and took off without the running lights. I had to make the voyage home without my passenger, and the trip seemed like an eternity! I *so* wanted to turn around and head toward Catalina Island, but I had no money and not enough gas to get there anyway. I thought of just racing out into the ocean until I ran out of fuel so when, or if, the Coast Guard found me, my parents would be more *concerned* about me than mad at me.

I was frantically trying to think of what I was going to say to his parents. I tried to conjure up a story before I arrived at our dock, but I couldn't focus. I felt dizzy. I realized that in a couple of minutes I'd be pulling to our dock without their kid!

Would I say, "Sorry, folks, but your son ran away. He told me to tell you he still loves you, but he needs some space." Or, maybe I could say, "As I was playing pinball, I saw a strange looking, black man standing near him, and when my game was over, I turned around and your son was gone--and so was the big black man!" Oh shit, what could I possibly say?

As I approached our dock, I could see my parents and the kid's parents standing at the railing, looking out over the bay, having cocktails. I felt like I was going to faint! I hopped out of the boat to tie up to the dock, and as I was securing the boat I heard the boy's father screech, "Where's my son?"

Now I felt like *swimming* to Catalina. I looked up, and with concern in my voice, I said, "You wouldn't believe it! While we were at the Fun Zone playing games, I somehow got separated from him. I was playing skeeball, and when my game was over I looked around and he was nowhere to be found!"

Needless to say, the mood of the party dramatically changed. All four adults had looks of horror on their faces. They all started talking and asking questions at once, but my dad finally interrupted everybody, and said, "David, go up to my office!"

I finished tying up the boat and then marched up to his office. I looked over the balcony and saw the man and his wife glaring at me. I wanted to tell them that their son was safe in the long arms of the law, but I was too scared. My plan was to run away before the cops brought the kid to my house, and I assumed that would happen fairly soon, so I needed to explain this away to my old man and hit the bricks, pronto!

When he closed his office door, he demanded, "Where's the kid?"

"I don't *know* where he is, Dad," I said.

This time with less patience, "David, what in the hell happened to that boy? You have to know something. You were *with* him, for God's sake!"

"Honestly, Dad, I don't know!"

At approximately the same moment I uttered those last words, the doorbell rang. My dad said, "Now I wonder who that could be?"

I shrugged, as if I couldn't possibly have any idea who it could be, and said, "I really don't know."

"Come with me. I have a feeling you *do* know," he said.

I thought I was going to throw up! It seemed like everything was moving in slow motion. We walked the very long walk to the front door and he said, "Open the door, David."

I opened the front door, and there stood two Newport Beach police officers with the kid standing between them. My dad nudged me out of the way and said to the cops, "Oh, thank God! We were about to report him missing. Where did you find him? His parents are here, and they're worried sick."

The big burly cop said, "Hi, Mister Wambaugh. Sorry to bother you like this, but it looks like this boy and your son were involved in some underage drinking. Obviously your son was able to evade the police which creates an additional problem."

My dad looked at the big cop and said, "So what exactly happened, officers?"

The second cop, a Mexican guy who was so tiny he looked like he could have been jockey, said, "Well, apparently your son had an adult purchase two six packs of beer, and then both boys proceeded to the beach. We patrol that area because it's notorious for underage drinking, so when we attempted to make contact, your son fled on foot."

The big cop said, "Mister Wambaugh, we're not going to make an arrest in this matter, but we strongly advise your son that nothing like this better ever happen again."

My dad said, "Well, thanks, guys! I really appreciate that, and we'll certainly deal with David on this matter. This won't happen again, I can assure you."

The cops wanted to personally hand the kid over to his parents and tell them what had gone down, so when they all met in the middle of our courtyard the kid ran to his mother, weeping like a baby.

The cops briefly explained to his parents what had happened, and after hearing some of the story, the kid's dad started screaming at me. My dad stepped in and ordered me to my room. My parents were so upset at that point, they really didn't know what to say to the departing guests. No matter where they moved me, no matter what they did, nothing worked. I was on a path of total destruction and it was coming fast and furiously.

We had a live-in housekeeper who was supposed to help monitor me when my parents were out, but I think she was afraid of me because I was always surly, and when she'd try to talk to me in her broken English I sometimes pretended not to understand her. However, she proved that she wasn't *too* afraid, because once when I was drunk, I called her a dumb ass in Spanglish, and she got so mad she chased me around the kitchen with a butcher knife.

When I went to my dad's office to tell him what Mary Lou did, he listened to my complaints and then went downstairs to get her side of the story. After speaking to her for a few minutes in Spanish, he knew without a doubt who the perpetrator was. After I was made to apologize he motioned for me to go upstairs, and I was grounded for yet another month.

———

One night when I was still supposed to be grounded, my parents went out to dinner, so I didn't think it would be a big deal if I went out for a couple of hours myself. When the coast was clear, I snuck out of the house, got in my car, and picked up a few of my buddies. We stole some booze from the parents of one of the boys and went joyriding. That was easy enough since all of our parents sported fully stocked liquor cabinets and the bottles would never be missed. The three of us drank two bottles of Cutty Sark in less than two hours, and on my way home that night I was involved in a horrendous injury accident.

I drove my '81 Chevy Citation right through a stop sign and was T-Boned by a VW bus traveling over fifty miles an hour. Somehow everyone survived, but the two women in the VW were injured. I didn't know how badly because I didn't hang around to get the details. I went into emergency mode, started my car and fled the scene. Seeing as how my car was bent like a boomerang and the back tires were jammed against the twisted metal, I was grateful that the car had front wheel drive. I was able to drag the back end, and limp slowly home down the Pacific Coast Highway, tire smoke billowing behind me.

After I got home, I realized I'd left a trail of breadcrumbs in the form of black rubber all the way to our driveway, so I thought I'd better take some action. I called the Newport Beach police, and hoped by the time they arrived, I'd appear to be sober. When the cops got to the house I was waiting outside, standing beside my wreck.

I explained that after I stopped at the stop sign, and started slowly through the intersection, the VW bus was jamming, and had T-boned my car. I told them that I thought the VW was leaving the scene, so I came straight home and called right away to report them for leaving the scene of an accident. The cops took a report, and amazingly, I wasn't arrested on the spot. I guess they didn't notice I was drunk.

When my parents arrived home that night, all I could hear was the yelling that came from outside the garage. They were hysterical. My car was sitting in the driveway, totaled beyond recognition. That time, I think my parents were just glad that I was alive, and after our long discussion about what had taken place that night, they decided to hold off any consequences until the police investigation was completed. As always, I was guilty as hell but went unpunished because I had the art of manipulation down to a science.

———

I maintained control for a short while after that incident, but only long enough to con my dad out of a new car. I promised my parents with all my heart that this time was different. I told them I would behave and go to school regularly. I said I would never drink again. I begged and harassed and nagged and begged and then begged some more. I reasoned that I had to get to and from school, and it was the only reasonable option. Eventually, when I had my dad on the verge of a nervous breakdown, he relented. I had him so crazy, and the salesman at the dealership was such a con, that we somehow talked my dad into buying me a beautiful Nissan sports car right off the showroom floor. At the end of that day, I had a tight ride and yet I was still miserable.

I hated waking up every day, being forever preoccupied with the next bottle I could get my hands on. My heart was heavy, my soul was empty, and I didn't like this game of life. Was I *that* different? Did I do something so bad that I deserved to live with this madness?

Within a couple of weeks after getting my new car, my parents caught me drinking and driving, so they confiscated my ride, and that was the end of that. But I still had my boat, and could go surfing every day. As I would cross the bay, I'd listen to the purring of the engine and fantasize about what it would be like to fit in my own skin. When I would pass by John Wayne's house on my way to catch the early morning glass, we exchanged friendly waves and hellos. During those few weeks I actually felt pretty good, and even had a couple of fleeting glimpses of hope, but that's all they were--fleeting glimpses.

Soon enough I was hanging out with the hardcore punks whom I'd become friendly with out in the surf. My new friends were from Newport Harbor High, the public school on the other side of town. That bunch was much more middle class and accepting of me right away because they could see I was crazy and had no fear out in the big surf. They had the best parties, the best looking chicks, and there was always at least one hellacious brawl thrown in for entertainment.

Throughout all those years, I'm not sure if I just wasn't aware, or simply didn't care about what I was doing to my parents. I don't think that I maliciously set out to hurt them, but they got in the way of my drinking and I couldn't allow that. I had literally pushed them to the point where they were making irrational decisions.

Soon after I lost my car, my dad was leaving on an international publicity tour for his book that had just been released, and on the day he left he told me that I was to be grounded until his return. That was an impossible thing as far as I was concerned, so when my dad took off, so did I. I knew that my mom was afraid of me by then and couldn't possibly keep me under control. That's one of the most shameful things I've ever done, scaring my mom like that. I didn't mean to, but I did it. I made her so crazy, that when I ran away, she kept my psychiatrist appointments for herself.

I traded in my polo shirts, khakis, and saddle shoes, for combat boots, torn up 501's and wifebeater T-shirts. To complete my new look, I dyed my hair with Lady Clairol pure white dye, pierced my ear and installed a big silver cross that hung almost down to my trapezoid. I ran the streets with my new gang, always looking over my shoulder for my mom or the police. I thought my dad was still out of town, so I was really surprised when he showed up one night at The Cuckoo's Nest, a popular Orange County venue that hosted the most well known punk rock bands from all over. My friend, Pate, spotted my dad wading through a sea of violent punkers, and they cleared the way without resistance. They must've thought he was a cop, because he sure *looked* like a cop. Christ, he *was* a cop!

Before my dad got too close, we hurried out to the van we came in, popped a few black beauties and washed them down with some Wild Turkey. After we polished off all the booze and drugs, we were ready to go slam dance to the sounds of The Circle Jerks. Within one day I'd gone from living in a multimillion dollar home with a bomb-ass speed boat docked outside my back door, to living under piles of dirty clothes in Pate's closet and stealing food and beer from the 7-Eleven down the street.

On my second morning in Pate's closet, my mom came to his house to see if he knew where I might be. He told her he hadn't seen me in days, but that he hoped I was okay. I remained under the dirty clothes until she left, but then a few hours later the cops arrived wanting to search the house. As they came in I bolted out the back door, over the fence, down the alley, and into the safety of a yacht that was dry-docked. I stayed there for a while, and when I felt it was safe, went back to Pate's house to make another plan of action. He thought his place had gotten too hot and didn't want the cops coming to his pad while his parents were upstairs watching Wheel of Fortune, so that meant I had to find other accommodations.

A miracle came just in the nick of time. My mom left a message with Pate's mother saying she wanted me to call some woman who supposedly was going to help me. She left the woman's name and phone number, but that was her only message--nothing more. I was suspicious, but I thought maybe my mom really *did* hire someone to help!

I called the number, and the woman who answered was the bringer of incredible news. She said that my mom totally understood how I felt about wanting my own apartment, some money until I could get a job, and that of course I needed to have my car back. The lady said that my mother didn't think those requests were unreasonable and that she would provide them for me. The lady told me that my mom wanted her to see me in person, just to be sure that I was healthy and doing okay, and following the physical inspection, she was supposed to give me a check to cover the things we'd discussed, and then hand over the car keys.

I told her to hold the phone, and consulted with my friend. I said, "Dude, you wouldn't believe it, bro, this lady on the phone is gonna to hook us up fat. Trust me, homey! Car, crib, bank account, all sorts of shit!"

Then I got back on the line, and said, "Ma'am, I don't feel comfortable meeting you because I don't trust you. But I'll tell you what, I'll be surfing at Thirty-Fourth Street tomorrow morning, and there's a bench there on the boardwalk. I'll be able to see you from the water, so if you're thinking of bringing anyone with you, I would see that, and then I'm gone, and the deal's off. My posse will already be in place watching you, so you're not going to get one over on me. I'll be there between ten and eleven, and as soon as you see that I'm physically okay, you'll give me the check and my car keys, right?"

"Absolutely," she said. "I'll see you in the morning."

The next day I had lookouts all over. We thought we had the whole area staked, so when I got the thumbs up from the guys, I approached the woman on the bench. She was sort of a frumpy middle-aged woman. As I got closer, she pulled a picture out of her jacket pocket, but didn't seem to recognize me at first, because the David in the picture looked like a clean-cut young man, and the guy standing in front of her looked like Billy Idol with a suntan.

She looked at the picture, and then up at me and said, "Oh, you must be David."

"Yeah, that's me," I said.

"You look a little different now than you did in this picture."

"Yeah, so?"

She glanced at it again and said, "It must be an old one."

"I wouldn't know,"

"Come on, have a seat, dear," she said.

I said, "No, I'm cool." So now that you can see I'm fine, I'd like my check and the keys 'cause I gotta get going."

She started to stammer, and then it happened. A cargo van came screaming down the alley in reverse, heading directly toward me. It came from out of nowhere and stopped just shy of my surfboard. When the van screeched to a stop, two big black guys flew out of the back and the chase was on! They earned their money that day since I knew the area like the back of my hand. Unfortunately, my escape route was blocked off by a Newport Beach police cruiser, with the cop standing outside his car waiting for me. I was tackled, shackled, and transported to the Newport Beach Police Department.

When my mom arrived at the station I was in a holding cell, still in my wetsuit. As she came around the corner toward me, her face turned the color of my hair. There I was, now looking like Billy Idol on crack! She broke down and cried, and once again I had rendered her speechless.

As my mom turned and walked away, a big bucktoothed old man approached my cell and gave me an idea of what was to come. He said, "Okay, listen up! We're gonna be taking a flight in our private plane to a school in Provo, Utah. Our school will help you learn to deal with life a little better, and we can teach you to *behave* better. We make *all* our boys behave better! You'll see."

I said, "Yeah? How're you gonna make me act better, dickhead? If you let me outta this cell, I'll show *you* how to act better."

"Oh, come on now; don't resist us," he said. "You're gonna be just fine!"

I said, "Yeah? Screw you, old man."

———

When we arrived at John Wayne airport in the van, I asked one of the black guys if he would loosen my shackles a little, and I couldn't believe it when he said no. Like I really would be able to overpower two big brothers and a hillbilly. Both guys had been starters on the BYU football team a few years back, and one of them even had a short career in the pros, so I doubted I could've outrun them. I was so angry at my mom, I was ranting and raving the whole way there. She'd set me up and then had the nerve to come with us on the plane. The psychiatrist that I'd been seeing before I ran away had recommended Provo Boys School to her as a possible solution for my chemical dependency and behavioral problems.

We flew into Salt Lake, and then drove about an hour to the school. When we were approaching our destination I noticed razor wire on top of the surrounding fences. I had arrived at Provo Canyon Boys School, and I could already see that the place was going to be a nightmare.

The hillbilly said, "Welcome home, son."

I looked at him and said, "Fuck you!"

When I got out of the van, shackles and all, I remember being very scared. I'd heard stories about these kinds of places, and they weren't happy stories. I had a feeling I'd be getting into a lot of fights, whether I wanted to or not. Provo Canyon Boys School was notorious for being a violent institution. The place was run by former members of the BYU football team. The former football players from the Y were huge, but some of the delinquents at Provo Canyon were beasts, so there were some hell raising fights in that school.

There were two populations there, one consisting of spoiled, rich, entitled assholes like me with major behavioral problems, and the other of thugs from CYA, the California Youth Authority, which is a state prison for minors. The state of California figured that the only hope left for some of them was forced behavior modification. And that's just what the place was all about: forced behavior modification.

Some of the guys would fight staff or each other until they got a shot in the ass, and then it was night-night until the next day. Thorazine is a powerful anti-psychotic drug that is sometimes used in mental hospitals to subdue out-of-control psychiatric patients. In large doses it's almost paralyzing. At least it was for me. Just seconds after the injection, the drug knocks your dick in the dirt and renders you totally harmless. After you started drooling on yourself they'd place you in a small, dark, rubber room with a little hole in the middle so you could relieve yourself if necessary. It was called the "P Room," and everyone had different ideas of what the "P" stood for.

It was hard to believe, but I encountered one of my childhood friends who'd also wound up in Provo. Bixbie greeted me upon my arrival, and I was really happy and relieved to see him, thinking it would be so much easier having an old friend there with me. He graduated from Provo six months before I did, and went back home to San Marino where his wealthy family still lived. He'd planned to spend the summer at home, go on to college in the fall, and then to work in the family business after college. He had it all worked out. He was going to be set for life. On the day before he was to leave for college, he blew his brains all over his bedroom with a twelve-gauge shotgun.

I was shocked by his suicide! It seemed as though he had everything to live for. His life was all set. I was never able to understand why he killed himself, and I've thought about him throughout the years, wondering how his life would've been if he were still here. I imagined he might've outgrown his problems, gotten married, had kids, but...who knows? I'm sure people thought the same thing about me that I thought about Bixbie, how I had everything in the world going for me, that I was set for life, but I chose to squander it away. How pathetic.

At least *something* good came out of Provo Canyon Boys School. I received my high school diploma and graduated with a B average. That was much better than my previous overall GPA which was probably somewhere between a D minus and an F.

I remember being so proud of graduating from high school with decent grades, and I thought I might have even made my parents just a little proud for once. What a hell of a thing to be proud of: Their kid just graduated from reform school! I wouldn't have been released until my eighteenth birthday if I hadn't fulfilled the requirements to graduate, so you bet your ass I applied myself for the first time in my life. My freedom depended on it. Regardless, it felt good that I was able to make my parents smile.

Because I was doing so well, I thought my parents might want me to come home, but that was the last thing they wanted. They were smart enough to know that if I came home it would be a complete disaster, so they insisted that I stay in Provo. They made that decision out of love, care, and sincere concern for their boy, but I took it as being rejected again. I felt like discarded trash, not welcome anywhere. That was the catalyst that sent me back to the dark side.

I was really bummed when my parents said it would be best for me to stay in Utah for a while with the Mormons, and away from my old crowd. I wasn't too keen on living around a bunch of Mormon cult members, but I guess I had no choice. I was depressed until I was able to get my parents to ship my car to me. I made them feel guilty for insisting that I stay in Utah, so after I got my car I told them that it would only be fair if I had season lift tickets to some of the world-class ski resorts around Salt Lake. They were so happy that I got a high school diploma, and had enrolled in some college classes there that they granted my requests.

———

In Provo, I drank and used drugs with the other guys who also weren't welcome back home with their parents. We all had wealthy parents, so we had nice cars, nice apartments, and skied every day. We hung out together as a posse until a couple of unfortunate incidents took place that eventually broke us up and sent one guy to prison. The first incident took place in Salt Lake when two of the kids got busted for selling acid and cocaine to undercover cops up at the Snowbird resort. One of them got a short prison term, and the other got probation for ratting out his pal.

The incident that finally split us up was a car crash that left one kid hospitalized with some injuries. We'd just polished off a batch of *Hop-Skip-And-Go-Naked*, a fruit drink mixed with 190 proof grain alcohol that takes you from buzzed to blacked-out in no time flat. We were joyriding in a '77 Caddy belonging to one of the guys, careening down a dirt road surrounding the lake where we water-skied during the summer, and the kid driving lost control of the car. We flipped over, landing upside down in the lake. We all got out of the car before it sank, but the accident left one kid with some head injuries. We dropped him at the hospital, and never saw him again. That's when we splintered.

I was enrolled in Utah Technical College, taking a few basic classes with the thought that someday I would be able to transfer to a four-year university. What a laugh! I got incompletes at every junior college I ever enrolled in, which eventually numbered five. The day finally came when my dad asked me to produce a report card from Utah Tech, and when directly asked, I fumbled and mumbled, and finally confessed that I didn't have one.

He was totally pissed, and said, "David, don't leave that apartment, and I mean don't even move. I'm going to call you back in fifteen minutes and you'd better answer that goddamned phone!" And he hung up on me.

Fifteen minutes later he called back, and said, "David, I want you to take a taxi to the Salt Lake International Airport where there will be a plane ticket waiting for you at the counter for a flight leaving at 3:15 this afternoon. Leave everything there in your apartment and just bring the clothes on your back. I'll arrange for your car and your things to be shipped here to us. And do *not* miss that goddamned plane! Do you understand me?"

"Yes," I mumbled into the phone.

Chapter Five

When I got off the plane at John Wayne airport, my parents actually greeted me with smiles on their faces. I was still traumatized from the first time I was set up, so I was waiting for another kidnapping to take place. I kept flashing back to the flight that had taken me to Provo two years earlier.

On the way home, my dad broke the news that I wasn't going to be staying with them in the Newport Beach house. Their plan was for me to stay in our newest San Marino home, which was a much smaller, more manageable house. They said I had to get a full time job, and take at least one course at Pasadena City College. Initially, they'd planned to divide their time between San Marino and Newport so they could monitor me to some degree, but they wound up staying in Newport most of the time.

Everything was good for almost a month, until I got an invitation to go skiing at Mammoth Mountain for a couple of days with an old high school friend of mine. Anthony told me he was a good Christian, and didn't drink anymore, so after relentless haranguing my parents gave me their okay. I neglected to tell them that Ziggy was also going, since my parents knew, for sure, *he* wasn't a good Christian who didn't drink. Anthony had a beautiful new truck with all the bells and whistles, so we were driving to Mammoth in style. After they picked me up, I think we stayed sober until we got to the end of my driveway.

Before we hit the slopes, we decided to get a couple of bottles of 100 proof Peppermint Schnapps to keep us warm throughout the day, so Anthony and I hopped in his truck and were off to the liquor store. While the stereo was blaring *Bang your Head* by the Twisted Sister, we hit black ice, flipped over two times and landed right side up, just like a cat! However, at the end of the weekend, we had to drive seven hours back home with no windshield. All three of us were wearing goggles, ski hats, and had scarves over our faces the whole way home in snow and rain.

As we neared my house I was praying my mom wouldn't see us, but I'll be damned, as soon as we pulled into our driveway, the garage door opened and she was starting to back out. She looked at us, did a double and triple take, shook her head and continued to back out before driving away. When she returned, she demanded that I remain around the house for observation.

But after a few weeks of observation, I convinced her that I should go to Lake Tahoe for a few days with Ziggy, where his parents had a house. I assured her that his parents would be there to supervise us, even though we were *supposed* to be adults, and should have been able to supervise ourselves.

Our first night in Tahoe was a disaster. My friend, Mike, and I were having a drunken wrestling match in the middle of Bally's Casino when some guys tried to break us up. They didn't identify themselves as police officers, so we wound up getting into a full beef with four off-duty cops. Three of us were booked into the Washoe County Jail for assault and resisting arrest. I knew it would be hopeless to call my parents, so I called my brother to bail me out, which he did. I never showed up to my court date, so I don't know what the final outcome was, but I figured I would have a warrant out for my ass. I do know that Mark lost his bail money but he never sweated me about it.

I enrolled in a refresher English course at Pasadena City College, and got a full time job bagging groceries at a nearby supermarket. I'm sure my parents thought I'd stay out of trouble, seeing as how I was busy with a job and school too. Unfortunately, a few of my screw-up friends who also hadn't gone away to a four-year university, came over almost every day and we'd drink beer, smoke pot, eat Domino's pizza and watch MTV.

Everything was going just fine until September of 1981, when I had a substantial hiccup in my program.

One night after drinking all evening, I was showing off my car to my friends, and as we were flying around one of the many winding roads of San Marino, I went too fast on a curve, and the back end of my car started to slide out. I knew I was going to eat shit before I could save the situation. I was sliding in one direction and overcorrected, hit the opposite curb, and then flipped upside down on the manicured front lawn of a very nice home. Green beer bottles were all over the street and in the yard where my car had turtled.

Somehow I had the uncanny ability to react very quickly after disaster struck, perhaps because disaster struck so often. There were no life-threatening injuries, just a few cuts, scrapes and bruises. Everyone had gotten out of the car safely, me first, when I heard sirens coming. I knew I reeked of alcohol so I was desperate to find something to disguise my boozy breath before I had to face the cops. I got up off the curb, walked past my turtled car and opened the unlocked back door of the house where my car was upside down. I crept in and went directly to the refrigerator, pulled out a half gallon of milk and started drinking straight from the carton.

An elderly woman, dressed in a bathrobe, startled me when she came into the kitchen and turned the light on. It was unreal because she didn't seem alarmed that some kid was in her kitchen at 11:00 p.m. drinking milk.

She sweetly asked, "What in the world are you doing in here, honey?"

"I'm just drinking some milk, ma'am," I said.

"Would you like a glass?"

"Sure, please," I said.

She opened a cupboard, got a glass, and asked, "What's going on out there?"

"Well, I had an accident in your front yard, and I'm pretty sure I'm in big trouble, so I guess I'd better go out there and face the music."

She walked over to the window and her jaw dropped. She said, "Oh, my God, that's terrible! Are you hurt? Was anyone else hurt?"

"No, no one was hurt, ma'am, at least nothing serious. Just my car, and well, your yard looks like it got kind of messed up. I'm really sorry about your lawn, ma'am. I ruined my mom's lawn once and she was really pissed." I headed for the door, then turned around and said, "And thanks for the milk, ma'am."

She had a look of puzzlement on her face and followed me outside to see for herself what was happening. By then it looked like a crime scene out of *CSI*. There was overkill with the amount of cop cars, ambulances, and fire engines that had arrived. Even a helicopter was circling above.

I talked the cops out of arresting me because I convinced them that the punishment I was going to get from my parents would be so much worse than anything that they could possibly do to me. I begged and pleaded with them to let me go home and face my parents, which they actually did! It was amazing that I pulled that one off. When he found out my parents weren't home, the sergeant said he would be contacting my father on Monday to give him the whole story of what had transpired that night, all the way down to the carton of milk.

My dad had been the most famous cop in America, so I'm sure that's why I got so many passes throughout the years from his admiring law enforcement brothers. Not to mention, they probably thought that my dad had endured enough heartache from his piece-of-shit son, so they tended to have mercy on me for his sake. I had learned early on that my dad's name was often a get-out-of-jail-free card for me.

My parents were at our desert house that weekend, so I wanted to call and tell them about my accident before they started the two-hour drive home. I wanted them to have plenty of time to cool off. I dialed the desert number, and my mom answered.

"Hi, Mom," I said, trying to sound casual.

"Hi, Dave. We were just talking about you. What's up, sweetie?"

"Oh, nothing much," I said, "but I just wanted to tell you that I got into a little accident last night. I hit a curb and my car got kind of got messed up."

"How messed up?"

"Pretty messed up," I said, sweating bullets.

"Was anyone hurt?"

"Not too bad," I lied.

"What do you mean, 'not too bad'?" she said, her voice rising an octave.

"Well, one of the guys had to get some stitches in his hand," I said.

"Dave, what happened?" she said. "Was there drinking involved? Hold on a minute. I want your dad in on this conversation."

My dad came on the line and said, "David, I don't even want to hear your story right now. We're on our way home, so do not move an inch. And you'd better be there when I walk through that door!"

My heart sank. When they got home my dad came into my bedroom, read me the riot act and told me hell would freeze over before he would ever buy me another car or anything else for that matter. But I didn't believe him. He always said things like that when he was mad.

———

I had stopped going to my bonehead English class at the junior college because it was way over my boozy brain, but I was still working full time at the store. I began dating a girl who also worked at the market, and after a few months of seeing her, I got her pregnant. We agreed that the best course of action would be for her to get an abortion, so I took her to a clinic to have the procedure done. And after that, she dumped me. I still had some papers from the clinic, stating that she'd had the abortion, so Ziggy and I left them on her parents' doorstep for them to see, a rotten and spiteful way for a scumbag like me to retaliate. When her mother found them, she was outraged and called my dad, saying she wanted me to disappear from her daughter's life.

My dad called me that very day with another ultimatum. My choice was to either move out to our desert house and away from the girl, or to be homeless--just as simple as that. I packed my things and was on my way to the desert. How bad could *that* be?

———

My parents had become hardened and desensitized by my insane behavior to the point that nothing I did seemed to affect them as it had in the past. Nothing seemed to surprise them anymore, and I'm sure they believed I was capable of almost anything.

They'd sent me to countless psychiatrists and psychologists hoping to find answers, with no success. There was no possible way for me to have ever been successfully diagnosed since I never gave accurate information, and I was always drinking. I lied, telling shrinks what I thought they wanted to hear so I could get the session over with and get the hell out of there. I had no idea what was going on with me, no idea at all. More than one doctor guessed that I might be bipolar and prescribed all sorts of psych meds that did me no good whatsoever. Of course I seldom took them as prescribed, and when I *did*, I washed them down with whatever booze was available at the time.

I had no plans or dreams anymore, not that I really had any to begin with, but at that point I didn't care about anything except where my next drink was coming from. I always found such amazing relief in booze. The feeling I would experience after the first few drinks is hard for me to describe. My mind would slow down, the tightness in my chest would dissipate and I could become someone else. When I was drunk, I was able to pretend things weren't as they really were. I wanted so *badly* to be someone else, a person who had a place in life, but of course that was only a fantasy.

Upon my arrival in the desert, I assumed I would be staying with my parents in their condo, but to my delight my mom informed me I would be staying in their other place, directly across the street, which they'd bought as a guest house for family and friends who might come to visit.

My dad made a couple of demands right off the bat, which I had to execute *pronto*. Either that or I would have to find another place of residence. All I had to do was find a full time job, and stay sober. Very simple, he said. That was it. I knew I could pull off getting a full time job, but the sober part was questionable. That time around, he didn't even require that I sign up for any college classes, because he knew by then it would be too much to ask of someone with my alcohol-addled brain.

I felt like I'd hit the jackpot. I was the luckiest guy alive. I lived in a beautiful condo all to myself at The Vintage Club in Indian Wells, the most exclusive country club in the desert at that time. I was able to play golf any time I wanted, and there were two amazing golf courses: the mountain course and the desert course. I practiced and played every day, so my game came back quickly. I was living a healthy life. I got a job as a host at TGI Friday's, and I even lost thirty-five pounds, thanks to my grandmother.

She and my granddad came for visits fairly often, and they'd sit around the kitchen table with my mom, chat, smoke cigs and drink coffee. One day when they were visiting, I walked into the kitchen to get a couple of cheese sticks and a coke from the refrigerator.

When I went over to give Grandma a kiss, she turned around, did a double take, and said, "Hi, honey. Boy, you've gotten chubby since the last time I saw you."

I thought I didn't hear her correctly, and said, "Excuse me, Grandma?"

She patted me on the belly, and said, "You've gotten pretty chubby in the last few months." She must've seen the ghastly look on my face because she quickly added, "But you're still just as handsome as ever."

I knew I'd gained a few pounds, but nobody had ever called me on it. I was totally shocked when she said it, but I knew it was true. I *was* chubby from all the boozing, but I just wasn't able to accept it, that is, until my grandma called me on it.

The following day I went on a diet. I worked out two hours every day, ate only Cheerios with nonfat milk, plain tuna, and chicken breasts, and lost thirty-five pounds in sixty days. Her words had an immediate effect on me, and was the first time I'd ever taken control of anything in my life and saw it through.

Two months into my new life in the desert things couldn't have been better. I looked great, felt great, and I was sober. I had my job at TGI Friday as a host, played golf almost every day, and even started an auto detailing business on the side.

I had the perfect clientele right there at The Vintage Club. Eli Callaway, owner of Callaway Golf and Callaway Vineyards was one of them, and Jim Nordstrom of Nordstrom's Department Stores, along with a few others around the club of that caliber. My detail package was the "Dave's Special." It cost me about twenty bucks for the supreme wash and wax at the Elephant Car Wash in Rancho Mirage who would actually do the work, and I would charge my client twice that. That was the "Dave's Special!"

Mr. Callaway and Mr. Nordstrom always seemed impressed with my work. I didn't consider it fraud; I just considered it my broker's fee. When I'd started the business I actually *did* the detailing, but it was a backbreaker so I'd just made a minor adjustment and outsourced the jobs. For the most part, things were going really well in the desert. My parents and I were getting along and I was doing what I was supposed to be doing, but shit hit the fan again in the spring of 1983.

My childhood friends were scattered all over the U.S. in different universities, but many of them were coming to Palm Springs for spring break. The desert was the hot spot in the eighties for college coeds, and one of my friend's parents owned a place in Palm Springs where all the guys were going to hook up and party for the week. They got my phone number from an old girlfriend of mine, and after they'd left several messages, I called them back to see what they were up to. Ten minutes later I was on my way to Palm Springs, and that same night I drove home in a blackout.

The following evening, at least ten of my pals decided to surprise me by showing up at my job at TGI Friday. They came in with their fake I.D.'s and ordered round after round of Long Island iced teas. They were yelling, throwing food at each other, and behaving inappropriately, especially toward the girls sitting at the next table. Ziggy was there, as inappropriate as Ziggy could be.

Finally, my bull dyke manager caught on to the fact that these were *my* friends, and brought to my attention that they were out of control and that I'd better get them *under* control or we were going to have a big problem.

I went over to their table, and said, "Listen you guys, this box-bumper is gonna fire me if you keep dickin' around in here. Please, for me, just chill. If I get canned from this job, my old man will completely go south!"

Ziggy laughed and snorted, "Fuck you, Wambuh. Drink a Long Island or I'm gonna tell that lesbo bitch you called her a box-bumper."

"Come on, Ziggy!" I pleaded. I'm gonna get fired because of your stupid ass!"

Then two other guys across the table started chanting, "*Wam-baugh, Wam-baugh, Wam-baugh!*"

I looked around, saw my manager glaring at me, and no sooner than that, Ziggy blurted out, "Wambuh, if you don't go into the bathroom with me right now and drink this Long Island, I'm gonna pour it over my head."

"Please, Ziggy, don't do that to me," I said.

"*Wam-buh! Wam-buh!*" Ziggy chanted.

I knew he wouldn't hesitate to dump the drink over his head, so I said, "Okay, Ziggy, let's go." And I followed him into the bathroom and powered the Long Island in two glugs. After four more trips to the bathroom, I got fired, told the lesbian to gargle my balls, and my friends and I were asked to leave the building. The lesbo told me I could pick up my check the next morning.

This was going to be ultra devastating for my parents because I had been showing promise there in the desert and had given them another glimmer of hope, and then I did it again and screwed everything up. I couldn't make sense of what I'd done, or why I was compelled to destroy myself.

I was much too scared to tell my parents that I'd been fired, so they assumed I was going to work every night. But instead, I was going to Palm Springs to drink with my friends. On the second day of the party my brother and one of his friends showed up unexpectedly. Mark never had much to do with my friends, but my friends all seemed to like him. Most everyone liked Mark. We drank, smoked weed, and tried to lure chicks to the crib for some Jacuzzi fun. My friends kept telling me how cool my brother was, and said we should invite him to all the parties. It was over the next couple of days that Mark and I actually bonded for the first time in our lives. He and his friend were the life of the party, and I was finally proud to have him as my brother.

Mark and I spoke on a level of feeling that was unprecedented. We talked about how we both had squandered our lives away with alcohol and drugs, and together, we tried to make sense of the events that led us to that point in each of our lives. We also talked about redemption, our comebacks, and how we would support each other every step of the way.

———

Two days later, as I was getting out of the shower the phone rang. I didn't want to answer it because I'd been drinking, and figured it was probably my mom or dad calling. As I was about to run out the door to avoid being popped, I stopped for some reason, turned around and picked up the phone. It was my dad, and I figured I was in trouble somehow, but that wasn't the case this time.

He said in a tone of voice that gave me shivers, "Dave, something terrible has happened. I need you to come over here."

It sounded as though he was fighting back tears, but I'd never heard or seen him cry before. My first thought was that my mom was dead. I thought, Please Lord, don't let my mom be dead! As I was crossing the street I saw my dad walking toward me, his head down, and he seemed to be shaking. It made me want to turn and run somewhere, anywhere. Again I thought, please don't let my mom be dead. What terrible thing was he going to tell me? God, not my mom! What would we *do* without her?

He slowly raised his head as if it weighed a hundred pounds, looked at me with tears in his eyes, and said, "Mark's dead, Dave. He was killed in a car accident down in Mexico. I'm sorry to have to tell you this, son, but he's gone."

Stunned, but relieved because it wasn't my mom, I said, "What happened?"

"He and his friend, Mike, were in Mark's Jeep heading back to San Diego from Ensenada, and I assume Mark lost control of his Jeep." He was silent for a minute, trying to gain control, and then said, "They were ejected when his Jeep swerved into the oncoming traffic. Both of them were pronounced dead at the scene."

We just stood there for a while, looking at each other. I didn't know what to say, but I kept thanking God it wasn't my mom. I didn't say a word and finally my dad put his hand on my shoulder and motioned for me to go inside.

I entered the den and I'd never seen anything like it in my life. My strong, courageous mother was curled up in a little ball, rocking back and forth on the loveseat, looking as though she'd somehow grown smaller. She was talking but I couldn't understand what she was saying. It was plain to see that part of my mom had died with my brother. I thought about how *I* should have been the one to die first, seeing as how I was far more out of control than Mark had ever been. And also, he was a much better person than I ever was.

Soon after my brother's death, my dad said to me, "Listen to me, Dave, my life is ruined. It doesn't matter how many bestsellers I write, or how many movies I make. That bullshit doesn't matter anymore. Remember that. It's over for me."

I didn't respond because I figured his life had already been ruined with all the pain and suffering that *I* had put him through, but this was different. This was final. I didn't really understand the depth of that statement until much later in life, after I'd spoken to other fathers who'd lost children. Their sentiments were always the same.

I was sent to Tijuana to identify Mark's body, sign documents, and pay the Mexicans to bring him back across the border for burial. I'm sure I was asked to go down there and deal with the situation so I could see how I might wind up if I didn't change my ways--a scare tactic that didn't work. Ziggy rode with me, and after I identified Mark's body and made the transportation arrangements, we went on a two-day bender with the money left over from what my dad had given me. I still don't know how or why I did such a terrible thing like that when my parents were grieving the loss of their oldest son, but I did it. I sure did.

On our way home after our binge in Tijuana, Ziggy and I decided to stop in San Diego and have a few drinks before continuing on, and make a game plan as to how we were going to explain the two-day bender. We decided on the downtown Manchester Grand Hyatt, and went straight to the Top of Hyatt Bar, forty floors above San Diego Harbor. We were hoping we might hook up with a couple of cougars that would like to take care of a couple of cute boys for a while, but unfortunately it didn't happen. We sat there and just got drunk, as the reality of our situation started to set in.

We decided we were both such losers, we should commit suicide for the good of humankind. While we sat there drinking Johnny Walker Black Label, I noticed that the windows of the bar opened up onto a ledge. Ziggy and I were crying to each other, saying how much we loved each other and how we tried our hardest at life, but it was plain to see that it was useless. We were born to lose. We agreed that our families would be much better off without us, and so would the world as a whole.

After the tears subsided a bit, I said to Ziggy, "You know what, brother? I think God made us come to this bar, because the windows open up to the outside. Look over there."

Ziggy just said, "Damn, Wambuh!"

"What do you think, brother?"

"I think that's *deep!*" he said.

"It is deep, Ziggy, but it's the best thing for us. Trust me."

"Okay, but that's fucked up. Aren't you scared, David?"

I said, "Of course I'm scared, bro, but we can power a bunch more Johnny Walkers and then just hop off the ledge. I'm sure we'll pass out as soon as we jump, so don't be too scared."

"Awright, Wambuh, let's go!" he said.

We sat there and got plastered, and then pussied out, agreeing that the building was just too damned high to jump from. Eventually, the bartender asked us to leave because we had become totally obnoxious, and when we tried to argue with him, we were escorted out of the hotel.

I'm not quite sure where we went from there, but the next day we decided to make the million mile drive back to my parent's house and turn ourselves in. When I arrived back home, my dad met me as I was pulling into the garage. He was beyond outrage and grief.

He said, "David, for all we knew, you were dead! That would be *two* sons dead! And Ziggy's parents are worried sick about him and have been calling here since yesterday. Where is that asshole, anyway?"

I shrugged, and said, "I don't *know* where he is."

My dad walked past me, out of the garage, and yelled, "Ziggy, your parents have been looking everywhere for you!"

I was praying that Ziggy wouldn't come out, but he immediately popped his head out of the bushes where he'd been hiding and said, "Uh... Hi, Mister Wambuh."

My dad looked at Ziggy, and said, "I suggest you go inside right now and call your parents. They think you and David may have been killed down there because no one has heard from either of you for the last two days. They're worried out of their minds."

As soon as Ziggy went inside the house to make his call, my dad turned to me and said, "Well, David, this is the worst thing that anyone has ever done to us. You have two choices. You can go to rehab first thing in the morning, or you can get out of my house. And mark my words, if you don't go to rehab, the way you're going you and your pal will both wind up on skid row before you know it."

I looked at my dad and said, "I can't go to rehab, Dad. I'd rather go to skid row."

He said, "Okay, come on, I'll help you pack." And then he stuck his head in the house where Ziggy was on the phone, and yelled, "Ziggy, come on, help us pack up David's stuff."

Ziggy obeyed, and we packed my car with the few belongings I had left. When we were finished, I motioned for Ziggy to get in, and we drove off into the night with no idea where we were going. Dumb and Dumber.

———

My brother's favorite restaurant had been the Panda Inn, a Chinese restaurant in Pasadena that our family had frequented for many years. We went there almost every Sunday night on our way home from the desert. My parents reserved the restaurant for Mark's memorial, and all of his friends came. I was surprised how many friends he actually had, definitely more than I had. Everyone ate and drank and told me what an incredible person Mark was. I had been so self-centered my entire life, I realized that I knew nothing about him, and had no idea how many true friends he had made in his twenty-one years on this earth.

The father of the boy who was killed with Mark asked me how I was doing, and I told him that my parents thought I should go to a rehab, and that when I'd rejected the idea my dad kicked me out of the house. As always, I was very selective in the bits and pieces of the stories I told, in an effort to depict myself as an innocent victim. He took pity on me and invited me to stay at his home with his family until I had some kind of a plan. I quickly accepted the offer and moved in the following day, right into their deceased son's bedroom.

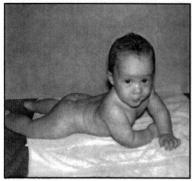

1965

Six-month-old David, upon his arrival into the Wambaugh Family. There was Mom, Dad, and a brother, Mark, who was two years and two days older.

Life in Walnut, California was simple. Dad was a cop at LAPD and my mom stayed at home with me and my brother.

We made newspaper hats and had fun playing with our pet snake.

I often carried this little case with my treasures in it, and when I got angry I would put some socks, underwear, and a snack in it, preparing to run away. Then I would sit at the bottom of our driveway, trying to decide what to do next.

Chapter Six

Right away, Ziggy and I got jobs digging ditches. We would drink every night, but woke up early each morning to dig ditches all day. It was a nightmare. Definitely a far cry from my life at The Vintage Club.

One night after work I went with a couple of buddies to a Mexican restaurant known for serving minors, but I had to work the next day, so after ten or twelve margaritas I decided to call it a night. It was pouring rain, and I could hardly see through my windshield. The roads were very slick, and when I was less than a mile from home, I rounded a corner too fast, hydroplaned, and lost control of my car. After going up and over a curb, I crashed through a tall wooden fence and down a steep embankment, right into someone's back yard. The mud was so deep at the bottom of the embankment, I tripped and fell face down, and was covered with mud from head to toe.

I got up, walked around to the front of the house and rang the doorbell. A man opened the door wide, took a step back and said, "What in the hell happened to you? Are you okay?"

I said, "Yes, sir, but I had an accident. My car went airborne and I somehow went through your fence, and my car's in your back yard."

"What? What do you mean?"

I slowly replied, "It was an accident, sir."

"Jesus Christ!" he said. "Let's go see what happened." Then he turned to his wife and said, "Honey, call the police and get them out here!" As I followed him through his house, he asked, "Have you been drinking?"

I said, "Oh, no sir. I'm in AA."

As he walked out the back door, he screamed, "Good God! Look what you've done to my property!"

I didn't say another word, and just waited in the rain for the cops to come. When they arrived, they started their standard investigating procedure, which included a field sobriety test that I failed miserably. As they were just about to arrest me, I told them what had happened to my brother, and that I had been very depressed because of it. I told them that if they would let me go this time, I would never do anything like that again. I told them who my father was. It's hard to believe, but they actually let me go. Another reprieve!

Ziggy and I drank and dug ditches all summer. Ziggy had somehow gotten himself accepted at a nearby university so he was going off to school, but at age twenty, I had no idea what I was going to do. He told me about the student loans and grants he'd gotten, and also told me that he wouldn't have to pay them back because he was exempt. He said someone had told him that, so it must be true. When I asked him who told him that, he said he couldn't remember but he was *positive* it was true.

I said, "Ziggy, why do you think you wouldn't have to pay back that money? It's not possible, bro."

He said, "Huh? It's free money, Wambuh. Come on, I'll get you accepted in there too."

And Ziggy did help me. I didn't receive any loans or grants, but I did get accepted into the University of La Verne. I couldn't believe it. We were actually students at a university! How he pulled that shit off, I'll never know.

We started school that fall, and my curriculum for the first semester was way beyond me, even though they were just the dummy entry-level classes. In less than a month into the semester, I sold my books for drinking money. I knew there was no chance I'd get anything above an F anyway, so I felt it was the smart thing to do.

It turned out that I didn't get F's, but close. Regardless, I was asked to withdraw from ULV, and the only thing I got out of that school was two STDs from a slut who would sleep with anyone willing to risk it.

Ziggy was eventually asked to leave the university too, but for different reasons. He stole a motorcycle belonging to Hurricane Hannah, the pioneer of Supercross racing. He snatched it right off the racetrack just a few miles from ULV. He got busted and was charged with a felony, but the charges were later dropped.

The coup de gras was when he attempted to sexually assault a girl in student housing. She happened to live across the courtyard from me, and one morning as I was on my way to my final class, I saw four sheriff deputies walking up the steps to her apartment. I knew in my gut that Ziggy had something to do with it so when I saw him at class, I said, "Ziggy, did you mess with those chicks across the way from my crib? The sheriffs were there this morning."

"Huh?" he said.

I said, "What did you do, Ziggy?"

"Wambuh, I swear to God, she wanted me!" he said.

"Is that why all the cops were up in her crib? Because she *wanted* you? Are you kidding me?"

"I'm telling you, bro, she wanted to milk my cow."

"What?"

He said," I'm serious, Wambuh, she wanted to suck my hog."

"It sounds like you got a whole farm in your pants, Ziggy," I said. "But I've seen you naked, bro, and what you got is more like an inchworm."

He said, "Wambuh, I'm just telling you she wanted it. Pete said he boned her in the ass the first day he met her."

I said, "So, did that mean she wants *you?*"

That confused him, and he said, "Huh? Whaddaya mean?"

"Forget it," I said. "Let's go get a drink, bro."

———

I didn't want to go back and live with the family whose son had died with Mark. Having to sleep in their dead boy's room was way too creepy. I just couldn't go back there.

Ziggy and I sat down together and weighed our options, of which we had none. We came to the conclusion that our only *real* option was to get welfare. We figured they would provide housing and food for us, but we just didn't know what part of town they would put us in. Anything was better than living in Ziggy's '65 Mustang which had no muffler, four bald tires, graffiti painted all over the body, and major dents everywhere.

Our first stop was the welfare office in Pasadena. After we filled out the necessary paperwork to get our hotel vouchers and food tickets, a buxom black woman approached the counter, and said, "I gotta ax you boys, you know where we're sendin' you?"

We both nodded our heads, and I replied, "Yes, ma'am. We're both from L.A.. We're good. We know what's up."

She looked us up and down, smirked, and said, "Good luck, boys."

She gave us directions to our new address, and chuckled as we turned to walk out the door. Our new home was on the corner of 5th and Wall Street in downtown L.A., right in the middle of skid row--and I mean *right* in the middle! There were cardboard-box homes all over the sidewalks, alleys and doorways. There were very few Caucasians, and none of them appeared to be under fifty.

On our first day there, we witnessed a brutal attack that took place right in front of us. Several young black guys ran past us on the sidewalk, knocked an old bum to the ground, and gave him a vicious beating that left him unconscious. They took everything out of his pockets and strolled away, as if it were just another day. We later learned that the welfare checks came on the first and third of each month, so those were the two days you didn't want to be running the streets. Everyone laid low on those two days.

The Panama Hotel was unreal. We gave our paperwork to the man behind the safety glass, and we were each assigned a room. The rooms were very small, and smelled like ammonia, urine and feces. The stench in the community bathroom down the hall was even more overwhelming. That first night, we decided to share a room for safety reasons. I woke up during the night to take a leak, and as I was approaching the bathroom, I saw what I thought was a huge, nearly naked black chick wearing a pink wig running toward me. It was a chick with a dick. He had huge fake tits and was wearing a teeny thong that only halfway covered his substantial piece. He blew right by me, and a couple of seconds later another tranny playfully trotted after him. They were apparently playing hide-and-seek. I didn't know what they were hiding or what they were seeking, and I really didn't want to know.

The next morning Ziggy and I walked over to the soup kitchen with our meal tickets, just in time for breakfast. We wanted to get a little nutrition before we started panhandling. We'd decided that after breakfast we'd go up to Broadway and panhandle from the people on their way to work. We were going to ask for spare change and cigarettes until we had enough money to drink for the rest of the day.

The food line was a block long, so I imagined they were serving some pretty good grub. As we stood in the doorway of the Pioneer Kitchen waiting to use our tickets, a mountain of a black man standing directly behind us bellowed, "Last night, I had a dream that all black men and white men were created equal." That's all he said, and the whole place erupted with laughter. Everyone roared--except for us. I wasn't able to make any sense of it.

The big dude stuck out a hand the size of a catcher's mitt and said, "My name's Shoefly. How you boys doin'?"

I cautiously replied, "Good, sir, how about you?"

"Lot better than you, lots better than you," he said. "For real! Whatchu boys doin' here? Ya'll don't belong down here."

"I'm not quite sure, sir," I said. "I'm really not *sure* what we're doing here."

Ziggy didn't say anything, and Shoefly smiled and just shook his head.

When I looked at my breakfast, I honestly couldn't figure out what the hell was on my plate. After making a sincere effort to stomach the food, I surrendered and gave the rest of the food tickets to Shoefly. He loved the Pioneer Kitchen food, especially neck bones, pig's feet, collard greens, chitlins, grits, and other unidentifiable slop. I told him that if he looked out for us and made sure no one tried to hurt us, I'd give him my hotel vouchers too. He liked that idea, and from that point on we had a tour guide, a bodyguard, and free entertainment. It was a great tradeoff, since I didn't plan to use that hotel voucher anyway.

Everything was going fine until Ziggy had to screw things up and damn near get us killed. We were getting comfortable and acclimating fairly well to our new surroundings, doing the same thing every day. After we panhandled all morning, we'd settle in on a street corner with Shoefly and drink bottle after bottle of rotgut wine, smoke menthol cigarettes, and swap lies.

One day while we were drinking with Shoefly on our corner, from out of the blue, Ziggy said, "Hey, Shoefly, you wanna know who David's dad is?"

"Who his daddy, Ziggy?"

Ziggy shot back, "His name's Joseph Wambuh. He wrote *The Onion Field* and all sorts of other things. He makes famous movies and everything!"

I assumed that the derelicts on skid row would have no idea who my dad was, until Shoefly turned, looked at Ziggy, and said, "Whatchu say, Ziggy?"

Ziggy blurted it out again, "David's dad is Joseph Wambuh, The famous writer!"

Shoefly turned to me, looked me straight in they eye, and slowly said, "Big D, is dat da trufe?"

I felt like strangling Ziggy. I turned to Shoefly and said, "Hell, no! Ziggy's crazy."

Ziggy looked at Shoefly and said, "Check his ID. He pro'ly still has an expired driver's license. You'll see, Shoefly. Check it out!"

Shoefly gently said to me, "Let me see your license, big 'D'. Dat can't be true. Is your daddy really Joseph Wambaugh?"

I looked at Ziggy who had a goofy expression on his face, and it made me realize just how crazy, stupid and retarded he really was. I finally answered, "Yeah Shoefly, he's my dad. It's true."

I could see his wheels spinning like mad, and I guessed that whatever he was thinking, it couldn't be good. For the rest of the day, Shoefly talked about all the different books my dad had written and the movies he'd made. He said he was a big fan, and that his brother, Wofeek, was even a bigger fan. He said that Wofeek had just done a stretch in prison, and all they do is read books, true crime being a favorite. The brother had been in prison for several years, so Shoefly was sure his brother must have read most of my dad's books by the time he got out.

Not much else happened that day, but Shoefly said that he wanted us to go with him to his brother's crib the next day so he could introduce us. I sort of went on high alert, because Shoefly seemed to have changed somehow; he was more sober and thoughtful. I didn't understand why the sense of urgency for us to meet his brother, but nonetheless, I had bad feelings about what might take place in the next day or so.

The next morning we piled into Ziggy's beater and we were off to Wofeek's house. We drove through parts of L.A. that looked very dangerous. Criminal element was on every street corner, and in the cars that cruised the streets. It all seemed to be either all ghetto or barrio. Not many whites at all.

As we neared Wofeek's dilapidated apartment building, Shoefly suddenly seemed distant. He had protected us during our days on skid row, and I'd grown to like him. He was our gentle giant who somehow reminded me of my brother Mark. But now I had the feeling that Shoefly was setting us up. We walked a couple of blocks to a dilapidated apartment building, up a rickety flight of stairs that looked like they could collapse at any time, and Shoefly gave a special knock on his brother's door.

A little black kid answered, and said, "Hi, Uncle Shoe! Momma, uncle Shoe's here!"

The boy's mother came out of the bedroom looking like she'd just taken a big old crack hit, and slurred, "What up, cuz? How you doin', Shoe? Feeky jist called, say he be back in a minute. These those boys Wofeek talkin' 'bout?"

Shoefly slowly offered up an answer, "Yes, ma'am. Dis Joseph Wambaugh's boy, and dis Ziggy."

She lit up, and said, "Mmm, mmm, mmm! Feeky be here in a minute. You boys want a brew?" We both nodded, and she gave us each a sixteen ounce Old English 800 malt liquor, and left the room.

Just moments after we cracked our brews, Shoefly's brother came slamming through the front door, ranting about his parole officer, saying he was a racist and was targeting him because he was black.

"I keel dat muthafucka if he violates me one mo time!" he snarled. "Jist 'cause I get a few dirty drug tests, dis dude gonna violate me again and put me back in prison? Hell no! He says I be smokin' crack. I jist *make* the shit, I don't *smoke* it! Man, fuck all those white muthafuckas!"

He surveyed the room, and acted as if he just noticed us for the first time. He turned to Shoefly, and asked, "Who Joseph Wambuh's kid?" He pronounced my name just like Ziggy did.

Shoefly turned, pointed at me, and said, "Dat's him, Feeky. Dat's Wambaugh's boy."

Wofeek zeroed in on me, and said, "So your daddy's Joseph Wambuh?"

"Yes, sir, my name's David. It's very nice to meet you." I was trying to look friendly, while wondering how we were going to get out of that dump in one piece.

He stuck out his hand, and said, "It's nice to meet you too," without paying any attention to Ziggy.

Shoefly interrupted his brother and said, "Feeky, Dave real cool, he real cool."

Wofeek looked at Shoefly and yelled, "Shut up, nigga! I know he cool, I know Dave cool. Me and Dave here, we gonna make some money, feel me nigga?"

Suddenly, the small black boy burst through the front door and said, "Daddy, Tavarius is gettin' beat by dat boy down da street!"

Wofeek yelled to his wife, "Shaniqua, go get dat little nigga up here 'fore I beat his black ass!"

She didn't waste a second and bolted right by us and out the door. We stood around the window and watched it all go down out on the street. As the mothers were trying to break up the boys' fight, they started going at it with each other, punching, scratching, pulling hair and screaming. I wouldn't have wanted to take on either of those chicks. One was the size of Queen Latifah, and the other one resembled Serena Williams.

Wofeek dismissed the squabbling, turned his attention back to me and slowly asked, "Does yo daddy like you?"

I answered politely, "Not really. Actually, not at all."

And then Ziggy blurted out, "Yes he *does!*"

Wofeek turned toward Ziggy, and asked, "So Ziggy, how much do David's daddy like him?"

"A lot," the dumb shit said.

I interrupted, and said to Wofeck, "Put it this way. If I were ever to get kidnapped, my old man wouldn't pay a dime for my ass."

"Yes he would, Wambuh!" Ziggy said. "You just think that, but he would." And then Ziggy looked over to Wofeek, and said, "Mister Wambuh's real rich. David's a total fuckup but his dad still loves him anyway."

Wofeek looked over at me with a big evil smile. I asked Wofeek if I could please have another beer, and he motioned for Shoefly to get me one. Shoefly reappeared with two beers, one for me, and one for Ziggy. I began thinking that this could be one of my very last drinks. Wofeek got off the couch and asked Shoefly to step outside for a minute. It was the only exit, so they didn't have to worry about us bailing.

As soon as they were outside, I said to Ziggy, "Dude, what the fuck is wrong with you? We are fucked, you idiot! Have you *not* figured out that this crazy asshole wants to kidnap us and try to get bank from my old man?"

"Huh?" he said.

I said, "You jackass! In the first place, I guarantee you my dad won't put up a dime for us, and in the second place..."

I stopped in mid-sentence, realizing that we were in *very* serious trouble. We were totally out of our league with this guy. That man, Wofeek, didn't have an ounce of humanity in his eyes. All kinds of shit was racing through my mind. I wondered what my parents would do if this crazy, violent criminal asked them for ransom money. Would they pay it? I wouldn't if I were them.

And I did feel bad for Ziggy too, because I was actually the one who got us to skid row in the first place. Ziggy was just dumb enough or loyal enough to join me on my most recent trip to hell. I felt sorry for him because he was basically a good guy, just dumb and misguided, but he had a big heart.

After considering our options, I whispered to Ziggy, "We're in serious trouble, bro. This isn't like all the other times we've been in trouble. This is *much* different. This isn't San Marino, Ziggy."

As I was about to continue, Shoefly and Wofeek reappeared and Shoefly was the first to speak. He said softly, "Awright, fellas, here's da deal. We gonna make some good, easy money from Dave's daddy. Dave gonna call and say he been kidnapped, an' he gonna axe for a million from his daddy. And den when we get the money, we split it fiddy-fiddy. We straight?"

In an upbeat voice, I said, "Okay, let's do it! It's a great idea. I'm down. Are you down, Ziggy?"

Ziggy said, "Sure Wambuh. Cool, let's go!"

Shoefly came back to his old self, and Wofeek even broke a smile. As we were getting ready to formulate a master plan, one of Wofeek's many children busted through the door and screamed, "Daddy, momma's getting her ass beat by dat woman down da street. She need help!"

Wofeek got a frustrated look on his face, and said, "Nah, nah, nah, dat dumb-ass ho. I keel dat bitch yet! Shoe, you chill wit da fellas. I be right back."

"Sure, Feeky," Shoe said.

Wofeek got up and walked out the door. As soon as that door closed, I said to Shoefly, "Please, Shoe, please listen to me. My dad isn't going to pay you guys a dime, and he'll have every cop in the LAPD looking for you if this goes down. You guys will have a BOLO up your ass, Shoefly. If you don't know what a BOLO is, it means, *Be On the Lookout For.* You will go to prison forever. The three of *us* are just alcoholics. Your brother's a criminal, but you're a kind man. Please Shoe, do the right thing. Let us go!"

As I was speaking to him, his shoulders began to sag and he was looking directly at the floor. I thought it was a sign that he was softening up. I gave a slight nudge to Ziggy, indicating for him to get up and walk toward the door.

He did, and when I got up to follow him, Shoefly stood up, pulled up his shirt, revealing his fat belly and a pistol, and said, "You gotta sit down now. You can't leave like dat. Feeky'll keel me. Why you trippin' anyway? You guys gonna be rich too. Feeky say so."

When we sat back down, I said with more conviction, "Shoefly, we ain't gettin' nothin'! You're gonna go to prison, and your brother will hurt or kill us! You love skid row. Don't lose your freedom over this dumb shit."

I paused and hoped he would come to his senses but I could see that my plan wasn't going to work, so I said, "Oh well, fuck it! You guys are gonna do what you're gonna do! But, may I please have another brew? All this bullshit has given me a headache."

A small grin came over his face, and he said, "That's a good idea. A brew sounds good to me too."

When he rose from the couch and rounded the corner into the kitchen, Ziggy and I looked at each other. I gave him a thumb up and we hit the door on the fly. We ran down the stairs and sprinted the two blocks to his car. We hauled ass back to skid row, dipped into a seedy skid row bar, found a phone booth, and called my dad for help.

———

I explained just enough for my dad to tell me, "Don't move from there, David. You guys stay right there in the phone booth. Stay exactly where you are. Someone will be there in a few minutes!"

I immediately disobeyed him by walking out of the phone booth and straight to the bar to order a couple of vodka-cranberries, but before we even had time to get the bartender's attention, four detectives came barging through the front door and converged on us. I recognized Dick Kalk, who had been my dad's old detective partner. He looked me up and down, asked if I was okay, and then escorted both of us out to the unmarked police car.

They saw Ziggy off, and drove me to Union Station where they bought me a one-way train ticket to San Diego after advising me to never come back to this part of town for any reason. I was told that my parents would be picking me up at the Solana Beach Station, and I was really nervous because it had been over a year since they'd last seen me. I looked like a skid row bum, and in actuality, I *was*!

When I got off the train, I was relieved to see that only my mom was there to meet me. When she saw me it was apparent that she was disgusted, sad, and exasperated. She said that my dad was too upset to come and pick me up, and I didn't blame him. That's all my mom said the whole way home, which made me real nervous about seeing my dad. I would've bet anything, that in his worst nightmares, he would've never guessed that someday he'd have to be calling his detective friends to pull his loser kid out of a kidnapping plot on skid row.

I'm sure my parents lived with the constant fear that they might someday receive the same call about me as they'd received about my brother. After Mark was killed, my dad told me about the recurring nightmare he would have for years to come. He said he'd often awaken at night in a cold sweat after dreaming that my brother was standing on a train track, facing away from a freight train that was rapidly approaching him. My dad would be screaming and yelling at the top of his lungs and running desperately toward Mark, praying that he might turn in time to see the train bearing down on him, but Mark never heard him. In the dream, Mark would always be demolished by the train. I think a part of my dad died along with my brother.

———

My parents had recently bought a beautiful condo overlooking the ocean in Solana Beach, near San Diego. As I walked through the front door, my dad was sitting in the living room reading the newspaper.

He looked up, and with no expression, said, "Hello, David. I'm going to make you the same offer you refused the last time, and give you the same choices I gave you the last time. You're very sick, Dave, and you need help. Either you go into treatment tomorrow, or you can live on the street again. What do you think? Are you willing to go?"

I'm confident my parents were sure that I was a sociopath, and I don't know if I was or not, but I do know that I behaved like one. I only cared about myself and about escaping. I had been chasing the drink from the time I was five years old, but I was never able to find what I was looking for. I always wanted so desperately to be someone else, but I didn't know who. All I know is that I despised the guy in the mirror.

I looked my Dad in the eyes, and said, "I can't go to rehab, Dad. I'm sorry, but I can't."

He said, "Dave, just go into treatment and complete the program, and then you can stay at home with us afterward."

So, all I had to do for another chance at a great life was to complete a treatment program. I'd be able to live in this beautiful home right on the ocean and start all over. Just go into treatment and see it through.

As I sat and contemplated the offer, all I could think about was getting a drink. I couldn't focus on anything else. My desire to drink was stronger than my desire to become a decent human being, and I said, "Dad, I ain't goin' to rehab. I'm sorry."

He got up, and as he walked out of the room, all he said was, "Good luck, Dave."

I turned to my mom and asked her if she would give me a ride back to the train station. She had tears in her eyes, and said, "David, please, are you sure you won't at least try? Can't you do it for me? You know your dad and I would do anything for you if you could just get it together. Please, don't pass up this chance."

I wanted to be a good son, and I wanted to do the right thing for my parents, but I just didn't have it in me. My spirit was bankrupt, and living in the sunlight just wasn't in the cards. It was only darkness for me.

I said, "Mom, I'm not going to rehab. I'll be fine. May I please just have a ride back to the train station?"

She turned and walked toward the garage without saying another word. I was relieved, because that meant I was only about twenty minutes away from a drink. When I got off the train, back in L.A., my trusty sidekick was waiting for me. Ziggy never ceased to amaze me, because within hours of *his* departure from skid row, he'd gotten himself a sweet living situation in an incredible guest house belonging to the parents of one of our old high school friends.

That night we drank most of the booze from the guesthouse, and then decided to go out to a bar and check out the Bettys. We thought maybe we could even hook up with a couple of barflies if they'd had enough to drink. Nearly broke as always, we went to a local watering hole in hopes of finding someone we knew who might sponsor us. We walked in, waved at a few people we recognized, and bellied up to the bar. We had enough money to buy a couple of rounds, so we had a good start. After two drinks each, we became creative. When people got up to dance, we'd go to their tables, swill their drinks, and walk away. After repeating this several times we went back up to the bar because Ziggy said there were a couple of chicks sitting there who had been ogling him. He always thought that.

As we were standing at the bar ready to make a move on the girls, I stepped on something hard down on the floor. When I lifted my foot, I saw that it was it set of car keys. I picked them up, waved them in front of Ziggy's face, and stuffed them in my pocket. We agreed that we would steal the car, but we didn't know how we were going to match the car with the keys. Suddenly, Ziggy came up with another one of his brilliant ideas. He said we should walk the parking lot, pushing the button on the car alarm transponder until we found the match.

After a short time, we found the match. The thing was a street legal, monster truck. The goddamn thing looked like *The Grave Digger*.

We flipped a coin to see who was going to actually drive the beast, and I lost. Like an idiot, I drove the truck over to Ziggy's new place and covered it with a tarp that we found in our friend's garage.

The next day when I woke up, I had a fuzzy recollection of what had happened the night before, but I was praying it was only a nightmare. Unfortunately, my nightmare became a reality when I walked outside and saw the monster truck.

I looked at Ziggy, and said, "What in the hell am I gonna do now? Do you think I could just take this thing back to where we found it?"

"Huh?" he said.

"Never mind, I gotta get the hell outta here before they have an All Points Bulletin out for my ass."

Ziggy giggled, and said, "Damn, Wambuh, you're crazy!"

I crawled into the driver's seat and headed for Tijuana, leaving Ziggy behind. I figured I could sell it down there for several hundred bucks, at least, and drink myself into oblivion for a few days. I didn't think I'd need a pink slip in order to dump that ride on some Southsider, looking to be the most high profile Mexican in T.J.

I stole a bottle of booze from my buddy's house when I was on the way out the door, so by the time I got to San Diego I was well over the limit. I decided to stop by a friend's apartment while I was passing through, a guy

I'd met about a year before when I lived on the streets of San Diego for a couple of months. He had section-eight housing and SSI, so he still had a roof over his head and enough disability to keep him in cheap vodka and generic cigs indefinitely.

After he greeted me, I said, "Dude, I stole this truck, and now I don't know what the hell to do with it!"

I led him back outside to show him the truck, and when he saw it he raised his eyebrows real high and said, "Yeah, right. You didn't steal this truck. Your parents hooked you up, huh? You musta finally got your shit together. This truck is fuckin' dope!"

I couldn't drill it into his head that I really had stolen it, so I said, "Yeah, my parents really hooked me up, but not with this truck. Later, bro." I got in the monster truck and drove away.

I was terrified, and didn't know what the hell to do, so I started thinking that the rehab my dad talked about didn't sound so bad anymore. I knew that if I got caught driving this thing, which inevitably I would, I was looking at a lot of jail time. I decided, Screw it. I'm not driving this monster another foot, so I got out right then and abandoned the truck in the Birdrock area of La Jolla.

I walked and took a bus all the way back to my friend's apartment, and again told him what I'd done. Eventually, when he finally believed my story was true, he drove me back to the truck and pilfered everything not bolted down, including the crucifix hanging from the rearview mirror. For that, I told him, he must buy me a bottle. We sat in his dingy apartment all night drinking whiskey, smoking generic cigs, and brainstorming about what I should do next.

We came to the conclusion that my best bet would be to call my parents and see if the option of rehab was still open. When I called them, they said yes, the offer was still good, and this time I jumped on it! I figured that now if I got busted for stealing the vehicle, I could plead insanity and try to convince the court to allow me to stay in rehab for as long as they wanted, or even a mental hospital for that matter. I was willing to do anything--except jail time.

When I told my dad I was going to be on my way to rehab as soon as I hung up the phone, he asked, "So, Dave, why the sudden change of heart?

Why're you so willing to get treatment now? Don't get me wrong, I think it's great, but I'm just really curious."

I said, "Honestly Dad, it's because I really want to quit drinking." Of course, that was the last thing I wanted to do, but I was going to *have* to quit drinking, at least until the dust settled.

I arrived at Centinela Hospital in Inglewood, which is located in South Central L.A., one of the most dangerous parts of Los Angeles. It was an all black neighborhood, and it was an all black hardcore rehab. I was one of only two white people out of thirty-plus patients. It was my first experience at treatment, and it was of the educational variety. We had lots of documentary films, movies, drug and alcohol classes, speakers who came to talk about various alcohol and drug related topics, and we had lots of homework.

In group therapy, everyone had to check in and say how they were feeling that day: mad, sad, glad, hurt or afraid. How *dumb*, I thought. Who gives a shit about that stuff? I didn't know what I felt or *how* I felt, so when asked, I just said I was glad. Glad that I was in rehab and not in jail. I went through the motions and talked a very good game for a novice, but the bottom line was, I couldn't wait to leave.

I didn't learn a thing about addiction or anything else for that matter, because all I could think about was the truck that I'd stolen. It never left my mind, and I couldn't imagine what prison would be like. I wanted to tell someone about my crime but I didn't know who I could trust. The only other white person in treatment was a middle-aged drunk named Ernie, who was a boat mechanic from San Pedro. He seemed trustworthy enough, so one night after an AA meeting I asked Ernie if I could talk to him about some trouble I was in, and maybe he could give me some advice.

When we were alone, I whispered, "Ernie, I think I'm in some deep shit. I don't know if you've ever been in trouble with the law, or if you would even know about this kind of shit, but I need some advice, man."

"Sure, what's up?" he said.

I sighed, and began, "Well not too long ago I got fully sauced at the local meat market and... Oh fuck it, Ernie, I stole a car, no actually a truck. A *big* truck. A monster truck!"

"Dude, I *love* monster trucks," he said.

"Yeah, that's cool, but what the fuck am I gonna do?"

"Is this your first case?"

"What do you mean?" I said.

Mildly frustrated, he said, "Is this your first felony case? Have you ever done time?"

I said, "Jail, but not prison."

Then Ernie said, "Well, let's see, if this is your first case, you'll get a pretty good deal. I say eighteen, two, or three."

What an incredible relief it was to know that the worst-case scenario would be ninety days in county jail. Three months. I could do that. It's a long-ass time, but I'd just have to man up and handle it.

I said to Ernie, "Thank God! I really hope I don't have to do any time at all, but if I had to, I could do ninety days. I'd have no choice, right?"

He laughed, and said, "Dude, not ninety days. Three *years*. You'll either be sentenced to eighteen months, two years, or three years in prison, but because it's your first term, you'll probably get the eighteen months. Just thank God you didn't take it across county or state lines or anything, because then you'd *really* be screwed."

"What do you mean *county lines*?" I said.

He was full of shit, but I didn't know it then, when he said to me, "Well, it's a federal crime if you steal a car and take it across county lines. You didn't know that? I mean, I don't know why it's a federal offense, I just know it is. It brings more time, but you'd go to federal which is much nicer than state."

"State what?"

"State prison, dude."

I gulped, and said, "Do you think I should turn myself in?"

He instantly replied, "I would, and the sooner the better."

I took a deep breath and said, "Shit! I guess I better call my dad."

Ernie said, "Good luck with that. What's that shit they say here? *'One day at a time, Let go, Let God. Easy does it.'* All that good shit."

I said, "Yeah, Ernie, all that good shit!"

My mom answered the phone on the second ring, and said, "Hi, Dave, how are you, honey?"

"Good," I lied. "Is Dad home?"

"Sure, what's up? Is anything wrong?"

"I just need to talk to Dad." He picked up the phone, and I started, "Hi, Dad. I think I'm in some trouble."

"What is it this time, David? And I want the all the details."

He never said a word during my whole story, which made me want to die. When I finally finished, he said, "Jesus, David!" He yelled to my mom, "Dee, get on the phone."

When she was on, he told her, "David stole a truck from a bar in Pasadena." Then, back to me, he said, "David, I'm afraid I can't help you on this one."

I didn't believe him. I knew he would try. I was called out of group later that afternoon and was directed to administration. There was an urgent message for me to call my dad.

When he answered, he said, "You need to call a detective at the Pasadena Police Department who is in charge of the auto theft detail. He's waiting for your call. Don't lie to this man. Absolutely no bullshit, because you're in serious trouble."

I called the number my dad had given me, but I learned that the detective was already on his way to Centinela Hospital to see me. I honestly thought about bolting, but I had no money, no resources, nowhere to go. I was stuck.

The guy looked like a detective. He introduced himself and we were led to a consultation room. In a detective voice, he said, "So what's up?"

I said, "Well, sir, it's a long story, but basically, I stole a truck when I was drunk, and I'm really sorry."

He didn't arrest me, but I had to appear in court upon the successful completion of rehab. And the charges for grand theft auto were never filed! However, my parents did pay the owner for damages. I learned early on that rehab is a fabulous place to go if you want to avoid consequences. Cheat on your wife, go to rehab. Steal a car, go to rehab. Sell crack, go to rehab. Don't pay your taxes, go to rehab. It worked for me!

Chapter Seven

After I got out of rehab, I moved to San Diego into a county-funded recovery home, primarily for alcoholics and addicts who are homeless. It's like the last house on the block, so to speak. However, I actually thrived there. It was a shock to everyone. I really gave my parents some hope again, and I even had a glimmer of hope myself. I stayed for ninety days, and only drank a handful of times with some of the other drunks who existed there.

It was November, 1985, and after my successful completion of three full months, my parents permitted me to live in their beautiful beach condo by myself. I was doing so well, they also allowed me to use one of their cars so I could get to AA meetings and look for a job. I hadn't been convicted of a felony at that point, and I had a high school diploma, so I decided that I'd become a cop. Surprise, surprise!

After the orientation to become a San Diego County Sheriff's deputy, I thought I'd found my calling. I honestly felt in my heart that I'd finally found something I wanted to do, and was confident that I could do it. I was twenty-one years old then, and I could envision a successful career with the Sheriff's Department. I would be a celebrity to other cops because of my dad. I'd probably get to meet all the hot cop-chicks. I was so anxious for the first day of testing to start that I didn't get any sleep the night before.

On that first day, we did some physical and written testing, and I don't know how I did on the written part, but I kicked ass on the obstacle course. I came in second out of about sixty people. I felt I was better qualified to be a cop than most of the wimps who were also trying to qualify. I'd even given up the fantasy that I'd someday be rich and famous. It was going to be okay just being a cop.

When I returned home after my first day of testing, I had a message from a couple of my old San Marino buddies saying they were coming to San Diego, and were going out on the town to look for chicks. I called them back just to see what they were up to, and agreed to meet up with them. I said I'd have a few brews with them but that was all, because I had more testing to do at seven a.m. the next morning.

It didn't work out as planned. I stayed until last call and walked out of the bar totally obliterated. I said goodbye to my friends, poured myself into my car and as I pulled out into traffic, a San Diego police cruiser fell in behind me, seeming to have appeared out of nowhere. I saw my law enforcement career go down the tubes in seconds flat. That dream was over. I couldn't believe it.

He lit me up right away, and I had to make a split-second decision of whether I should pull over or haul ass. I was screwed either way, so I tried to outrun him. It was fruitless because I was driving a little four-cylinder Toyota Corolla station wagon and the cop was driving a Crown Vic with a high performance V-8 and special suspension. I shot up and down a few alleys trying to lose him, but he was right on my ass so I decided to pull over and surrender.

It was like slow motion as the rachets of the handcuffs tightened on my wrists, one slow ratchet at a time. I saw my dream, the only realistic dream I'd ever had, slip right through my fingers. As we drove away from the scene of my arrest, I looked out the windows on both sides and saw bystanders straining to see the dirt-bag in the back of the cop car who is surely on his way to jail.

I didn't say a word to the cop. I just bowed my head and began to cry. I wasn't crying tears of sadness, I was crying tears of loathing, hot tears of self-loathing. I wanted to hurt myself. I wanted to kill myself. These were the kind of tears I had shed countless times throughout my life. The only other thing going through my mind, other than how much I despised myself, were the questions I always wound up asking myself. The recurring questions were, what the fuck did I do? How could I have done this again to my parents? I was almost close to making them proud. What is wrong with me? Dear God, what in the fuck is wrong with me? And the answer to these ever-present questions was always the same. I didn't know. I simply didn't know.

My parents kicked me out of their condo, confiscated the car, and dropped me back off at the home for derelicts. I always blamed my parents for everything wrong in my life, and of course I was hateful toward them for making me go back to that shit hole. I'd been doing so well up until then that I thought I should have another chance to stay in their house and look for a job. Wrong. So it was back to the house of the drunks and bums, but this time it was only for a few days before I bailed. I caught a ride from one of the guys who'd just relapsed and was getting kicked out. I bought the gas and a couple of bottles of booze with the last of my money and we headed to L.A.

I guess Ziggy was on to bigger and better things because I couldn't track him down, so that meant I had to be homeless on my own this time. It really sucked, being homeless without Ziggy. I slept in bushes, on park benches, under bridges, in stairwells, alleys, and any other spot that would give me shelter. Sometimes I'd buy bottle after bottle and ride city buses until the drivers would ask me to get off. I panhandled every day for drinking money, and I was steadily failing, mentally and physically.

I drank myself into oblivion every single day. Each morning I would wait outside one particular liquor store until it opened at 6 a.m. I'd have the shakes by then, so when I'd give the man the bills for booze, he knew to keep the change because I had tremors so bad, it would've been impossible for me to grasp the coins.

I had a duffle bag full of my worldly goods consisting of filthy clothes that smelled of a drunk, and that was all. My life consisted of nothing. At that point I was accepting the reality that I'd probably die on the street. I was hoping it wasn't going to take too long and didn't think it would, seeing as how I drank a half-gallon of vodka every day.

My mental illness took on a life of its own. I didn't even *need* alcohol or drugs to fuel the rage inside me. My madness was so intense that I withdrew into a world of delusion. I didn't know the truth about anything any longer. I headed south to Oceanside, but I can't remember why.

Nana, my dad's mother, died after a long bout with cancer, and my parents somehow got a message to me telling me that she'd died. Surprisingly enough, they said I could come back home if I wanted to, that they were willing to give me another chance. I couldn't imagine why they would offer, but they did. I was really tired of living in the bushes at the Oceanside transit station, waking up every morning to a gardener spitting dirt and leaves all over me with his leaf blower.

So, I went back out to the desert and moved in with my grandfather, Pappap. After Nana died, my parents bought a nice condo for him, not far from theirs so he could be near them. His place had two bedrooms, so it was a perfect setup for him and me. It wasn't The Vintage Club, but it was really nice. I started working out every day, eating well, going to AA meetings, staying sober, and spending time with Pappap. Like always though, it was short-lived.

Things were going well until another spring break came around. My old drinking buddies flocked to Palm Springs once again and were staying in a popular hotel that was packed with coeds. That time I didn't even *try* fooling myself that I'd stay sober if I hooked up with the boys. I hadn't seen Ziggy in a long time, and I'd never been sober around him in the past, so I didn't think it would be any different this time. The night they arrived I told Pappap I was turning in early, went to my room, out the sliding glass door, and off to see the clan.

Also staying in the hotel, was the USC football team. Even the punter was much bigger than anyone on our crew, but you'd be surprised what six or eight shots of 151 could do to a guy. We had plenty of liquid courage, so much so that we challenged them to a game of tackle football.

We didn't get a chance to find out who'd be the victors because on the first snap, it was a completed pass to me, and that was the end of the game. The guy who tackled me drove me into the ground, shoulder first. The sound was like a tree branch snapping. My head was spinning, I threw up all over the place, and everything went fuzzy. My shoulder was demolished. My friends put me into Ziggy's car and he rushed me to the ER at a nearby hospital, and on the way there he blew through every red light and stop sign along the way. He thought that by waving a red T-shirt out the window, it was legal for him to act like he was an ambulance driver.

After sitting in the emergency room for hours, the attending physician finally told me that I had a severe shoulder separation and would need surgery. I was searching for a story I could tell my parents about this one, but the truth was, no matter what I could've said, it wouldn't have mattered.

Just as I thought, my parents weren't surprised when I told them what had happened. I explained that the doctor said I needed to have surgery immediately, so they did some research and got the name and phone number of an orthopedic surgeon that I was to call for an appointment. After my surgery, I was laid up for weeks with a two-inch screw through my AC joint. I became really depressed from having nothing to do but pop pain pills and watch MTV.

A short time later, one of my friends who'd been at the spring break fiasco, called and invited me to his place in San Francisco. I went, and within six hours after the tires touched the tarmac I was involved in a car accident that left me with two broken fingers on my only good hand, and deep scrapes and bruises all over my face and body.

What happened was, my friend's roommate and I were rushing to the liquor store before closing time, since we thought we hadn't had enough to drink yet. We were hauling ass to beat the clock, but we didn't make it because the guy missed a turn and drove directly into a concrete post. We were in his VW Bug, and when we collided with the piling I hit the windshield. It shattered into shards, leaving me with tiny cuts all over my face, and two black eyes.

I didn't get out of the emergency room until late the next morning, and when I got back to my friend's apartment, I knew by his expression that I didn't look so good. I went to the bathroom to survey the damage and when I saw myself in the mirror I was hardly recognizable. I figured I'd be screwed when I got home.

I flew home the following day and my mom was there to pick me up at the Palm Springs Airport. I'd called her that morning before I boarded the plane to tell her that I'd been in a minor traffic accident with my friend and got a little scraped up. When the plane landed, I even needed help with my little carry-on bag. I had no use of either hand, so the porter followed me out to my mom's car with my bag. Both of my arms were in slings and my face looked like raw hamburger. The lacerations and bruises all over my body were even more painful than the fractured fingers.

When my mom saw me she slowly shook her head with no expression. That's another time I remember feeling bad for her. I knew she didn't even want to look at me, but I had no choice other than to ask her to give the porter a tip since I couldn't reach into my pocket.

We drove away in silence and after a very long thirty minutes my mom finally asked, "So what are you going to do now, Dave?"

I said, "I don't know, Mom. I really don't know."

She carried my bag into Pappap's house, set it down, and walked out the door. She said no more about it and neither did my dad. I had rendered them speechless once again. It was a recurring theme, and I didn't know how to stop it. I was on a merry-go-round of craziness and I couldn't get off.

Many years earlier, Pappap had broken his hip and needed his wheelchair or his electric scooter, so there we were, one with no hands and one with no legs, but somehow we managed together. Except that after I got my cast off, I started drinking again with a friend I'd worked with at TGI Friday's. He'd bring over a couple of twelve packs every day, and we'd down them in the hot sun to intensify the effect.

My parents didn't come by too often during that time, as I'm sure they thought I wouldn't be drinking because I was laid up. They were wrong. I wasn't drinking as much as usual, but I didn't really need to since I'd pop ten or twelve Vicodin and nod off for most of the day, pain free.

Eventually, my mom walked in one day and caught me drinking, so they gave me another ultimatum. It was either go to Betty Ford's rehab or get out of Pappap's house. I wasn't willing to go to treatment, so I left the desert and went back to L.A. where I couch-surfed with friends for a few months. Soon I became unwelcome everywhere. My old pals got tired of me eating their food, drinking their booze, hitting on their girlfriends, and generally being a drunken pig. I was a daily blackout drinker and spun out on opiates, with my arm in a sling, no money in my pockets, and not a pot to piss in.

I once told my dad that I needed to drink to the point where a switch would just turn off and I would be in happy oblivion. I never knew how many drinks it would take to do it, but I always found it. He told me that it was described just like that in Tennessee Williams' *Sweet Bird of Youth*. Of course, I wouldn't know about that. It had always been all about me.

After a few months of couch surfing, I called my mom and said I was totally motivated to get sober this time. My motivation came when the friend I had been staying with informed me that I was no longer welcome at his house, so I sold my mom another bill of goods. She desperately wanted my words to be true, but they never were.

Arrangements were made for another rehab program, this one at The McDonald Center in La Jolla. My mom drove me there and left with some renewed hope that this time it would do some good. I successfully completed the twenty-eight day program, and when I left, she helped me settle into a little studio apartment at Windansea Beach in La Jolla, a world famous surfing spot.

Unfortunately, I only made it a few days or so out of rehab before I drank again. Soon after my mom left, I hooked up with my roommate from rehab and we started drinking. We'd been planning to work our AA steps together, but instead, we skipped the steps and went straight to a bar.

As crazy as it sounds, I had myself fooled into believing I could drink just one time, one night. I believed that because I had the education about alcoholism and addiction, there was no possible way I could slip back into the rapacious creditor's iron grip. I honestly believed that I could drink for just one night with impunity. That belief was in my heart and soul, until the second I was about to take that first slug of my screwdriver. In that split second when the powerful scent of 100 proof Vodka was filling my nostrils, a fleeting glimpse of truth came flooding through my mind, and in that split second I instinctively knew I was fucked if I brought that glass filled with poison, up to my lips. I knew inherently that my demise, my parents love, and my hope for a decent life would be only another lost dream if I swallowed the venom. I wanted so desperately to set the glass down and walk away, run away, but I found a mental blank spot that I only came upon when I was about to throw my chances of decency away. I closed my eyes, took three deep gulps, and was on my way to oblivion. From that moment, I stayed in oblivion until I was later confronted by my parents. My roommate headed to northern California the next day but I continued boozing for a few more days after he left.

When that party was over, I got sober for a couple of weeks because I had to get a job in order to pay the rent on my little crib. I found a job making sandwiches in a liquor store deli for a hairy Iranian guy, but quit when my cash settlement came through from the San Francisco car accident. When I received my settlement check, I thanked the Iranian for the deli job, bought a fifth of Jack Daniels and bounced.

After I got that cash I kicked back, surfed every day, and would drink until I blacked out. Eventually I was arrested on a warrant for not completing the court ordered program for one of my DUIs, and had to go to jail, but I wasn't locked up for long. After I was released from custody I had to report to the sheriff's department every weekend for three months to wash their patrol cars.

———

My drinking was again escalating to the point where I needed booze first thing in the morning or I would be sick. During that time I don't think I drank more or less, I just more or less *drank* when I could because I had DT's, and would shake uncontrollably until I had some booze in me. One night I overdosed on alcohol and Valium, and was rushed to the emergency room at Hillside Hospital. When I came to, I was told that my blood alcohol reading was so high they were amazed I wasn't comatose or dead. Upon my release from the ER, I was transferred into their drug and alcohol treatment program, and after thirty days I felt great physically and emotionally. I had hope again, and I think my mom had some hope too, but my dad knew better.

I had pissed away my small settlement and didn't have much to go back to, so my mom said she'd help me get started again. She was seeing a positive change, so she informed me that I had a trust fund that had been set up years earlier. It was meant to help make my life a little easier when I got older, however she felt that if there was ever an appropriate time for it to help me, this would be it. Knowing I'd need financial help until I could pull myself together, they gave me access to my trust fund in 1988, when I was twenty-three. Bad mistake.

Things were great for a while. I stayed sober for 236 days, the longest period of sobriety I'd had since I was a little kid. It was by far the happiest time in my life. I was very close with my parents, saw them often, and they seemed to be pleased with the new me. I looked good, and felt great physically, but I didn't feel good in my soul. Maybe I looked like a million bucks but I felt like monopoly money. I couldn't get a good job because I didn't have any job experience or education. I used my trust fund money to pretend like I had it going on, but I knew it was only a matter of time before my house of cards would collapse.

I went to AA meetings every day, and tried to work the program, but it was useless. I couldn't connect with the people in the AA meetings, and I really didn't like the fact that they tried to control me, especially some old shot-out reformed drunk. I could never understand the concept of following people who were once as scummy as I was. My common sense told me that if I really wanted to get well, wouldn't it be better if I followed a man who's never cheated on his wife, always paid his taxes, didn't miss his kids dance recitals? But what did I know?

So, once again, I believed that I didn't fit in anywhere, and once again, my need to find relief from my emotional pain was growing stronger by the day. In my whole life, I'd never felt like I fit in anywhere. I even felt alone when I was in a room full of family and supposed friends.

D-day finally came when I received a call from a lady who was the editor of a local publication, *La Jolla Magazine,* whom I'd met a couple of times at a coffee shop frequented by many of the locals. She asked if I was single, and if so, would I like to participate in the "Bid For Bachelors" charity event benefiting the Muscular Dystrophy Association. The men who were participating in the event were supposedly some of the most eligible bachelors in San Diego. I agreed to do it, although I didn't know how I would fit in, since I surely wasn't one of them.

On the day of the event I was really nervous. When it was my turn to walk down the catwalk, I was so stressed I thought I was going to faint. By the time I got to the end of the runway, Ted Henderson, the ex-Oakland Raider who was the emcee, said, "This is the son of author, Joseph Wambaugh. Joe's a good friend of mine, and Dave here, lives in La Jolla, but I'm not quite clear on what he does for a living."

Everyone used to say they were good friends of my dad, but half of them he'd never even met. What an asshole! I was totally humiliated. He just threw me straight under the bus. The other bachelors were local celebrities and sports figures, and then there was me. I was never more embarrassed for myself in my entire life.

The poor woman who had the misfortune of bidding on me paid $850 for the date, which was the second to lowest bid, the lowest going for a bald little guy who looked like Beetlejuice. She was a nurse, and was engaged to a dentist. She said she wanted to have a little innocent fun before getting married, so this way she was able to make a tax-deductable donation and buy some fun at the same time.

We never left the limo during the entire evening, and we wound up getting sloppy drunk together. If her fiancé knew just how much fun she'd bought at that auction, I doubt if a marriage would be in their future. I know my girlfriend wasn't happy when she walked into my apartment later that night and caught the nurse and me swapping spit on my futon.

My parents didn't know for sure that I'd gone off the deep end yet, but I was becoming suspicious. I was able to hide it for a week or so until an incident took place that was impossible to explain away. I'd gone out to the desert to visit Dennis, my old Mexican dishwasher buddy from TGI Friday, and after we downed a few brews, he wanted to show me how fast his old Datsun B-210 could do a quarter mile. He said he souped-up the engine and had done some other things to the car that I couldn't understand. There were no decent straightaway roads anywhere near us, so we drove to Desert Hot Springs, a small city on the outskirts of Palm Springs, where the roads were long, straight and desolate.

That crazy Mexican popped the clutch and we flew up and down those roads until some concerned citizens called the police. The cops pulled us over right in front of the police station and I knew Dennis was going to jail that night. I just thanked the Lord that, for once, it wasn't going to be me.

The male cop asked Dennis to get out of the car and the female cop approached my side of the car, asking me to provide her with some ID. I handed her my license and she walked away for a minute, then came back and said, "Mister Wambaugh, is your father the author, Joseph Wambaugh?"

"Yes, ma'am," I said.

"Would you please step out of the car?"

"Yes, ma'am," I said as I got out.

"How many drinks have you had tonight?"

I didn't know why it mattered since I wasn't driving. I said, "I don't know. Maybe six."

Ten seconds later, she had me sucking on a Breathalyzer. When she saw the results she raised her eyebrows, and said, "Mister Wambaugh, please place your hands behind your back. You're being placed under arrest for being drunk in public. I'm going to have to take you to jail tonight."

I yelled, "I wasn't in public! I was in his car!"

She said, "Not anymore. As soon as you stepped out of that car, you were in public."

"You bitch!" I said, as she smiled and read me my Miranda rights.

The following day it was in *The Desert Sun*, the local paper covering the Coachella Valley:

Wambaugh son arrested by police

DESERT HOT SPRINGS -

David Paul Wambaugh, 24, of La Jolla, son of author and part-time Indian Wells resident Joseph Wambaugh, was arrested early Monday on suspicion of public intoxication. Wambaugh was a passenger in a car that was stopped in front of the police station at 6:42 a.m. after police received calls complaining of erratic driving.

The driver of the car, Dennis Martinez, 24, of Desert Hot Springs was arrested on suspicion of drunken driving. Both men were taken to the Riverside County Jail in Banning, where they were released after being cited.

The timing was really shitty because my dad had just written *The Secrets of Harry Bright*, a story of fathers and sons that was based in the city of Desert Hot Springs. Just weeks earlier, he had been given the title of Honorary Mayor. Out of all the towns in the world, I had to get popped in that one! My phone started ringing off the hook the next morning, and I had a pretty good idea who was trying to reach me, but there was no way I could face my parents, so I did the only thing I knew how to do. Drink and run.

Within a month, I was back in treatment. I had been in and out of blackouts for a few weeks, and was having health problems. My liver enzymes were dangerously high and my white blood cell count was so low they thought I had full-blown AIDS. When I started feeling a little better and the shakes went away, I decided to leave rehab--against medical advice. Without telling anyone, I packed my things, called a limo, and had the driver take me directly to a liquor store.

After a couple more months of drinking, I thought I was losing my mind. I called my parents and said I wanted to see an independent psychiatrist, not some quack from rehab who's probably in AA himself. My dad found a psychiatrist who specialized in dual-diagnosis patients, and I liked him immediately because he gave me his home phone number in case I had an urgent need to speak to him. I'm sure he regretted giving it to me, seeing as how I had four or five urgent needs every night.

After months of having no success with me, he suggested that I go across the country to a rehab in Jackson Mississippi. I liked the guy, but I couldn't believe the bastard wanted me to go all the way back there. Yet it was obvious that I had to go somewhere, because I was so screwed up on pills and booze I could hardly even dress myself.

By that point in my life, I had seen dozens of psychiatrists and psychologists, and had been treated for several different psychological disorders, but all the treatment had been unsuccessful. There had been some talk about bi-polar disorder, but I'd never been given a concrete diagnosis. You name it, I was labeled it at one time or another.

No one ever said, "Hey, I know what's wrong with this clown. He's a self-centered bastard who lives in fear and discomfort and the only medication that's effective in treating his disillusionment about life and its requirements, is a bottle of booze. Or several, in his case. What's wrong with this asshole is that he's so emotionally retarded, he's unable to effectively deal with situations that healthy people handle instinctively, without the need for anesthetic. He's actually a funny guy, and seems to possess a boyish charm that can be endearing. He's polite and, believe it or not, likeable, but what's wrong with him is that he can't distinguish the difference between objective reality, and *his* reality. He has a disease of perception."

No one ever said, "The truth about him is that he feels ashamed because he was rejected at birth. But the reality was that he became wanted by loving parents who specifically chose him. He was literally a "chosen one." And he feels inferior because he's short. He's 5'8", so not *too* short. Tom Cruise is shorter. He feels insecure because he thinks he's chubby, but he's actually in top physical condition. He feels stupid because he thinks he's not as smart as the rich kids, although he's been tested and has an above average IQ.

He feels unattractive because he has a baby face, unlike the chiseled faces of the rich kids he has competed with. But actually his face is just fine. He's cute, not GQ cute, but enough to attract his share of Bettys. He feels ashamed because he sniffed his maid's panties and liked it. His foundation is built on shame."

The shrinks didn't seem know what to make of me. The truth is, none of them had any idea what the fuck was wrong with me. They had to come up with something for the exorbitant prices they charged.

I was so drunk and loaded on pills I couldn't keep it together long enough to make my connecting flights, but after a few days of fading in and out of blackouts, I finally arrived at Pine Grove Hospital in Hattiesburg, Mississippi. I could tell right away that it was a total behavior modification boot camp. After five days, I bailed, AMA (against medical advice), as always.

Of course, I called a limo, had him drive me to a liquor store and then to a hotel. Somehow, I hooked up with a cute southern belle who was working the front desk and she became my girlfriend for the next few days, but she finally tired of me when I nearly drowned her in her bathtub.

She had prepared a romantic bubble bath with candles, wine, body oils, and bath beads, and when it came time to enjoy the tub, we both got in. But I immediately passed out on top of her. She was a tiny little thing, and I was 175 pounds of dead weight, so thank God her roommate came home and was able to help drag me off her and out of the tub.

I got dressed, called the driver, and asked him to take me to the airport. I had the same problem getting home as I did getting there. I kept missing the damn flights. When I arrived home several days later, my parents were frantic. I was really screwed up, disoriented, and totally out of touch with reality.

My shrink had done some research before I got back, and had a facility lined up to admit me upon my arrival--that's if I ever *got* there. I went directly into Rancho L'Abri in San Diego County, a beautiful place. I was then twenty-four years old, and I liked it so much I wound up going there *eight times* over the next few years! Eventually, the owner told me that my money wasn't good there anymore. She said it wouldn't be the right thing for her to do, to take my trust fund money again and again, knowing I would never stay sober.

As always, I was in violation of my probation, so I turned myself in after I discharged from treatment and was sentenced to more time in work furlough. By now, I was a regular in rehabs and jails and I was becoming well known in the recovery community as a habitual fuck-up, a relapser who just couldn't stay sober. I was blowing through my trust fund, renting limos regularly so as to not get another DUI. That's how I rationalized it. Truth is, I was a grandiose son of a bitch and thought I deserved to ride around in limos like a rich guy. You notice that I used the term, *thought,* not *felt*. I *felt* like I should be put to sleep like a rabid pit bull.

I couldn't find the desire to stay sober again. I just didn't have it in me, yet I wanted so desperately to *want* sobriety. The only desire I had was the desire to drink. I lost everything I ever had because of my desire to drink. I just wanted to drink myself into oblivion every day of my life, which mostly I did.

Chapter Eight

For the next few years I was in and out of rehab, wasting the last of the trust money, and when I had all but pissed it away and was fresh out of another rehab, my dad decided to come back into my life. I told him I was willing to do anything to get my shit together--even get a job! I think that impressed him. So much so, that he said to me, "Son, would you like me to get a place in San Diego where I could be near you and help you get it together?"

When he asked me that, it made me sad and grateful at the same time. I was grateful that he would even want to be anywhere near me, but sad because I knew in my heart I would let him down again. I mean, my dad was willing to pick up his life and move close so he could help me. How amazing, after all the terrible things I'd done to them.

"Sure!" I said excitedly. "I would love you to be here as my support system."

After a couple of months of my dad commuting between Newport and San Diego, my parents wound up buying a beautiful home in Rancho Santa Fe, one of the most exclusive neighborhoods in San Diego County.

As soon as I was settled into a very nice sober living home, my dad was ready to get down to business. He told me we had to attend to first things first, and the first thing was for me to find a job. I thought, Holy shit! This is going to be like boot camp. He's reliving his Marine days! He told me to be outside my sober living home the next morning at seven a.m. sharp. I did as I was told, and was waiting at the curb when he arrived. I could see that he was getting pumped up for our job hunt, and I really didn't share his enthusiasm, but I faked it.

When I got in his car, he handed me the yellow pages and a pencil.

I said, "Why're you giving me this? I don't know how to do this stuff. I don't even know what I'm supposed to look for!"

He said, "You're looking for a job, dummy!"

"But I don't know know what I'm capable of doing," I muttered.

"Well, probably not much," he said, "but let's think about something you'd *like* to do other than drink and waste my money." He snatched the yellow pages from me, flipped it open, and said, "What about selling fitness equipment or working at a gym? That's something you might like, since you enjoy working out."

I said hesitantly, "That might be something I could be interested in. Maybe."

He handed back the yellow pages and said, "Here, look 'em up."

I said, "Whadda you mean? We don't even know if these people are hiring."

He said, "That's why you're going to call and *ask* them if they're hiring. Jesus, David!"

I reluctantly said, "Uh, okay, but what am I gonna say if they ask me why my work history is almost non-existent?

"Dave, just con them like you do everyone else," he said. "You know you can talk your way into a job, so don't bullshit me. We know you can *get* the job. We just don't know if you can *keep* it."

I thumbed through the fitness equipment section of the yellow pages and there just so happened to be an upscale fitness equipment business just blocks away from my sober living home. I did as my dad told me to do and conned my way into a job at the very first place we tried. I walked out of the store, gave my dad thumbs up and got into his car.

He asked, "So? What happened?"

"I did what you said to do. I conned the manager into giving me a job, and I start full time tomorrow morning!"

He grinned, and slowly shook his head in disbelief.

The store catered to the La Jolla crowd, therefore handled high-ticket fitness equipment. We sold stationary bikes imported from Germany that cost just under $5,000 and treadmills that cost about the same. It was a two-man show, but my manager eventually let me take over making all sales because it was apparent to him that I was better at selling than he was. But he was smart and didn't let his ego get in the way. Another bonus for him was that it freed him up to smoke dope in the back room, and play Lion King with his twenty-one year-old mistress.

I was doing very well and things were really coming together. This was the first time in my life that I was almost a legitimate person. My parents were getting hopeful at that point, and my dad and I would have dinner a couple of times a week so I could check in and tell him how everything was going.

One night at dinner he asked me if I would be interested in living in a home of my own. He thought it would be good for my emotional and mental stability if I had a permanent address. I said what he wanted to hear, and I wished I believed it myself, but I knew in my heart that I was nothing but a well-versed bum.

———

Within a couple of weeks we found a four bedroom, three-and-a-half bath, single family home in a newly developed area bordering Del Mar. My surroundings were amazing. I looked at my neighbors in awe, wondering how they were able to afford and manage these nice homes. And how is it that they've built these great families? They all had an inner fortitude that I was unable to tap into, or simply didn't possess. Maybe it was a flaw in my DNA, who knows? But I guess it didn't matter.

My mom gave me a check for the full purchase price, and I walked into the bank, handed it over, signed a few documents, and walked out a proud homeowner. It was amazing! I couldn't believe it. However, there was a stipulation in our agreement that if I drank, I would relinquish the house back to my parents and vacate the premises.

Although I didn't feel worthy of being in the company of my yuppie neighbors, I thought I could learn from them. The day after I moved into that dream home, I bought a light golden retriever puppy that was just eight weeks old. I named him Jake because prior to my last attempt at sobriety, I frequented Jake's in Del Mar, an oceanfront restaurant and bar with excellent double vodka cranberrys. I'd get hammered and fantasize about someday having a son, and when I did, I was going to name him Jake, just like the bar. I loved the name, and felt in my heart I wouldn't live long enough to have a real son, so this was as good as it was going to get. It was just me, and Jake the dog. He had beautiful brown eyes, very kind, yet sad. His eyes were like my brother's eyes: Thoughtful, kind, and sad.

Maybe Jake had sad eyes because he somehow knew I wasn't going to be able to take care of him. Maybe his animal instinct knew what I was: A total loser that he wouldn't be able to count on. Maybe Jake knew all those things about me the moment we met.

He certainly knew more than I did, because I had felt that this time there was no possible way for me to screw things up again. This time I had way too much going for me. I would have bet my puppies' life that I was through drinking. It was over. My days, months, and years of emptiness, loneliness, and hopelessness were now going to be replaced with fulfillment, hope, stability and security. At least that was my new fantasy.

I felt that I had finally arrived. I had a great job, a nice car, a beautiful puppy, and a home that most people only dream about owning. I couldn't have been more fortunate, and I was only twenty-four years old.

I was doing well for about a month, commuting back and forth to work every day with Jake on my lap. I was very happy, and felt I was getting healthier in every way. My mind didn't race as much anymore and I felt some peace for the first time that I could remember. Unfortunately, I received a random phone call that would wind up changing everything.

A woman called regarding an award that my dad was supposed to receive from The San Diego Criminal Lawyers Association at The Del Mar Hilton. She told me that he'd had to decline and couldn't be there, but I'm sure he didn't *want* to be there since he's not crazy about making public appearances or being honored. She said there were over three hundred invitations with his name on them, and she would be forever grateful if I would accept the award on his behalf.

I said, "Of course. I'd be honored to accept the award." And then, jokingly, I said, "You wouldn't be kind enough to cover the cost of the tuxedo rental, and maybe send a limo to pick me up, would you?"

"I'd be happy to take care of those things, David," she said. "And also, it would be fine if you want to bring a date or a friend."

"Really? How kind of you," I said. "That would be terrific. I'll certainly look forward to the evening."

I could really *be* somebody that night! I wanted to share the limelight with someone, so I called a friend and told him we'd be going first class in the back of a limo to a black tie event where I was certain there would be plenty of MILFs in attendance.

The guy I invited was from my most recent rehab, a heart surgeon who'd practiced medicine in Arizona, but lost his license due to cocaine and alcohol addiction. However, he was able to practice in California so he relocated to San Diego. He was a good ol' southern boy, and as slick as they come. He was a handsome older dude with plenty of bank.

The doctor showed up at my house about an hour before the limo was to pick us up, and he brought with him a twelve pack of Coors Light and a bottle of Cuervo Gold. He was supposed to have been coming to this event as my *support* system, not my drinking companion, but he cracked the bottle of Tequila, handed me a brew, and that was the beginning of the end--again. I knew that if I took that drink, the curtain would soon go down, and I would soon lose my house, my job, my puppy, everything.

I knew *all* those things, and yet when he handed me the bottle of tequila, I took three deep gulps and washed them down with Mr. Coors, another of my lifelong friends, in addition to Mr. Anheuser and Mr. Busch. I was really scared at first, but after several shots I tricked myself into believing that I'd be okay, that I wouldn't crash and burn this time. I could handle a few drinks. There would be no possible way I could go down because I had way too much to lose.

By the time the limo picked us up we were pretty drunk and I was totally shit-faced by the time I accepted the award for my dad. After receiving the award I was told by the lady who'd invited me, to gather my friend and go home a little early. And that our limo was waiting out front.

The next day I woke up to my mom's voice shouting my name, and she was shaking me. I thought I was imagining it, but when I opened my eyes, there she was. I had passed out, fully dressed, on the living room floor, and she was looking at me, not with disgust or anger, but with deep sadness once again. All I could think about was getting a drink. I'd bought a 1.75-liter of vodka on the way home the night before, so I knew I had some left.

My mom said that I reeked, and ordered me to shower and change my clothes. She said we had business to take care of, and that I was to come with her, no matter how sick I felt. When she walked outside to look for Jake, I downed some of the vodka to settle my nerves and then did as I was told.

We went to the bank where I had to sign the papers, relinquishing any claim to my dream home. When we got back to the house, she took Jake in her arms, and with tears in her eyes, said she'd find him a good home. I agreed with her that I couldn't take care of him. Hell, I couldn't even take care of myself. She was certainly good as her word. My parents raised that beautiful puppy until he died about thirteen years later.

When my mom walked out the door that day, I was too numb to cry. I got out the bottle of vodka and drank myself into oblivion. I couldn't believe how my life fell apart so fast, and how I broke my mom's heart again. I didn't have the answer to *why*. I can't describe the self-loathing I felt. If I'd had a gun, I believe I would've killed myself.

———

Shortly after I moved out of the house, I stopped going to my job selling fitness equipment, but I was able to support myself for a while with the money I'd saved while I was there. When that money ran out and I got tired of sleeping in the backseat of my car, I called my parents and begged for help. They gave me the option to return to the sober living home where I'd been before or I could remain homeless.

I reluctantly went back to the sober living home, but I didn't stay sober long. It was easy to get away with drinking there because most of the other guys drank too. The guy that owned the place didn't care if you drank or shot dope, as long as you paid the rent, and my parents thought I was staying sober. Eventually, the owner's partner got himself into some kind of legal trouble, couldn't deal with it, and blew his brains out. Two days after that, a sheriff came and told us we'd have to find other accommodations.

My mom said she'd help me rent a two-bedroom condo that I could share with one of the other guys from the sober living home, so I went to the Coldwell Banker office in Pacific Beach and spoke to a rental agent who said she could help us find the perfect bay-front condo.

However, my AA sponsor thought there would be way too much temptation on the bay, with the endless parade of hot chicks rollerblading by in bikinis all day long. He said he thought that could very well lead me back to the bottle. I told him that *anything* could lead me back to the bottle. Against my sponsor's strong suggestion to move somewhere more conducive to sobriety, I proceeded with the bay front idea anyway. I had a hard time listening to the advice of the AA people because I figured most of them had major issues of their own. It's like fishing in a dirty pond, I thought.

The rental agent who showed me property was a hot little spanker named Tobi with huge fake jugs. She was noticeably older than I was, but still hot. Tobi said that she used to work nights as a waitress at the Playboy Club when she'd attended UCLA, and then after graduating, worked in Beverly Hills as personal assistant to Elaine Young, the famous real estate broker-to-the-stars.

Well, I never got the bay-front pad, but I did get a date for the evening. I picked her up in a stretch limo and the lies began. That night, I was the David who had boyish charm, charisma, and the fake confidence to wiggle the pants right off her. Somehow I neglected to tell her that I had been institutionalized for most of my adult life, and I also didn't tell her that I was paying for the limo with my deceased brother's trust fund. I'd pissed his money away too. After Mark's death, what was left in his trust after his condo was sold was divided between my sister and me. I told this chick a boatload of lies and fantasies because I *lived* in a world of fantasy.

Sometime during our second date, I asked Tobi to marry me, so on July 4th, 1990, two weeks before my twenty-sixth birthday we flew to Las Vegas and sealed the deal. When I came out of my blackout, I had a wedding band on my left hand, a marriage certificate in my right, and a wife I'd known less than forty-eight hours. My new wife probably thought she'd found the golden egg. Little did she know that it was scrambled!

I didn't even know what a 401k was the first time I heard it mentioned by my new wife. I knew what a 647f was (drunk in public), a 23152a (DUI), a 5150 (a danger to myself or others) or a 187 (murder), and many other codes and numbers. I figured that 401k was probably the lewd and lascivious code or something raunchy like that, but I hadn't been picked up on one of those charges just yet.

When I called my parents to share the good news about my marriage, my dad just said, "Congratulations, Dave. Good luck. Actually, good luck to your bride."

I asked if they would like to meet her, but he said maybe sometime in the future.

A couple of days later, my dad called, and said, "Oh yeah, Dave, by the way, your wife's name is bogus. Her name's not Tobi Coleman, it's Julia Miller, and I doubt that she has a degree from UCLA. Just thought you might want to know. Take care of yourself, Dave." And he hung up.

Apparently, he'd checked her out through one of his old cop buddies, but at least my dad sounded upbeat, probably because I was going to be someone *else's* problem for a while. I'm sure he wanted to know who she was so he could get a more accurate picture of someone crazy enough to marry me. It was hard to believe that anyone would even consider marrying me, but I must have promised her the family fortune.

———

Tobi talked incessantly about the deep love and devotion she had for her grandmother, and that's really the thing that attracted me to her. Sure, she had big fake breasts, but her devotion to her family was very impressive. I had no devotion to *my* family, so I thought she was my little Christian soldier who'd come to save me from myself and reunite me with my loved ones.

She often talked about her childhood. Her real father and his twin brother owned a deli in New Jersey. He was a workaholic who was never home when she was a kid, and her mom had been in and out of psychiatric wards for years. Her sister was a closet dyke and her brother was as invisible as he could make himself.

Being a lesbian, Tobi's sister had suffered for many years, and when she finally came out of the closet as an adult, her mom went sideways, winding up in the psych ward again. Her sister was able to separate herself from the madness by moving in with her longtime partner and relocating to Yucca Valley, California where she bought her own home and worked for many years as a driver for FedEx.

Tobi said her brother escaped the insanity when he went away to college, vowing to do well so he'd never have the need to return to that madhouse. He'd become a successful finance guy and was the one who had started the family's migration to California. His mother left their father back in New Jersey and she and Tobi followed her son, all three settling in La Jolla. A few years later, Tobi's crazy mother married a wealthy old man and moved into a beautiful oceanfront high-rise in downtown La Jolla.

My new wife was overly eager to introduce me to her family, but I wasn't looking forward to this meeting at all because I knew they were going to drill me with questions, and I didn't have any good answers. At least none that were true. To relieve my anxiety I swilled a pint of 100 proof Smirnoff Blue Label before I visited their home. As soon as I walked through the front door the questions began flying at me from all directions. At one point in our conversation her stepfather asked if I was of the Jewish faith, like all of them. For the life of me, I *thought* Tobi had told me she was Catholic! I thought, Holy shit! I married a goddamn hebe!

We'd come in separate cars to that visit because I had wanted my own ride in the event that I couldn't handle her family, but I drank enough to suffer through the evening. When were ready to leave, I told her to follow me because I couldn't see straight. I figured that if a cop came up behind us, she'd be the one to be pulled over. I was thinking it'd be better if she went to jail instead of me, because I'd had too much trouble in my life already.

It didn't matter though, because I only made it a couple of blocks from her parents' house when going about forty miles an hour, I smashed into the rear end of a parked car. My car ran right up the back end of the parked car and stayed there. Our cars looked like two turtles humping. The collision was very loud, and a small crowd gathered.

I quickly got out of my car, walked directly over to my wife's car and got in. Her eyes were popped, and she didn't say a word.

I said slowly and deliberately, "Sweetie, listen to me very carefully. I cannot afford another DUI because I would most certainly have to go to jail for a long time. I love you very much and I don't want to be without you. Now, let's get the fuck out of here! Immediately! *Drive!*"

I called my Dad at 1:30 a.m. to tell him what had happened and to ask what I should do about it. He said he thought I should turn myself in right then and there, but I decided I'd rather be a fugitive.

The next day when I was sober I called the police to report my car stolen. A woman answered and as I started telling her my story she stopped me, told me to hold on, and patched me right through to a detective who was expecting my call.

When he picked up, he said, "Good morning, Mister Wambaugh."

"Good morning, sir," I replied.

He said, "Mister Wambaugh, your vehicle was in an accident at 939 Coast Boulevard in La Jolla last night at approximately 10:45 p.m. You were identified as the person driving the vehicle and leaving the scene of the accident. I'm not gonna play games with you. You can either come here and talk to me, or I can come talk to you."

"Okay, I'm on my way, sir," I said, "I'll be there soon."

When I arrived at the station an hour later, I was terrified because I definitely thought I was going to jail and would probably have to do some time. I couldn't believe it, but I talked the detective into letting me go without placing me under arrest. He did have me sign paperwork stating that I would make restitution for the car that I wrecked, and that was it. One problem throughout my life was that I looked so boyish and innocent that I *always* got another chance! And, of course, my dad's name always helped.

There I was, sharing my new wife's one-bedroom apartment, with no car, no job, no money, and no plan. I knew I had to find a job--any job. I thought about an old man I used to sometimes drink with at a bar in La Jolla who said if I ever needed a job he'd hire me to dig ditches for him. He'd been kidding of course, because he, like everyone else, thought I had money.

The following day I met him at the bar and asked if the position was still available. He laughed, but when he realized I wasn't joking, he got a serious look on his face and said, "Sure, son, you can dig ditches for me, but I hope you can speak some Spanish. I got all wetbacks diggin' holes for me.

I said, *"Muchas gracias. "*

"See you at six a.m," he said. "And don't be late."

"Hasta mañana," I replied.

The next day I sold my Rolex for a painfully low price, bought an old pickup, and started digging ditches full time alongside undocumented Mexicans who thankfully spoke enough English for us to communicate. I actually liked digging ditches next to the Mexican guys because they knew I was a lame-ass white boy with no digging skills, so they always picked up the slack for me. Even though I drank every afternoon after work, usually with my boss, I kept that job for almost a year, which was the longest time I'd ever held a job, but digging ditches was not for me, so I decided to expand my horizons.

In the spring of 1991, I got a license to sell life insurance, and after lots of interviews, I got a birddog position for a top producer at Mutual Benefit Life Insurance Company. My plan was to become a big-time financial planner, so I sold my truck to one of the Mexicans I'd worked with, and got myself a Jeep. With the extra money left over, I bought a couple of suits and I was ready to roll.

I often had good fortune come my way but I was never able to capitalize on it, and this time was no different. As soon as I got started at Mutual Benefit, I blew a life insurance deal that would've netted me over twenty-five K. In the beginning I wasn't even close to making any money, so at the end of each day, I 'd get a twelve-pack of beer and go to a bench in Del Mar that overlooked the ocean and the train tracks.

I'd sit there and drink, and wonder what the successful people in the world were doing at that moment. I'd look out at the ocean and dream about how *wonderful* it would be if I were ever able to become stable and healthy.

While sitting on the bench one afternoon, an older couple approached and asked if they could join me, so I stood up and offered them the whole bench, but they insisted we share, so we all sat back down and made small talk. The man saw the beer in my hand and asked if I had any extras.

"Of course," I said, and I walked back to my Jeep, bringing the old guy a cold one.

He introduced himself and his wife, and as we chatted about the beautiful coastal area, he told me his story of how he'd attained financial success. He explained that he was an ex-Marine, and many years ago had bought several acres of the Oceanside coastline when it was only $10,000 an acre. He talked real estate for quite awhile, and he educated me on some basic real estate principles, and I told him about my new job, and how I was getting a little frustrated with it because I wasn't making any money.

He turned to his wife, and they started talking about their life insurance agent. He mentioned something to her about his displeasure with his guy, and how the guy was mis-managing their affairs. Then the old man turned to me and said to call him the next morning and he'd have his assistant set up an appointment for me and my boss to come and see him. He was willing to give me a shot at getting them a better policy through our company. He said that I was a nice young man, and they would be happy to help me along in my new career. And then he added that I seemed to be "a sincere and honest lad." If he only knew.

I called my boss to give him the basic information the couple had provided, and he called me back thirty minutes later to say the deal looked really good, and as soon as it closed, I would most likely net about 25K. He thought it would be a slam-dunk.

I met some friends that night at a bar to brag about how great I was, and about all the money I was going to make. After several drinks, a few pills, and a whole tray of vodka Jell-O shooters, I attempted to drive home. I had the top down on my Jeep Wrangler, and the tunes were blaring. I was in the left turn lane at a busy intersection when I passed out. The next thing I knew, a San Diego police officer was shaking my shoulder, trying to wake me, while my stereo was blaring *Sweet Child of Mine* by Guns and Roses.

Unfortunately, I had a big bag full of syringes, enough to pacify all the junkies in La Jolla for a month, and enough steroids to pump up all the freaks at Gold's Gym. I also had a large Ziploc bag filled with tranquilizers.

I didn't think my wife was going to be happy about this so I didn't call her.

The judge convicted me of my third DUI, dropped the felony drug possession charges, and sentenced me to the multiple-offender DUI class, formal probation, and long-term residential treatment. I stayed in jail until they released me a couple of days later.

When my wife got home from work the day I got out of jail, she gave me an ultimatum. I would either have to get some help or we needed to separate for a while. I had nowhere else to go, and my parents weren't about to cough up any more coin for me, so I wound up going to a county funded facility in downtown San Diego that was just a step up from living on skid row. The problem was, I needed to arrive sober or I wouldn't be accepted. I had never in my life heard of such a thing! Why would anyone go to rehab sober? If you were sober, why go to rehab? I just didn't get it. I was always either blacked out, or so inebriated that I didn't know where I was until a couple of days into treatment. I don't remember how I managed to show up sober, or even *if* I showed up sober, but somehow I was able to get admitted.

I stayed for a week, and then promised my wife that I'd be good and would stay sober if I could come home. I even promised to take Antabuse, a drug that makes a person violently ill if they drink alcohol while on it. I was willing to get a prescription and take it to please my wife, because some of the old-timers in AA told me that it's not all *that* bad drinking on Antabuse. They said I might feel a little sick at first, but after a couple drinks I'd be okay, so that was my ace in the hole. I'd be able to please her, and please myself at the same time. A win-win situation.

After a few days of sobriety I got *really* thirsty, so one night I told Tobi I had terrible heartburn and was going to run to the store to buy Rolaids and a newspaper so I could look for another job. I picked up a pint of 100 proof peppermint schnapps and the paper, but forgot all about the Rolaids. When I got back to our underground garage, I sat in my Jeep, downed the pint of schnapps, read the obituaries, feeling relieved that I didn't find my name there, and then went back up to our apartment.

While I sat watching TV with my wife, I started feeling hot, and I mean engine-overheating kind of hot! I excused myself, went into the bathroom, and was shocked at the sight in the mirror. My face looked like an overripe tomato and I began having trouble breathing. I stumbled into the bedroom and crashed on the bed, hoping it would pass. I finally came out of it, but with three fireman, two paramedics, and a cop hovering over me.

A young fireman who was obviously brand new on the job looked at me and then over to Tobi, and asked, "So, what happened?"

She said, "Uh... uh... he takes Antabuse. Maybe he drank some alcohol or something."

He said. "You can't drink while you're on that. It could kill you."

The middle-aged cop chimed in, "Yeah, that's the idea. But some idiots drink on it anyway."

The young fireman looked down at me and said, "Dude, what were you thinking?"

I couldn't respond because I had an oxygen mask over my face.

They took me to the emergency room for a few hours, then wanted to transfer me to the psychiatric ward on a seventy-two hour hold because they thought I was a 5150, which is the Welfare and Institutions code for a person determined to be a danger to himself or others. I talked my way out of it, saying I must have swallowed some mouthwash when I was gargling. They didn't believe me, but they cut me loose anyway.

I stayed mostly sober for the next few weeks, mainly because I was flat broke and couldn't buy booze. My wife was tired of giving me gas money for my job search every day, especially knowing the gas money was going for something other than gas. The job never materialized, and I was drunk every day by the time she walked through the front door after a hard day's work.

One night I started a fight with her, just so I could storm out the door and stay the night with a girl I'd been boning, one who always had a full liquor cabinet. The following morning when I got home and walked into our apartment, I was expecting my wife to kick me to the curb, but she didn't. She didn't say a word, but her eyes were darting all around the room in every direction but mine. I sensed that something really bad was going on, something much more than just my disappearance.

The phone rang and Tobi jumped. She picked up and said, "Hi, Mister Wambaugh. Yes, he's right here." And she handed me the receiver.

My dad sounded like he was really sick, and he said, "David, you've really done it this time! Now, you've *really* ruined your life! What in the hell were you thinking? Are you *totally insane?*"

I interrupted him, saying, "Dad, I *know* I've ruined my life. But I have no idea what you're talking about.

He screamed at the top of his lungs, "You robbed a *bank*, you idiot! Goddamnit, David! This is something I *never* saw coming! How *could* you? What were you *thinking?*"

"Dad, I didn't rob a bank!" I said. "I swear to God!"

"You did, you *did* it! Where were you yesterday morning?"

He had me so scared I went totally blank and said, "I don't remember."

"David, you robbed a Wells Fargo Bank on La Jolla Village Drive yesterday at 10:47 a.m. Now you need to tell me the truth because I'm your only hope here!" He paused for a moment, and then said, "Your mother saw the newspaper story with the description of the bank robber. She went to your apartment today and found the green suit and the briefcase. I'm sure the sunglasses in your possession right now match the ones you were seen wearing in the bank. So where's the hat? And what did you do with the money?"

Before I responded, I thought really hard. I couldn't have robbed any damn Wells Fargo Bank! Could I? I wasn't positive. Not good. Oh my God, I thought. Oh my God!

I finally said, "What hat? I don't *have* any money! I swear to God, Dad, I did *not* rob a bank."

"Your picture's on the goddamn front page of the San Diego Union!" he yelled.

I almost fainted. I had to use the kitchen counter to hold myself up, and cried, "That's crazy, Dad!" Then I thought, It *can't* be! *Can* it?

He said, "You have the identical brief case, the same olive drab suit that's on the floor of your closet, and the matching Ray Ban sunglasses the robber wore, so it's either you or your twin. The only thing your mother didn't find was the Oakland A's baseball cap you had on. What did you do with it? And where's the money?"

"Dad, please!" I said, "You've got to believe me! I *didn't* rob a bank!" And I was hoping to God, that it was the truth!

He gave me the name of a detective who was in the bank robbery detail downtown and advised me to call him and turn myself in. He said I should tell the detective the truth about everything that had happened, that it was best for me to just get it over with.

I hung up the phone and bolted out the front door with only the clothes on my back and drove to my girlfriend's apartment to have a drink and make a plan. I called my drinking buddy to tell him what had happened and asked for his advice. He figured I was guilty, and said I should haul ass away from there before I got picked up. Everyone seemed to think I did it, so shit, maybe I *did!*

A couple of days later, when I was hiding out in Orange County, that friend called and gave me some great news. "Hey, bro, you're all good," he said. "They caught the guy the press called 'The A's Bank Robber,' and they said he's robbed at least seventeen banks in Southern California. The dude does look a lot like you, bro. You better tell your old man in case he doesn't already know."

My Mom answered on the first ring, and I said self-righteously, "Well, Miss Marple, did you hear they caught the real bank robber? I told you I could never do anything like that. I can't believe you guys would've thought that. Jesus, Mom!"

She was quiet for a few seconds and then said, "David, what do you expect? We don't know *what* you're capable of doing, and that's what's so frightening. There's *nothing* you could do that would surprise us at this point."

After sixteen months of marital hell, my wife finally had had enough. She called my mom early one morning to tell her that I had become physically abusive, and that she had me arrested. While I was in jail, she found another apartment and moved out, leaving my clothes in a pile on the floor of the vacant apartment we had shared. And then she filed for divorce.

Chapter Nine

My parents allowed me to stay with them for a while at their house in Rancho Santa Fe, but the requirements were that I couldn't drink and I had to get a job, the same old things they'd asked of me over the years. Soon after I settled in, I started a business as a personal fitness trainer. I didn't have any formal training or education, but I was really good at improvising. I got a few clients, wealthy women from The Ranch, trained them as best I could, and earned some decent money for a few months. Eventually though, I was confronted about my drinking by a couple of my clients when I showed up drunk for training sessions, so after a few of those, I hung up my personal trainer's hat, went to a bar, and within a week I was homeless again.

My mom kicked me out of their house, but was willing to help me get into a sober living home again, but that was it. The place I moved into that time was really nasty. The residents overdosed regularly, and sex was rampant. However, it was better than sleeping in the park or in the backseat of my Jeep. It brought another glimmer of hope for my parents because I seemed to be thriving there. I worked out six days a week, was going to AA meetings again, and really worked the program.

I was twenty-eight years old and had already been in so many rehabs, hospitals, psych wards, and sober living homes, my dad said I could probably *run* a sober living home. He suggested that I look at properties in Pacific Beach, and we could see about buying a triplex or a small apartment building and turning it into *Dave's Sober Living*. I would've been great at running a sober living facility if only *I* could have stayed sober. If only!

A couple of days later, after looking at apartment buildings all day, I went to the gym at my usual time. I exchanged pleasantries with Sarah, an attractive gym rat with an uncanny ability to make friends. She was slender and buff, her long dark hair pulled into a ponytail, a sparkle in her eyes and had a ready smile. She was thirty years old and got plenty of attention from all the middle-aged guys who worked out there. During a conversation she invited me to a Christmas party she and her sister were hosting. I thanked her but declined, knowing I shouldn't go where there would be holiday booze flowing. I did want to see her though, so I told her I would like to take her out somewhere in the daytime. I joked that I changed into a monster after dark, but of course she had no idea how true that was. She said she had never been to Mexico, and had always wanted to go. I suggested we go to Laguna Beach for the day, but she was dead set on Mexico.

Sarah had been into introduced to the San Diego scene by her sister, who had moved there a few years earlier. She admitted to being a party girl, and told me about the time she danced on top of the bar at *The Beachcomber* in Mission Beach, dressed as Pocahontas. I told her that it was okay, because I was a little wild myself. When she said it was probably the craziest thing she'd ever done, I was waiting for a punch line, something like, ...*except for when I ran naked on the beach in broad daylight*. Or, *except when I flashed my boobs at a priest*. But dancing on the bar was the craziest thing she'd ever done? I was in love!

She had worked as a library assistant in Phoenix, Arizona, and had shelved my dad's books countless times, so she knew of his fame and wealth, and must have assumed, regardless of my checkered past, that directly or indirectly, I meant money.

When I arrived to pick Sarah up, she opened the front door and those sparkly eyes were full of excitement.

She said, "Here we come, Mexico! My friends told me we have to go to a place called *Papas & Beer* in Rosarito Beach. Everyone says it's so much fun!"

My heart sank. Every time I'd been to Papas & Beer, I either wound up in a fight or a blackout, or both. I wasn't too optimistic about my chances of coming back to San Diego with my sobriety intact.

We drove across the border and down the coast to Rosarito Beach, straight to Papas & Beer where she ordered a margarita and I ordered a diet coke. For the second round, she ordered a margarita and I ordered another diet coke. For the third round she ordered a margarita and I ordered a double margarita.

She said, "Oh, I thought you didn't drink!"

I said, "Well, sometimes I do." I didn't tell her that sometimes I drank for years at a time.

She smiled, shrugged, raised her glass, and said, "Well, cheers! Here's to this incredible day, and thank you so much for bringing me here! This is wonderful!"

My brain was spinning, knowing I was two seconds away from throwing away another great opportunity. I raised my margarita glass to hers and said, "Here's to success. Bottoms up!" And then I faded into a blackout.

My dad busted me the morning after I got back from Mexico. He took his car away from me and dropped me back at the sober living home. I still had some money, so I left the place and went on another tirade. I snorted heroin, ate Valium like they were Skittles, drank like a derelict, smoked speed, and took anything else I could get my hands on. One night I got so sick I nearly died, and was taken by ambulance to the ER. My liver enzymes were way up again, and my kidneys felt as though someone had bashed me in the lower back with a baseball bat.

After I was discharged from the hospital, my parents paid for another rehab, the *Exodus Program* at Daniel Freeman Hospital in Marina Del Rey. It's famous for treating rock stars, like Axel Rose, Kurt Cobain, Flea, Stevie Nicks, and many others. I stayed just long enough to get fairly healthy, and then moved back to San Diego where I rented a room from two guys who had been my childhood friends from San Marino.

The divorce from Tobi was final in December of 1992, and by then I was seeing Sarah on a regular basis and spending most nights at her house.

We had a great time together because she drank right along with me while listening intently to all of my farfetched stories. I even think she believed most of them.

———

My parents were hoping my sister, Jeannette, would move away from her party-time friends in Pasadena, come to San Diego, and invest what was left of her trust fund in a small house or duplex. She had already pissed away most of her trust money by turning her apartment in Pasadena into a buddy hang-out.

I offered to help find a property for her in the San Diego area, but after a few weeks of looking, she decided she wasn't willing to make the move. Nothing came of my search, but I *did* manage to get a generous fee out of her for wasting my time. One thing I was consistently able to do well throughout my life was hustle money. Over the years my parents would ask how in the hell I always had money, and the truth was that I was always able to stumble in and out of very short term jobs and keep some money in my pocket. And on more than one occasion, I'd hook up with a sick co-dependent girl who would wind up taking take care of me for a while.

With the help of the money I hustled from Jeannette, I decided to buy myself a car, a Porsche 928. It was a beautiful car! It wasn't too fast off the line, but it could fly on the top end. My driver's license had been suspended since August of 1992 so I wasn't able to *legally* drive or register a vehicle, forcing me to become creative. I would only buy cars with current tags that had several months left before they'd expire, and I'd always give false information to the seller so no one could track me down in case something went sideways, which usually did happen. Nobody selling a car for cash demanded to see my driver's license when I waved a stack of Benjamin Franklins under his nose. When the tags were about to expire, I would sell the car to a shady Iranian I'd met down in San Diego. He bought all my cars when I needed to get rid of them, no questions asked.

One night, I'd gotten into a high-speed police chase, so I had to dump that car the next morning. I thought I should tell the Iranian what really happened, just in case the cops tracked the car to his lot. I was going to pay him to make up some story, or pretend he didn't speak English if the cops came.

After I expressed all of my concerns, he simply said, "And on this day I am blind and deaf, one hundred percent."

He handed me three thousand bucks and I hauled ass.

Sarah referred to the two of us as "Bonnie and Clyde," even though she'd never broken a law in her life. One day we decided to take my new Porsche out to Palm Desert, catch some rays, and pound a few margaritas. We took the scenic route over the mountains and then down into the desert below. It's a beautiful drive and a perfect road on which to test a high-performance sports car. I was pretty mellow on the drive there, but on our way back the next day, I was thinking about really testing my new ride. While Sarah took her shower that morning, I drank most of a bottle of vodka that I had stashed in my overnight bag, and then we went to a champagne brunch before heading back to San Diego.

There were a couple of long stretches of two-lane highway where I could put the pedal to the metal, so I punched it. That Porsche could go140 miles an hour, and the ride seemed very smooth. I couldn't hear Sarah's terrified screams over my new Mary J. Blige tape that was blaring. Seeing as how I didn't have a driver's license, I thought I shouldn't push my luck, so I slowed down, but two jarheads in an IROC- Z were right on my ass, and I was getting irritated, so I stepped on it again. Next thing you know, we were both flying down the two lane highway, going over 125 miles an hour.

Way up ahead, I spotted a car in my lane with its left turn signal on, just sitting there. There was an opportunity for the driver to turn, but he didn't. I was bearing down on him, and when I down-shifted into fourth gear, I was still going about 80 miles an hour, so I down-shifted again and the rear end of my car got all squirrelly. When I regained partial control, I crashed straight into the rear of the car.

The sound was deafening, and the windows exploded. We were covered with shards of glass but at least we were alive. Both doors were jammed, so I climbed out of the driver's side window, went around the car and helped Sarah out through the side window. I ran over to the car I had rear-ended and saw an old man and his wife sitting in their seats, looking straight ahead. It appeared as if they were in shock.

I said, "Sir, are you and your wife okay?"

They both shrugged, and nodded.

Then I said, "Sir, I'm very sorry I crashed into you but I don't have a valid license, so I really need to go."

As I said that, a woman driving a Beemer in the oncoming traffic lane, yelled out her window, "Don't worry, honey. I've called the police. They'll be here in a minute. Are you okay?"

The jarheads were pulled over to see if they could help, and boy, did they ever! I turned into a boot camp drill instructor and yelled at my new recruits, "Hey, listen guys, I've been drinking and I got a warrant out for my arrest, and the bottom line is, I don't wanna go to jail today. I really need your help."

They threw our luggage into the back of their IROC-Z and we hopped in. They drove us all the way to a Shakey's pizza on Pacific Coast Highway in Oceanside. Then we took a cab from there to my favorite Chinese restaurant in Pacific Beach where I could have some Bacardi 151 mai tais and think about what I was going to do next.

I soon discovered that I'd completely screwed up when I bought that car. I'd been too drunk that day, and had given the seller my real name, address, and phone number. I don't know what in the hell I was thinking.

I got a call from a California highway patrol officer the next morning. After he introduced himself, he told me that the car I had recently purchased was involved in a hit and run accident the previous afternoon.

I said to him, "Are you serious? I can't believe it! I loaned my car to my brother yesterday because he wanted to impress his date. He really left the scene, huh? Jesus! I can't believe he'd do that. What a dummy!"

The chipper chuckled and said, "Yes, he did leave the scene. And yes, he is a dummy who happens to be in serious trouble. So you tell that dummy to call me back within one hour with the real story, or we'll have a big problem. I know you're gonna help me get to the bottom of this, right?"

"Right," I said, deflated.

Needless to say, I didn't call him back. So when my phone rang later that afternoon from an unidentified number, I had a pretty good idea who it might be. I answered the phone, "Dave Wambaugh speaking."

"Hello, Mister Wambaugh," the caller said. This is Lieutenant Simpson. I spoke to you earlier today."

"Yes, Lieutenant?"

"Here's the deal," he said. "Your brother died in 1984, so he's not the dummy who was driving your car. A witness identified you as being the driver of the vehicle and you need to come down to the California Highway Patrol substation in Hemet and give me a statement."

"Okay, sir," I said. "I'll be there sometime this afternoon."

"We'll see you then," he said.

"Yes, sir," I said.

Did he really think I was stupid enough to think I wouldn't be arrested if I went to the CHP station? I knew if I showed up they would take me into custody immediately. No way, I wasn't that dumb! A statement? *Sure*, he wanted a statement!

I talked to Sarah, aka Bonnie, into letting me to move in with her. The poor girl had never broken a law in her life and there she was, saddled with a fugitive wanted by the law. She had a master's degree in education, had been employed somewhere since she was thirteen, had never had any negative police contact in her entire life--and then she hooked up with me, an outlaw. What on earth was *she* thinking?

When I moved into her apartment we agreed that we should slow down on the drinking, and that I would get a job. Well, Sarah slowed down on the drinking, but mine only escalated, and a job was not in the cards. In a short period of time I got really sick again and had to be hospitalized, back in the ER with both physical and mental problems. My parents were there to help me into a rehab program once again.

The CHP lieutenant never called. A warrant wasn't even issued, as far as I know. That would have been another felony, but somehow it slipped through the cracks. Another get-out-of-jail-free card? I led a charmed life.

I left rehab after a few weeks, and went back to San Diego. I wanted to show Sarah how serious I was about getting my shit together, and let her see another side of me, one she'd never seen. Some months later, I showed her a third side that she also had never seen. To make amends and to prove my resolve, I asked for her hand in marriage.

On May 16, 1993, which happened to be Ziggy's birthday, Sarah and I headed to one of the many little wedding chapels on the strip in Las Vegas. Sarah was so happy, and looked beautiful in her wedding dress. I rented a tux and hired a limo, which she paid for on her credit card, and we were off to the chapel to exchange vows. It was my second trip down the aisle in Las Vegas, and I was hoping it would be my last, but you just never know.

After about a week, Sarah sent my parents a wedding announcement with a picture of us sitting in the back of the limo. With the announcement, I enclosed a letter saying that I hadn't phoned them about the marriage because I figured they would just laugh and let me know how crazy I was. I went on to brag about the length of time I'd been sober since leaving rehab, and how supportive Sarah was regarding my sobriety. So supportive, that even though I was broke, had a warrant for my arrest, and had other legal problems, she still wanted to be my wife. My mom wrote back, and said that instead of laughing, she felt like crying. Seeing the pretty girl in the picture, sitting in the limo and looking so happy, made her sad because she knew she wouldn't be able to stay that way for long. My mom congratulated us, and then didn't meet Sarah until five months later.

It seems that the common denominator with both of my wives was that they *found* me, the bad boy, drunk, insane, a loser, and yet they both married me without a second thought. They were so starry-eyed by my dad's money and fame they probably thought they'd hit the super lotto. Neither of them could possibly have loved me, nor did I love them. I'm sure I led them both to believe I was heir to great wealth.

They must have been color blind to mistake red flags for greenbacks, or they may have tried to apply the mathematical formula used by the hot gold diggers in Newport Beach who *aren't* colorblind. Those hotties gamble that the money and prestige will outweigh the grief they will suffer by having to live with the disgusting asshole. Their mathematical formula is called, *"The grief-to-dollar ratio."*

I stayed sober for a month or so after we both said, "I do," but then

I started drinking and snorting heroin with a flamboyant queer from New Orleans whom I'd met in my most recent rehab. He was a hilarious character, and although it seemed unlikely, he and I became friends. He was way crazier than I was, and showed it. My wife wasn't too happy about me drinking and snorting heroin with some crazy butt-pirate in her house, but she came to like him as much as I did. He was actually a generous and good soul and he was constantly buying my dad's books, getting him to autograph them, and then would send them to his friends and relatives in New Orleans, telling all of them he was a very close friend of Joe Wambaugh's.

He didn't come around for a month or so, and wasn't answering his phone, which made me worry about him. Then one day my mom called to say she'd read in the newspaper that my friend had been found in the backseat of his car, dead from a heroin overdose. He'd died all alone.

I kept drinking, and things were only getting worse between Sarah and me, so eventually she'd had enough of my shit and jumped on my parents' bandwagon, pressuring me to go back to CRI-HELP, a long-term rehab in North Hollywood. I'd been there before, but had left after only four days. I agreed to go again.

When I walked through the door of CRI-HELP, it felt about as hopeless as it had been the last time I was there. I could see that it was going to be as bad as, or worse, than Provo Canyon Boys School. The patient population consisted of parolees, AIDS cases, rich kids, rock stars, and a few out-of-work actors. Robert Downey Jr. was sentenced to that program after he was busted for crawling into his neighbor's bed and passing out. I guess the program didn't stick, because after that, he got busted again for driving nude up Laurel Canyon with a pistol between his legs.

Corey Feldman was a recent graduate who would come to the place fairly often and share about how he had been sexually molested when he was a child. I thought it was creepy how he seemed to like talking about that shit all the time.

I had enrolled in the nine-month program, but left after only thirteen days. I couldn't handle all the confrontational bullshit that took place, and during one of the process groups, I'd had enough! I was told to sit in a chair in the middle of the room and the others proceeded to make a circle around me. They began yelling at me, saying, "Who the fuck do you think you are? You're a fucking loser! What makes you think you're better than everyone else?"

I stood up, and said, "I've been through this fucking bullshit before in Mississippi, but I was on psych meds, so it was almost tolerable. I'm really sober now, so what that means is that I'm gone!" I walked out and didn't look back.

I packed my belongings and called Sarah, begging her to pick me up immediately. After I thoroughly browbeat her, she drove from San Diego to get me. My parents were livid, seeing as how the rehabs I'd been admitted to were always paid in advance, and when I would walk out against medical advice, the advance payment was forfeited.

I swore to them and my wife that I would get a job, stay sober, and hopefully make them all proud of me. I really meant it at the time, and that's the insanity of it all. I tried the same thing over and over again, and expected different results. I knew somewhere in my distorted mind that I would fail again. That I was destined to continue to let my parents down until they would have to lay me to rest after all my chances ran out.

Chapter Ten

Sarah's sister was very creative, and typed up a resume that made it appear as though I actually had had a life. I saw an ad for a job that looked like it would be right up my alley. It was for a venture capital group looking for a highly motivated salesperson. I didn't even know what a venture capital group was, but I *did* know what a highly motivated salesperson was and that was me!

The next morning, I was interviewed by the president of the company in his beautiful La Jolla office. He called a couple of his partners in and introduced us. They were all wearing expensive suits, and looked successful. I liked that, and right away I saw myself fitting in. The president was an attorney who had had a successful law practice in New Jersey, but he'd felt there was a lot of opportunity and big money to be made here on the West Coast, and that he was ready for a change of pace. How lucky was I? I walked out of that interview with a job, and even my own beautiful office.

To start, I was paid $500 in cash each week, and my cell phone was paid for. I was given a very nice, full-size Ford Bronco to drive. My new boss also told me that after I closed a couple of deals for him, he would upgrade me to a Mercedes, which he did only two months later. He said that I would be dealing with multi-millionaires who notice things like suits, shoes, ties, and watches, and he said he wanted me to look the part. He took me to Neiman Marcus and bought me three Italian suits, some shirts, several ties, and two pairs of dress shoes. He also gave me signing privileges at two upscale restaurants, one in La Jolla and another in the Gaslamp District of downtown San Diego. The greatest thing of all was the stretch limo he bought for the company. He got it for the purpose of entertaining potential investors, and closing deals. All *kinds* of deals.

My job consisted of selling investment packages to people who were able to make a minimum of a $100,000 investment toward the development of a historic building that our company owned. At least I *thought* we owned it! The Gaslamp District of San Diego was still in the early stages of urban renewal, but was being rapidly developed. My boss thought I should educate myself on its history so that I could better entice my investors. It was amazing what I could learn when it came to money. I *loved* that job! It was sort of like being in the Mafia. Everyone had names like Jimmy, Bobby, Pauley and Tony, but he called me Butch. There were a lot of secret meetings in his office, and a lot of secret meetings outside the office too. I was never a part of any of those meetings, but I could smell a criminal conspiracy in the air and I found it exciting.

One time I became a little unsettled when I overheard my boss talking to someone on the phone about losing $70,000 in one night of gambling in Vegas. Shortly after that conversation, he was all over me to get more and more investors. I had a bad feeling he was gambling the money away, but I didn't say anything about it since I was getting paid and had great perks. At some point, Sarah told my parents about all my great perks, and of course my dad got suspicious and did a little investigating. After a few days, he called me to say that my boss *was* an attorney from New Jersey, but had been disbarred and sent to federal prison for seven years after being convicted on several white-collar felonies.

A few days after I got that news, I was pulling up to the underground parking structure and saw a lot of men wearing FBI raid jackets walking in and out of the building, carrying boxes and computers. A plastic surgeon from the office next door, who was standing outside the building, looked at me, shook his head frantically, and made the throat cutting gesture. I got the hell out of there immediately.

That night I had a friend follow me back to the office and I dropped off the Mercedes, leaving the keys on the floorboard. I found out through an attorney who had worked for us that my boss had gone on the lam, and was hiding somewhere in the Palm Springs area with a federal warrant out for his arrest.

I had to give up the Mercedes, my income, my signing privileges, and the limo that I loved so much. I was going to be a nobody again. And with no car, I was going to have to borrow my wife's little bitch-box to get around in. The party was over.

I never saw any of those people after that, but a couple of years later, a mutual friend told me that my former boss was killed in a car accident in Palm Springs. He'd been living in a studio apartment and driving an old piece-of-crap car. He'd gotten in a head-on collision while driving drunk, and also caused the death of a young mother who was driving the other car.

———

Shortly after I lost that job I started drinking every day, but I stayed at home so I wouldn't get myself into any more trouble. My wife remained loyal and was always hoping, just like everyone else, that I would grow up. Eventually, Sarah insisted that I go back into rehab, so I did.

My roommate in rehab turned out to be an ex-con junkie whose only reason for being there was to avoid prison. On his first night there, his wife snuck in a ball of heroin the size of a plum. He shot dope all night and talked about the good old gangbanging days.

During that evening he offered me a marble-size ball of brown tar and I caved in pretty fast. He showed me how to "chase the dragon" by taking a piece of tin foil about twelve inches long, crease it, and place a piece of the tar at one end. Then he showed me how you stick a straw in your mouth, light the foil from underneath, tip it upwards toward the heroin, and it slowly streams down the foil like a river of death. That's when you inhale the thick and billowy smoke. I was nauseous at first, but thirty minutes later, all of my emotional pain went away. I chased the dragon all night long while pretending to listen to his stupid stories that he kept repeating over and over.

I smoked a little too much dope before process group the next morning and was confronted by the counselor after I nodded off while sharing during the group session. I refused to take a drug test, so they told me I would have to leave. I called Sarah, and she reluctantly came to pick me up. On the ride home she asked me what my plans were, and for once I told her the truth.

I said, "I have absolutely no idea."

I was home from rehab just in time to join my wife on her company vacation. She worked in sales for a very large defense contractor that had big-time employee parties, and an annual company weekend getaway. The vacation was going to take place at a hotel and golf resort about an hour south of the Mexican border, and on one of the days they planned to have a golf tournament, so that was pretty cool.

On the night before the tournament, all the guys were bragging and carrying on about what great golfers they were, what low handicaps they had, and how far they could drive the ball. They were all college graduates with various degrees, and the only thing I had in common with them was the tequila we were drinking. I really didn't talk too much, but when the guy organizing the foursomes asked me what my handicap was, I explained that I hadn't played golf for so many years that I didn't even *have* a handicap anymore, but maybe I would shoot in the high eighties, or even ninety, I didn't know.

The next day, I stayed in the hotel room powering Coronas for a couple of hours before the tournament to get rid of the shakes from the night before. By the time I teed it up, I had just the perfect buzz to take the edge off and was ready to compete against the frat boys. I played lights-out golf that day. It was almost an out-of-body experience because I couldn't make a bad shot, and my putting was deadly. I don't recall what my score was, but I came in one stroke behind the winner. At the awards dinner that night, some of the guys were pissed off, claiming I was a sandbagger and must not have given them the correct handicap. I bounced from that party, and told Sarah I was going to the hotel bar to get away from those guys before I did something that would jeopardize her job.

There was another company party shortly after the Mexico trip, but that time I drove there alone in a cheap car I'd bought from a junkie. It was the employee Christmas party that was being held at the U.S Grant Hotel in downtown San Diego, and Sarah couldn't go. She had previously made plans to spend Christmas with her family in Arizona, but she encouraged me to go. The booze was free, so of course I went, and of course, got ripped to the gills.

When the alcohol stopped flowing, I stumbled out of the hotel and onto the sidewalk when two young black males approached me. Even drunk, it was easy to see what was happening. They asked for my money and I told them to go fuck themselves, and then I woke up in the hospital emergency room with a serious concussion and numerous stitches in my forehead. One of them had smacked me with a beer bottle, and the lights went out.

The ER physician just so happened to be a friend of mine from AA. While he was stitching me up, he said, "How're you doing, Dave?"

"Obviously, not that great," I said

"You gotta get sober," he said. "You had a bad concussion, brother. I'm scared for you. Come back to AA, Dave. I'd be happy to be your temporary sponsor." Then he handed me a card with his cell number on the back.

I said, "Thanks, John. I'll give you a call in the morning and we can start working the steps, and going to meetings together."

"Cool, Dave," he said. "Talk to you tomorrow. Let go, let God, bro."

And I said, "Yep, one day at a time."

Of course, I shined him.

That head injury took the wind out of my sails for a while and I was lying low until one day an old buddy called and asked if I wanted to meet him for drinks. He said he was buying, so you can bet your ass, I was flying. He bought me drinks all day long, so I was really sloppy by the time I left the bar that afternoon.

Just as I was pulling away from the curb, I'll be damned if a cop didn't pull in right behind me. I couldn't believe it! I was on the same street where I'd already had two previous DUI's. I figured that street was just bad luck for me.

I wasn't too surprised when the cop turned his lights on because the tags on my unregistered car had just recently expired. My car wasn't registered, I didn't have a drivers license, and I reeked of booze, so I knew if I pulled over I was going down for sure. I knew the streets and alleys around there, so I downshifted into first gear, and the chase was on. I thought I would have an advantage that day because there had been a light rain and the roads were slippery. The Crown Vics were much heavier than my Mustang, but they had the same engine and suspension, so I figured I could outrun him.

If I couldn't ditch him quickly, I'd be screwed because no one can outrun the radio. I pulled off the main drag and shot down an alley that opened onto a street that would lead directly to the nearest escape route. I came out of the alley a little too fast, lost traction and spun out. I came nose to nose with the patrol car, and my car stalled.

The cop jumped out of his car, and with his hand on his gun and yelled, "Freeze! Don't move, asshole! Do not move!"

The next thing I heard was someone shouting my name. It was my AA sponsor who screamed at the top of his lungs, "*Oh my God! WAMBAUGH!*"

I craned my neck, and amazing as it may seem, I saw my longhaired hippy sponsor standing on the front porch of a nearby house, holding his newborn baby. I was hoping the cop didn't hear my name or see him. I hoped he would just go back inside and keep his mouth shut.

I had to get away, so I started my car, looked at the cop, shook my head, put it in reverse, and the chase was on again. When I finally lost him near Mission Bay, I drove the back roads to a watering hole near my house, put the cover on the car, and called Sarah to come and pick me up. That whole chase was so surreal and unbelievable, it was even hard for me to believe it had happened, but it was absolutely *true*!

The next morning, I called the Iranian guy who bought my discards, and he sent one of his flunkies to meet me. He handed *me* $2,500 cash and didn't ask any questions, and I handed *him* the pink slip with someone else's name on it.

———

My wife was pissed when I wanted to borrow her Honda again, but I told her it was imperative that I have my own wheels if she expected me to find another job. I convinced her to use her good credit for me, and finance a Mustang 5.0 GT. I don't know if she really believed I would get a job, but she *wanted* to believe it.

Around five o'clock on Halloween afternoon, I figured I had plenty of time before I had to go home and get ready for the costume party that Sarah and I were going to that night, so I stopped for a pitcher of brew at one of my favorite spots. It was a cheesy strip club with thrashed dancers, but it was a good place to drink. I wanted to catch a buzz before going to the party, so after a couple of hours, powering down vodka crans, I had the perfect glow. That wonderful, perfect glow.

I was ready to pick her up and go out for a good time, and as I was making a right turn out of the parking lot of the strip joint, a cop rolled right up behind me. I couldn't believe it. I could *not* believe this was happening again! I'd only had this new ride for a few days, and wasn't about to lose it. So when he turned on those lights, I downshifted into first, and left burnt rubber in my wake. The main thing going through my mind right then was that I didn't want my wife to find out I got busted pulling away from a titty bar in the new car she'd just financed for me.

The chase lasted well over thirty minutes and reached speeds in excess of a hundred miles an hour. The CHP, the San Diego County Sheriffs, and the San Diego Police, including the Eye in the Sky, were in hot pursuit. I almost escaped before the copter arrived, but once it had me in its spotlight, I had no chance.

It was very foggy that evening, so I felt my only chance would be to find a surface street shrouded in fog, and escape on foot. If I could lose the cops on the ground and become invisible to the copter long enough, I thought I might have a shot. As I was flying down a surface street through the dense fog, it suddenly lifted and I saw that I was headed directly toward a concrete barrier that had been put there to indicate a dead-end. I was going about 70 miles an hour and there was no possible way I could stop in time. That was the first time in my life I thought for sure, I was going to die.

The next day, November 1, 1994, the San Diego Union Tribune ran an article that I'm sure made my parents cringe.

Wambaugh son, 30, is arrested

University City

The son of cop-turned-author Joseph Wambaugh was arrested early yesterday by San Diego police on suspicion of driving under the influence and evading arrest, after leading officers on a high-speed chase and crashing his car at the end of Governor Drive near Interstate 805.

David Wambaugh, 30, was taken into custody about 12:50 a.m. after his vehicle crashed into a barrier. He was taken to Scripps Memorial Hospital in La Jolla for treatment of a bloody nose and then booked into County Jail.

Police said officers attempted to stop Wambaugh's gray Ford Mustang near University Towne Centre after he ran three red lights and refused to pull over.

When I woke up in the hospital, Sarah, my wife of only six months, was sitting by my side. When I tried to reach out to her, I realized I was cuffed to the gurney. She told me that I had been on the eleven o'clock news that night, and the footage showed the firemen cutting me out of my car with the Jaws of Life. She said that my new car looked like a ball of twisted metal. It was reported that I had a bloody nose but actually it was broken, and I had cuts and bruises all over my body. Everything hurt, but nothing was life threatening.

While she was telling me about the eleven o'clock news, an old cop walked in the room, and said, "Young man, I've been a CHP officer for a lot of years and I've seen a number of people die. You're very, *very* lucky! You should take it as a sign. It's a minor miracle, and I'm shocked that you're not dead."

A few minutes later, a San Diego police officer entered the room to say that I was being charged with two crimes: A felony DUI and felony evading. It was beginning to seem as though every time I drank, I broke out in handcuffs.

I looked up at him in disbelief, and yelled, "Felonies? No one was injured. That's bullshit!"

He said, *"You* were injured."

"Well, check this out," I said. "I don't want to press charges on myself so you can just take that felony away! Now I only have *one!*"

As he walked out the door he turned, and said, "I'm just here to tell you what you're being charged with, and it doesn't look good for you."

"Great," I said, relieved that no one told Sarah where the chase had started.

I was placed in protective custody, where the high-profile criminals, child molesters, arsonists, and rapists were housed, so at least I had interesting neighbors. In the cell to the left of me, was the Pacific Beach Rapist, one of the most notorious criminals in San Diego. And to the right was a guy who was on trial for the killings of a San Diego police officer and an innocent motorist.

At my arraignment, I was assigned to a public defender who sported a ponytail that nearly reached his ass and had hoop earrings in both ears. He was telling me to plead guilty to all charges and he promised he would do his best to get me the lowest prison term he could negotiate.

I tried to tell the asshole that I didn't want to do prison time at all, but he wasn't hearing me. I impatiently said, "Forget about it, guy, I'll talk my way out of this shit on my own."

As I was thinking about what I was going to say to the judge, another lawyer sauntered in, introduced himself, and excused the tree hugger. One of my good friends, whose sister was mayor at the time, saw me on the eleven o'clock news the night before and was kind enough to call his family attorney for me.

Their lawyer had more boyish charm than Justin Beiber, and was the smoothest attorney I'd ever met. I told him what the public defender had said about me going to prison, and he assured me that it wouldn't be the case. And he was right. He got me sentenced to rehab for a year instead of having to do hard time. I had a doctor friend whom I'd been in rehab with a few years earlier and just so happened to own a court-approved rehab facility in San Diego, and my attorney managed to have me placed there. It worked out perfectly.

After I did my time in rehab, I was thirty-one, already had a couple of felonies under my belt, and had done a fair amount of jail time. I was miserable and my wife was supporting the household and still holding out hope that one day I might man up.

It was surprising that Sarah so much as *considered* having a child with me, given my genetic predisposition to addiction, but I guess her biological clock was ticking, and I did have an impressive last name and rich parents. She was thrilled when she became pregnant, but I was in a panic about what kind of role I could play as a father, and how I could possibly contribute to the support of a kid who would be coming soon.

I didn't have a car, so I had to learn to navigate the public transportation system. I took a bus every day to and from a job brewing coffee at a coffee cart in San Diego's Old Town. I had gone from driving a top-of-the-line Mercedes to riding Bus Number Four every day. I went from sporting expensive suits to wearing a red apron with a goofy nametag that said "David" with a smiley-face sticker next to it. I hated to be seen at the bus stop, so I would stand about fifty feet from the bus bench pretending to be doing something other than waiting for public transportation. The only good thing about that job was that I could keep a bottle or two stashed on the cart and drink throughout my shift, easing my humiliation of being there.

Our parents made an attempt to introduce Mark and me to other cultures with extensive travel: Cairo, Athens and Paris, 1975
You can see the excitement on our faces.

Chapter Eleven

Late in 1995, Ziggy came back into my life shortly before my son Jake was born. I don't know how he was able to contact me, but he appeared. He told me that he'd started a business a couple of years earlier doing outdoor sign advertising, and was doing incredibly well. I could never imagine him running a business. I explained that I was married, had a baby on the way, and desperately needed a decent job.

Ziggy gave me a great position in his company, and for the first time I would be following my best friend instead of him following me. It was so hard to believe, that after living on the street together, Ziggy actually had become a financial success. He was a pioneer of outdoor sign promotions, and at one point had at least a hundred people working for him. He hired a bunch of addicts and losers like me, giving us jobs that we would've never gotten had we not known him, and he paid all of us more than we deserved. He was generous with everything he had.

While I worked for him, I traveled fifty weeks out of the year and was in a different city every couple of weeks doing liquidations for furniture stores or new car dealerships. For each liquidation, we would order a few hundred signs, staple each of them to a stake, and plant them in strategic places near the businesses and freeway off-ramps. Then I would hire a dozen down-and-outs from local sober-living homes, supply them with clown costumes, and put them out on street corners with signs to wave and twirl. I would also grill cheap hot dogs to give away, and rent large Bouncy Houses to keep the children happy while their parents shopped for furniture or cars. I became good at creating a circus-like atmosphere, seeing as how I was a natural-born clown myself. I was drunk most the time, and sometimes didn't even show up at the job, so poor Ziggy had to put out several of my fires, yet he never fired me.

———

I flew home from New York about the time Sarah was to give birth to our son. In the very early morning, just twelve hours after my plane landed, Sarah went into labor. I had been out until 2 a.m. drinking, so when her labor started I was still drunk and too hammered to drive, so she took the wheel and I rode shotgun. We checked into the hospital and got her settled into her room. The nurse said they were going to induce labor soon, so I asked if she thought I had enough time to find a twenty-four hour pharmacy where I could buy a disposable camera, to be sure we got back-up photos of Jake's birth. She said I had about an hour, so I figured it was plenty of time to find a liquor store, buy a couple of pints of vodka and get back in time to see our baby being born. When I got back to the hospital, Sarah asked me where the camera was, and I told her that I was so excited about the baby coming, I must have left it at the store. She didn't believe me, and I didn't really care. I had the vodka.

On February 9th, 1996, Sarah produced an unbelievably beautiful baby, and we named him Jake David. When I laid my eyes on that innocent little boy I had mixed feelings. I was floored at how beautiful he was, like a little doll. I felt an instant bond when I held him in my arms, and I couldn't believe that God saw fit to give me such a gift. I was overcome with gratitude, but I started crying. These were not tears of joy, but of sorrow and despair. I suddenly felt so sad for this innocent little angel because I knew he was going to grow up without a father, maybe with the same abandonment issues that possessed me. I was frantically searching my mind, my heart, my soul for an answer to the question. Was there any possible way for me to turn my life around for this gift from God? I already knew the answer, and the answer was *no*. My head was swimming with contempt for myself. No matter how many different ways I posed the question to myself, the answer didn't change. My son was going to grow up without a father, and there was nothing I could do to change the outcome. At least that's what I thought.

When Jake was about a year old, Sarah's suspicions about my infidelity were confirmed after I came home from a business trip and I had *OWS* all over my clothes and person: *Other Woman's Smell.* She accused me, and I finally admitted that she was right. I was a cheater. A couple of weeks after that she filed for divorce. Infidelity was nothing new to me because I'd never been loyal or faithful to any girl in my life. I judged most women like the woman who discarded me at birth: disloyal, unfaithful, cheating whores who would give you up if it suited their fancy.

———

Over the span of my lifetime I had used truckloads of alcohol and street drugs, but on one of our business trips to New York, Ziggy turned me on to crack cocaine. When I took the first hit, the rush was so powerful that I nearly busted a nut in my shorts. That head rush was so good, I had a bad feeling that crack was going to become a real problem for both of us. Luckily, I didn't become a total crack-head, but Ziggy did, and he had the resources to keep himself flying, day and night--for a while.

Soon after we started smoking crack, I was back on the East Coast working a job when, out of nowhere, Ziggy called to say that he was in Tahoe, and had just bought a brand new, $65,000 Air Nautique. It was a beautiful, top-of-the-line ski boat. I think he was trying to get off crack, so he wanted to pursue healthy activities. I was on the next flight. When he picked me up at the airport, we hit the liquor store, stockpiled some booze, and water-skied all afternoon.

Along the way, Ziggy had gotten married and had a baby right away. His wife didn't like me, and I didn't like her either, so it was good that she wasn't interested in boating that day. After a day of skiing, drinking, and checking out the babes on the lake, we went back to Ziggy's pad, freshened up, and then went out on the boat that evening for more fun. Most of the restaurants and bars on the lake have guest docks, so we motored from place to place, hitting damn near every bar on the south shore until they were all closing. After last call, we had to navigate our way home, and it was so pitch black out on the lake we could barely see fifty feet in front of us, but Ziggy wanted to show me how fast his boat could go on glassy water.

We were going full throttle when we hit the stern of a moored ski boat, after which, Ziggy's boat was catapulted through the air for at least thirty feet. The sound was deafening! Thank God the boat we hit was unoccupied. We were both ejected into the water and I saw that Ziggy was barely conscious. I had fractured a couple of ribs, so it was really hard to swim or breathe, but I got us back to the boat. Unfortunately it was halfway submerged, and slowly sinking, so we screamed for help. When the Coast Guard finally came to our rescue, we were hauled into their vessel and given blankets. One of the Coast Guard guys said we would've died from hypothermia within fifteen minutes if we hadn't been pulled from the icy water.

As we were thawing, an officer approached us, and asked, "Who was driving the boat?"

Ziggy looked at me with a stupid look on his face and said, "Come on, Wambuh, tell him."

"Tell him what?" I said.

"Tell him. *You* were driving!"

I looked dead straight at the man and said, "Sir, this dude right here was driving the boat. I did *not* drive the boat. *He* drove the boat. And fuck you, Ziggy!"

Ziggy said, "Well, maybe I *did* drive."

He talked himself out of a BUI, which is *boating* under the influence, but he lost a very expensive boat and also had to pay for the other boat he wrecked. And, he had a really pissed-off wife. She'd come to L.A. in the first place to meet a rich guy, and she did just that, but she didn't know that the rich guy she married was also completely insane. He wasn't fun crazy; he was *crazy* crazy.

After my ribs healed, I was back on the road. I tried to get home as often as possible to see my son who was about eighteen months old by then, but the visits were becoming fewer. I missed him and wanted to be there for him, but I just wasn't capable. I wasn't capable of *anything* worthwhile. I always told my family that I loved them, and I believed I did, but love's a responsibility. I was a terrible son, a terrible father, and I didn't even know how to be a friend. I didn't know what family and friends were for, other than to use. I had no hopes, no dreams, and no future. Only a past full of regrets.

———

In July, 1997 I decided to try it one last time, to give rehab a real shot for the sake of my son, so I went back to Cri-Help. This would now be my third time there, so hopefully it would be the charm. Maybe I could pull it together for Jake's sake. My dad thought I might be able to do it for my boy who was only a year and a half old at the time, but I left after doing only four months of the nine-month program.

I went back to work locally, and rented an oceanfront apartment near my son so we could spend time together, and his mom was cool enough to drop him off for a few hours at a time. Jake and I had access to all sorts of beach fun, so she didn't think there would be any threat of me driving him anywhere, but I was sneaking drinks during our visits. It's ironic because I would've died for him but I couldn't *live* for him.

Because of my inability to stay sober, Sarah took me to family court and got an order forcing me to have only supervised visits with Jake, or none at all. She knew that I would drink and drive with Jake in the car without thinking twice, so she did the right thing. At first, I was angry about the supervised visits, but in my heart I knew it was the best thing for my son. I couldn't even see my kid without having to pay big bucks to a court-appointed woman hovering over my shoulder, taking notes.

Because of the supervised visits, I sobered up for a while and was doing fairly well, traveling only to the neighboring states for work so that I could be more available for Jake. I was beginning to establish a little consistency, and my relationship with his mom was improving. She was just about to let us have sleepovers, and I was excited and grateful. I never fought her on visitation, especially after I challenged her once in court and she buried me. Her lawyer had so much dirt on me I was afraid they were going to take me into custody straight out of family court. Halfway through her lawyer's Wambaugh bashing, I walked out of the courtroom and told my attorney to just send me the paperwork to sign.

I was really looking forward to my son's second birthday because Sarah was going to let us have a sleepover that night, and it was going to be the first we'd had in a long while. His mom and I had a great party planned for him. Our little cub was going to celebrate his second birthday at Chuck-E Cheese, and for once I was going to be there. I was so happy, and I wanted it to stay like that forever. On the night before his birthday party, I was arrested for another DUI and possession of crack cocaine. I missed Jake's second birthday and didn't see him again for many months.

———

In November, 1997, I was able to con the Judge into sentencing me back to the rehab owned by my doctor friend, so my time wasn't really like *doing* time. The doctor always welcomed me back--for the right price. One time I told him that I would pay him double if he would let me continue to work, since I had incurred some serious attorney bills trying to stay out of prison. He accepted my offer with the stipulation that I couldn't drink, which was one hell of a stipulation. That quack knew damn well I wouldn't stay off the booze, but he took my money anyway.

A few weeks into my stay at his rehab, I was on one of Ziggy's sign jobs in Detroit and decided to go home for the weekend. I got drunk on the flight home, and when the cab dropped me at the rehab, the manager was standing at the front door waiting for me. He asked to smell my breath and I told him to blow me. He told me I had to leave the property, and in order for me to come back, I would have to go to detox for three days. I told him to blow me again.

As I was gathering my belongings, a little Persian girl peeked around the corner into my room and asked who I was, where I was going, and what I was going to do. She said she'd arrived at the facility while I was out of town, and was surprised when I showed up there in that room. She had a beautiful face and dark inquisitive eyes. She said her name was Mithra, and as she spoke I could hardly take my eyes off her full lips and shiny brown hair that reached just past her shoulders. I asked her where she was from, and she said her parents emigrated from Iran before she was born and settled in Northern California, near Stanford, where she grew up. Her dad was a rich businessman that had something to do with the dot.com industry.

As I was waiting for my ride, I told her I would answer all her questions in the back of the limo if she cared to join me. When the manager realized what was happening, he tried to convince her not to go, but she piled in the back of the limo right along with me. I'm sure her dad wasn't going to be too thrilled when he learned that his daughter took off with some drunk in the back of a limo during her first week in rehab. I told the driver to take us to the first bar he could find.

I got fully tossed, and when I came to, I found myself in the back of the limo, but had no idea where we were or what had happened during the previous hours. When I came around, Mithra was petting me and lightly kissing my lips.

When I was able to focus, I looked at her and said, "What happened? Where are we? I need to roll down the partition and talk to the driver."

Before I could hit the partition button, she flung herself at me and said, "Baby, I'm so happy! I've never been this happy in my life!"

"What do you mean? What happened? What..." I was lost for words, since I didn't know what the hell was going on.

She cuddled up close to me, and said, "I love you so much, and just like the lady said, we'll take care of each other in sickness and health. Forever!"

I almost shit myself! I rolled down the partition, and said, "Hey, sir, would you please pull this car over immediately?"

He had a grin from ear to ear, and it made me wonder what the hell was so funny. He said, "Sure, Mister Wambaugh."

When the limo pulled over I got out, and said to the driver, "Bro, what the fuck happened?"

"What do you mean, Mister Wambaugh?" he answered.

"Please, call me Dave."

"Dave, you're one of the funniest guys I've ever met," he said.

I said, "Come on, bro, don't do that shit. Tell me what happened!"

He said, "When you two insisted that I drive you to Vegas, I cleared it with my boss, and then after the wedding ceremony, we picked up some ice and a bottle of champagne and headed back. We're in Barstow now, gassing up."

"I can't believe it! This is a nightmare," I said, feeling sick.

"Well, Dave," he said, "after you married Mifra, Mirtha, Meetra, whatever her name is, you told me you were already married. Is that true?"

"Yeah, it's true, bro. Oh, my God!"

"For real?" he said. "You were already married?"

"For real," I said. "So, what happened?"

He said, "You were so funny last night during that little wedding ceremony. I called my fraternity brothers and told them what happened, and now you're a legend at the SAE house at State. You gave your old wedding ring to some bum, and bought a pair of matching bands for you and Mifra, or Meethra, whatever her name is."

I looked at my hand and it was confirmed that he was telling the truth. With a knot in my stomach, I said, "Oh, Jesus! Listen to me, homie, get me back to Pacific Beach immediately and I'll figure out what to do with this Iranian when I get there!"

He said, "Hey, Mister Wambaugh, I mean, Dave. If you don't mind me asking, what was her last name before she became Mrs. Wambaugh? It was some Middle Eastern name, like twenty letters long. I know it started with a "K" and ended with an "I". Anyway, I guess it doesn't matter, because she's Mrs. Wambaugh now."

My third wife and I checked into a hotel back in San Diego where I had to make the dreaded call to my attorney, Brian McCarthy. When he answered, he said, "Dave, I'm assuming because you're not calling collect, you're not in custody for once. What's up?"

"Brian," I said, "I got fucked-up the other night, and wound up getting married to some Persian chick!"

He said, "Dave, I'm real busy today, I gotta go. Call me later, or tomorrow." And he hung up.

I hit redial, and when he picked up, I said, "Brian, I'm serious, please listen to me! I think I'm in trouble!"

"Yeah, Dave, what's new? Hurry up."

"I got kicked out of rehab the other night for showing up drunk, and when I left, this little Iranian left with me. She checked into rehab last week while I was out of town, and I'm not totally sure what happened, but somehow I got married to her!"

He said, "Well, good job, you dumb shit. I'm sure Sarah will appreciate that. What's your new wife's name?"

"Mithra, I think."

"That sounds pretty good, Dave. It has a nice ring to it. Mithra Wambaugh."

"Thanks," I said.

He said, "You're in trouble, alright. First of all, you violated your felony probation by getting kicked out of the program, and secondly, you committed another felony by marrying the Iranian girl while you're still married to Sarah. It's called bigamy, Dave. You're on a fast track to prison, and you ain't gonna like it there."

I hung up the phone and told my new wife that I'd be right back. I walked out of the hotel room, straight to the nearest bar, and drank, seeking oblivion.

Mithra said she'd always wanted to go party down in Mexico, just as Sarah had when we first met, so I told her I'd take her there, and that we could hang out for a few days. My plan was to check into the Rosarito Beach Hotel, have some drinks with her, excuse myself to go to the bathroom, and drive back to San Diego as fast as I could. Alone. She spoke Spanish, so I didn't feel too bad about the fact that I was going to dump her ass in Mexico.

On our way south to Rosarito, I let her drive because I was so drunk I couldn't see the road, but she was loaded too, and driving way too fast on those shitty Mexican roads. Sure enough, a moment after I yelled at her to slow down, she lost control, drove off an embankment and into a ditch. My airbag deployed, but I still got a lot of scrapes and bruises. When the cops showed up, they took us both into custody. My car was totaled.

I stayed in a holding cell while they took Mithra out for questioning. After a couple of hours, she reappeared, walking around the corner toward my cell clad in only her bra and panties. There were five Mexican cops following behind her with shit-eating grins, and it was obvious that she had just been gang banged by a bunch of third-world greaseballs. I was repulsed.

As they put her back into the cell next to mine, she said, "Baby, everything's gonna be okay. They're gonna let us go. Now, all they want is for you to go with them to an ATM and get the maximum amount of cash you can take out, and then they said they'll drive us to the border."

"Is that all?" I said.

"Yes, baby, I love you," she said.

"Yeah, I love you too," I said, "So, did all those guys bone you?"

"I did it for you, honey."

"Thanks, I appreciate the gesture," I said.

As soon as we got back across the border, we checked into a seedy hotel in San Diego and I told her that I was going to the liquor store to get some booze. I hit the door running, never looking back, and never saw Mithra Wambaugh again.

Thank God my friend, the doctor, who owned the rehab was able to help me escape this train wreck by telling the authorities that I was mentally incompetent at the time I married the other nut job. With his help, and Mithra's wealthy father, the marriage was annulled, and the man from Iran swept it all under his magic carpet.

Not long after my third marriage was annulled, I violated my probation again by testing dirty for coke. The court gave me the option of doing one calendar year in county jail or one calendar year in rehab. The catch was that if I chose rehab and screwed up at any time during that year, I would lose the time already spent, and *still* do a calendar year in county jail. My attorney strongly advised that I take the jail time and get it over with. He encouraged me to be realistic about my chances of staying sober for a whole year. He said that, from his experience with me, I couldn't stay sober for one month, let alone a whole year, but I chose rehab anyway. I was willing to do anything but jail time. I agreed with my lawyer about my slim-to-none chance of completing the year successfully, but I decided to gamble.

Before I checked in to start my year of rehab at COBAR House, I went on a big bender and wound up in the hospital again. It was July, 1998. I finally got there two days late, but the owner of the place was real cool and gave me a break by not reporting me to my probation officer. She was a very kind, but strict, older black woman named Connie Henderson.

As soon as I walked through the front door, she started, "Listen to me, Dave Wambaugh, you two days late, and I should call your PO and tell him what you done. You got time hangin' over your head, and you show up two days late? What's wrong with you? You already on thin ice 'round here, and you best not be screwin' up 'cause I'll put you in jail! You feel me?"

"Yes, ma'am," I replied.

She got up, came around the side of her desk, hugged me and said, "You be okay, Dave Wambaugh. You be jist fine."

"Thanks," I said, as I looked at her in bewilderment.

She was so cool it was unbelievable. She allowed me to work every weekend, and she even allowed me to fly out of town on Friday evenings, and be back in my bed by 6:00 a.m. on Monday for bed check. The black guys at COBAR were jealous of the way she treated me and they started calling me *The Golden Child*.

When I worked locally, I hired a guy from COBAR to drive me since I didn't have a driver's license and Connie wouldn't let me drive without one. We called him Daddy Rich, and he and I became pretty good friends. He was an older white man who suffered from depression and alcoholism, but he was a real gentleman, and had been financially successful at one point in his life. He came from a wealthy old La Jolla family, but because of his addiction and mental illness, he'd lost everything, including his wife and kids.

Daddy Rich and I worked a job up in Orange County, and every Sunday after our job was finished I'd take Daddy Rich to a nearby strip club and get him some lap dances. I'd spend a couple hundred bucks and watch him light up when the strippers would bump and grind on his lap, and bury their melons in his face. I'd just sit there and drink as much as I could while Daddy Rich was surrounded by strippers. It was excellent entertainment.

One Sunday night after we got back, Connie called me up to her office at midnight, and I thought I was going to be in deep shit for drinking that day. When I walked in she gave me a sad look, and said, "Richard's dead. He killed himself."

I was totally shocked, and could only say, "How?"

"He walked out in front of an Amtrak train tonight," she said. "He dead, sweetie! I'm sorry. You can tell everyone at group tomorrow."

"Okay," was all I could say.

"Were you drinkin' with Daddy Rich today?" she asked.

"Yes, ma'am," I said truthfully.

She patted me on the cheek and said, "Go to bed, honey." With nothing more said about the drinking.

I felt guilt that I might have had something to do with Daddy Rich killing himself. He was my friend, and I spent lots of time with Daddy Rich, but I never noticed anything wrong with him. Was I *that* out of touch that I could only see things that pertained to me? Was I really *that* selfish?

After his funeral, I went to the liquor store and didn't return to the facility. When I didn't come home that night Connie sent out the posse. It consisted of her husband and some of her kids, and they were ordered not to come back without me. Two days later, her husband and a guy named Lynwood found me in a motel with some shot-out crack whore drinking a forty, waiting for more rocks to arrive. Larry, Connie's husband, begged me to go with him because he was tired as hell, and he said he couldn't go home without me.

I asked him, "Am I kicked out? Did Connie call my PO? Is there a warrant out for me?"

"Come on, now," Larry said, "you know better than that! Connie wouldn't do you like that. She jist wants you home. If you come back, she said you can detox in my room, and jist start over. She said she'll forget about it."

Relieved at that news, I said, "Okay, let's go."

When I walked into her house, Connie looked at me and asked, "You okay?"

With my head bowed, I said, "Yes, ma'am."

She snapped, "Don't you ever fuck with me like that again! I'm so mad at you, I could spit! I don't even want to look at you right now, Dave Wambaugh!"

I detoxed in Larry's room for a few days and then I was back in action. There was one guy named Big Bill in the facility who was making a huge stink about the fact that I wasn't kicked out for my bender, when others had. I told Connie about him running his mouth and getting the others on his bandwagon. She simply said to her assistant, "Pigpen, go tell Big Bill to come up to my office and then you go back downstairs and pack his shit." Thirty minutes later Big Bill was escorted off the premises and into the hands of his probation officer. I don't think Connie liked people to mess with me.

Connie showed me big-time love. She should've violated me several times, but didn't. She let me slide, signed my completion papers, and faxed them to my Probation Officer on my 365th day. I was always blessed like that--or was it a curse?

Chapter Twelve

I was thirty-four years old when I left COBAR house in May of 1999, and for the next year and a half I traveled all over the United States, still doing sign promotions for Ziggy, and drinking more than ever. But Ziggy was finally too messed up on crack to keep the business going, and when he eventually had no accounts left, he folded.

I had to get some kind of a job, but the only way I could think of to earn decent money was to do my own sign promotions. I figured if Ziggy did it, running on only three cylinders, I could certainly do it. So, I bought half a dozen clown suits, printed up a supply of business cards and brochures that my mom helped me design, and I was in business. *Sign Me Up Productions* was born. Unfortunately, I had to do all my business on a cash basis since I didn't have a bank account, which had been seized by the IRS.

I'm sure I'd done some serious brain damage to myself over the years and lost my ability to function at a very high level, but I was a good self-promoter and salesman. I got several accounts right away, learned how to design signs and get them printed, knew where to find the clowns, and I was willing to work all night assembling signs for each job. I made a lot of money, but didn't have a clue about keeping records, or reporting income and paying taxes, and that's when my IRS problems really began to accelerate. Of course for the past several years, while being an "independent contractor" for Ziggy, I was constantly on the move, and had no permanent address, but any correspondence that *did* find its way to me, usually by way of my mom, I just ignored. I figured, why should I pay taxes? I never had before, and besides, it was way too much red tape for me to even think about. My belief was that if I made the money, I should be able to keep it.

While working one of my jobs in Los Angeles, I met a stripper who'd recently moved from North Carolina to Hollywood to become the next Angelina Jolie, just like the other two million girls wanting the same thing. I knew the strip club wasn't the best place to find a girlfriend, but I wasn't too picky at the time, and obviously, neither was she. It was love at first lap dance. Before I knew it, I was in the VIP room where she wound up smoking my pole, so I was in love. She became my girlfriend that very night.

I moved into her West Hollywood crib with her and two other strippers, and abandoned my place in San Diego. I lived in a whorehouse. I guess you could say that we had a tumultuous relationship because we were both drunks, and both abusive. She was physically abusive and I was verbally abusive. She assaulted me a few times and once even sliced my back with a butcher knife. I should've gone to the hospital to get stitched up but I didn't want any negative police contact, so I treated it as best I could. The cut was pretty deep, so I'll always have a nasty scar on my back to remember her by. All I would have to do to put her in a rage was to call her a *stripper,* which was the truth, or call her by her stage name, *Ginger,* which also was the truth. I gathered that the truth hurt. Either name would initiate a reaction from her, sometimes violent.

One time I was attacked by some of her regulars from the titty bar whom she'd invited to her birthday party. I couldn't believe she had the nerve to invite *customers* from the titty bar to her birthday party at my house. I always got stuck paying the rent, so I did consider it *my* house. After I was good and drunk I called her a whore, and one of her clients blindsided me. He hit me so hard in the jaw that it must have fractured because I could hardly open my mouth for weeks.

———

The following day, I moved back to my mom's house in the desert. While she was nursing me back to health, she was also looking into long-term rehabs that might work for me. The Betty Ford Clinic had just started a ninety-day program specifically designed for professionals. It was called PRP, the Professional Recovery Program. There were physicians, judges, pilots, attorneys, business executives, professional athletes, and me. We were a class of sixteen, and of that sixteen, thirteen have since died, all of alcohol and drug related causes.

I was accepted into the program because my mom told the person in admissions that I was the president of my own advertising company. She neglected to tell the woman that I was the president of an unlicensed company that consisted of one broken down drunk who had no driver's license, no bank account, and a felony warrant out for his arrest. I imagine they accepted me on the strength of our last name. Just as my wives had!

My roommate was the best. His name was Dave Smith, an ex-professional baseball player who'd been an all-star pitcher for the Houston Astros, and definitely the most laid-back and easy-going of all the guys there. He was the current pitching coach for the San Diego Padres, but the coach, Bruce Bochy, made Dave go to rehab because he'd been showing up drunk to practices and games.

We had luxurious accommodations, off campus at a luxury resort, and Dave and I were able to play golf every day after our group sessions were over. I had a really good time hearing about all the incredible experiences he'd had as a major league player. As usual, I left rehab a few weeks early and did not graduate, but we stayed in touch for a while. We met once at a restaurant in Del Mar after we were both drinking again, and it just wasn't the same. The devil had come back into each of our lives, and we were both much different. A few years later, I heard he'd gotten married and had a beautiful little boy, and a year after that, I got another call from the same friend informing me that Dave recently drank himself to death. He was fifty-two years old, and his son was barely one.

Another rehab patient I became close to was a young physician named Jim. He was probably one of the smartest people I'd ever met, and was the most complete package I'd ever seen. Talk about an eligible bachelor. He was brilliant, good looking, well spoken, had good manners, played collegiate football for four years, and he was even funny.

Jim had a lot of unresolved issues with his father, and from what he told me, his dad was a real ball-buster and had put too much pressure on him when he was growing up. His parents came out for family week, a time that allows the families to participate in the treatment by addressing pertinent issues in a controlled environment, and start up the healing process. He told me that he and his dad had opened up an excellent line of communication and he was confident that it would continue after treatment. He also said he'd gotten resolution on other things that in the past had driven him to self-medicate.

Although I left prematurely, I talked to Jim almost every day. The day before he left, I remember him telling me how excited he was to go be going home, hoping to make everything right. He could hardly wait to start his new life, and was planning to resume his medical practice as soon as he got back to St. Louis. He said he was also looking forward to restoring other relationships that he'd damaged prior to treatment. He had everything going for him, but the morning after he arrived home, the police found him bludgeoned to death and stuffed into the trunk of his car like trash. The cops said it was a drug deal gone bad. Apparently, as soon as he got off the plane, he went to East St. Louis to buy some crack and was murdered by drug dealers.

There was tragedy after tragedy with almost all of the PRP guys who'd been there with me. They died terrible deaths, one after another, and yet somehow I stayed alive, or at least I *existed*. One of the three survivors is currently the medical director at the Betty Ford Center, and we have remained very good friends.

After I left treatment I stayed with my mom for a while. She had recently moved into a house that she'd built, which was even more grand and impressive than any of their previous homes, even with an eight-passenger Otis elevator. It was like an MTV crib. I started seeing a local psychiatrist, and he was the first mental health professional who appeared to be worth anything. It seemed as though he actually cared, and that was good enough for me.

I still don't trust shrinks, and think they sometimes do more harm than good. I feel they create just enough confusion to keep you coming back. If the patient gets well, the patient wouldn't need the doctor anymore. That means the doctor would lose a patient, which translates into a substantial loss of income. I'm sure the wives of the head shrinkers *really* don't like it when patients are cured. God forbid if the new Beemer, Botox injections, or breast augmentation should have to put on hold until some new whack-job shows up for therapy.

For the next five years I bumbled through life, functioning at about two percent. I was in constant trouble with my PO, never following the rules long enough to ever get off probation. I almost always had warrants out for my arrest and was in a revolving door of jails and institutions. I was seen by more psychiatrists, but they just put me on more medications that did absolutely no good.

I couldn't rent an apartment legitimately because the cops always seemed to be closing in on me, so I stayed in motels, hotels, or vacation rentals at the beach. In September 2002, about a year into my hotel hopping, I became very sick and my dad came to my rescue once again, always showing up when I was in critical condition. He set me up in a cheap sober-living home about ten minutes from their house, and after doing well for a couple of months he said he would help me rent an apartment. I planned to have a roommate from AA, so my Dad figured it was a pretty safe bet, but first I had to do a month in jail for a probation violation. After that, my probation would be reinstated, giving me a clean slate.

The month I spent in jail seemed like an eternity. At that point, I thought thirty days in jail was a long time. The time went by so slowly that I started to forget what it was like to breathe fresh air. Initially, I was booked into the downtown San Diego jail, and then transported to George Bailey Detention Facility in Otay Mesa, about twenty-five miles southeast of the city. Donovan State Prison was directly across the canyon from George Bailey, and I had nightmares about someday residing there, becoming a *real* convict.

The Bailey Detention Facility was called "Thunderdome" because of the violence it's known for. When you check into Thunderdome, you best be prepared to fight because that's exactly what's expected of you. At least seventy men of various ethnicities are housed in each tank, so there's constant racial tension. The whites aren't supposed to play games, share food, or have too much interaction with any non-whites, especially the blacks.

The food was so gross I usually gave mine to one of the other white guys, but one night a black guy asked if he could have my Jell-O if I wasn't going to eat it. Without thinking, I gave it to him, and the white shot-caller happened to see me hand it to the black guy, so immediately, several of the whites beat me up. The sheriffs came in, and seeing that I was bruised and had a fat lip, asked if I wanted to go into protective custody, but I declined, and told them that I was okay, that I had just fallen down. From that day on, I always ate my Jell-O.

The ever-present smell of urine, feces, farts, and stinking feet was nauseating, and the screaming and yelling made it impossible to get any decent sleep. One night, when I was in and out of a disturbed sleep, I felt something tugging at my shoes. It was a little Mexican Southsider, trying to steal the shoes right off my feet.

I said, "What the fuck're you doing?"

"Hey, let me have those shoes," he said.

I said, "Sure," and scooted down my bunk toward him and kicked him flush between the eyes.

He flew backwards into a concrete pillar and crumpled to the ground. It nearly turned into a riot, but the white and Mexican shot-callers quelled it.

Toward the end of my thirty days, I told myself I was finished with breaking the law. I never wanted to be back there again.

———

Upon my release from custody, my slate was clean, and it had been a long time since I'd had a clean slate. But a few weeks after I moved into the new pad, I relapsed and started smoking meth, so the guy who'd been sharing the apartment with me quickly moved out. I became so paranoid, I would peek out the window for hours, my arm getting sore from holding the curtain open, waiting for the cops to break the door down and arrest me. The meth made me stay awake for several days straight. I couldn't eat, and my hair was falling out. The paranoia was horrible.

About the time I was about to lose my apartment and become homeless for the umpteenth time, I met a little hottie named Brooke at a coffee house in Point Loma, and wound up moving in with her before my eviction notice came. Actually, she only lived a couple of miles from parent's San Diego house.

When I told my dad about her, and that I'd met her in the coffee house near his home, he asked me her name. He called me a few days after that and told me that a friend of a friend told him to tell me to stay far away from that woman. She was known to have a multitude of issues. Right up my alley!

I'm sure Brooke had a major panty splash when she heard my last name. My name's probably golden in that neighborhood, seeing as how my dad lives there. So, once again, another girl was willing to overlook my sordid past, and hope to cash in on my family's money. I didn't even have to tell this one that she was first in line for the gold; she assumed it.

Of course I didn't heed my dad's advice. I jumped right in with both feet, moved in with her right away, and we played house for a couple months. She had a six-year-old daughter with Travis, a local trust fund drunk who got sucked in by her, and she also had a ten-year-old boy whose dad was a professional dancer. Eventually, the dancer found he had more interest in his male dancing buddy than he had in her. She said she was shattered when he told her that he liked "*man*-gina instead of *va*-gina."

Travis had financed the beautiful Jaguar she was driving because she used to give up some ass every now and then, but now that I was around, she'd stopped. He didn't want to pay for no lay, so he contacted me and asked if I'd be interested in taking over the payments on the car. He said he'd already made payments for over a year, so I agreed. He also said he wanted to do it legit, but I didn't have a driver's license so I continued to stall until I could think of a way to get the car without having a license. Finally, he called me and said that we needed to take care of it that day or he was going to take the car back, and then *I* would have to be responsible for supplying the little money grubber with a ride.

I met him at the San Diego Yacht Club where he was a member, and when I walked into the club, I went to the bar and told the bartender I was there to meet a certain gentleman. He directed me to a table out on the deck where a guy, who looked like the late Chris Farley, was sitting. I approached the table, and said, "Travis?"

He stood up, stuck out his bloated hand that had no idea what a callous was, and said, "Hey Dave, what's up? So have you caught Brooke getting banged by any of her old Johns yet?"

I actually laughed out loud. I liked this guy. I said, "Actually, I haven't.

He said, "Just wait, sport, you'll see." Just as he said that, Brooke rushed up to the table with their six-year-old daughter in tow.

She said, "Travis, what the fuck are you saying to him?"

He said, "Oh, I was just telling David here that you're a whore, and he agrees."

I said, "Travis, I didn't say that!"

"Well yes, you did in so many words," he said. Then he looked over at his daughter, and said, "Honey, I have to get away from your mommy now because she's really sick again and needs to go back to that place where they help her with her problems so she can get better." He then turned to me, and said, "Oh, by the way, David, you know she's been in the nut house several times for her eating disorder, right? And you know what they say about chicks with eating disorders?"

I curiously said, "What's that?"

He said, "They're all sex addicts. There's no question that she's a whore."

He got up and walked away, but Brooke and her daughter followed. She was yelling at him at the top of her lungs, but finally was smart enough to tell the kid to go back and stay with me until they were finished.

Travis and Brooke were standing on the dock next to the side entrance of the yacht club, and as their daughter and I were looking on, the last thing I heard Travis say was, "You're a skanky whore, and I'm calling CPS as soon as I get home, and I'll get her taken away from your tramp ass!"

He then proceeded to palm her face like a basketball and throw her right into the drink, purse and all! She may have drowned had it not been for the sailors nearby who were rigging their boats, because I wasn't planning on going in after her. All four of the sailors jumped in the water to save her. Her cell phone sank to the bottom.

Everything was fine and dandy with her until I started smoking the meth pipe again. Like all things in my life, this episode ended badly. Brooke dressed like a high-class prostitute, she looked like a high-class prostitute, and her phone rang at all hours like a high-class prostitute's, so I was suspicious from the very beginning, but my paranoia from the meth certainly didn't help.

During one of our blowouts, the one that got me arrested, I was accused of calling her on her cell phone and telling her that I was going to kill her. After she'd he called 911, there were at least six cop cars outside the house. A female officer got on the bullhorn demanding that I come out of the house immediately, and when I didn't come out they came in after me. When they found me, I was clad in my skivvies and hiding underneath the bed, too toasted to get out without their help. I was placed under arrest and charged with making a terrorist threat after I called her cell phone and told her I was going to kill her. Because I was in a drug-induced psychosis, my ability to be rational was out the window. Upon sentencing, I was convicted of the felony, put on probation *again*, given a strike, and had a three-year prison sentence hanging over my head. I never saw Brooke again.

When I checked in with my new probation officer, I immediately knew I was in for hell. He looked like of one of the flamers who cruise Santa Monica Boulevard looking for love. He had bleached blond hair, wore tight T-shirts, tight jeans that showed a little bulge where his package was supposed to be, and wore pansy shoes.

The first time I met him, he looked me up and down and said, "So, are you Joseph Wambaugh's kid?"

Yes, sir," I said.

He gave me a fruity little smile and said, "Personally, I think you should've done some prison time, so if you fuck up, your ass is going down. Do you understand me?

"Yes, sir," I said.

His smile broadened, and he said, "Good. We're on the same page."

"Whatever," I mumbled, trying to go along.

He said, "Mister Wambaugh, you're going to be on my car program. You are a Pinto. Do you know what a Pinto is?"

"A horse?" I said.

"No," he snapped.

"A bean?"

"No. It's a *car*, Mister Wambaugh. You will call in every night after 7 p.m., and if the recording says *Pinto* you'd better get your ass in here by seven a.m. the next morning to take a drug test, or I'll violate you and recommend to the judge that he put your ass in prison. If you get one dirty test, you will be on your way. So, Mister Wambaugh, do you have any questions for me?"

"Yes."

"What's that?"

"Can I go now?"

He said, "Yes, Mister Wambaugh. Go."

———

In 2003, a few months after I was convicted of making the terrorist threat, I'd sobered up for a short time and met Suzy, a very nice girl I'd known from AA. She was in her mid twenties and was very beautiful. The only thing I didn't like about her were that she smoked like a chimney, and had countless tattoos and piercings all over her body.

I started drinking again two days after we met, but she still liked me. She *must've* liked me because only *three* days after we met, before we even had an official date, I asked for her hand in marriage and she accepted. We spent that day in La Jolla, and I let her pick out a beautiful one-karat diamond engagement ring, for which I paid $3,500 cash at an upscale jewelry store near the La Jolla Cove.

I kept two pints of Jack Daniels strategically stashed in my car and snuck drinks throughout the day, so by nightfall I was pretty drunk. When we were back at my apartment, making the wedding plans, I had to close one eye so I could see the notes she had been making on a tablet. When she asked me what was wrong, I told her that one of my contacts was bugging me, even though I didn't even wear them.

She moved in with me that day and I promised that I would stay sober, especially now that I was going to be married. Unfortunately our engagement was short lived, because when I went out of town the following week to do a sign job in Las Vegas, she up and left me. I'd called her from Vegas the night I arrived, and confessed that I drank again, and that I was sorry. She hung up on me, and wouldn't pick up when I called back several times. When I came home the following night, she was gone, and so were all her belongings, except one thing. Her engagement ring was sitting on the dining room table with no note or anything. She was obviously a smart girl and she got out just in time.

I took a shower and drove over to the strip club that I occasionally patronized, and after a couple of lap dances, I stood up to pay the girl, and when I reached into my pocket to get money, the ring fell out onto the table.

The stripper asked me what the deal was with the ring, and when I told her the story, she asked to see it, and then didn't want to give it back. She gushed about what a beautiful ring it was, and said, "What a dumb girl! Who would want to break off an engagement to *you?* You're *adorable!*"

I would've asked her to marry me right then and there, but she'd already told me she had two babies, and that she was trying to get back with the daddy if he could just get off the meth and successfully finish parole. That was way too much for me to deal with, so instead, I told her that if she'd stay the night with me, I'd give her the ring in exchange for sex.

She was elated, and so grateful. She said she would use the ring when she married her boyfriend since he was in no position to buy her one, so it made me feel really good to know I was doing a real kind thing for someone. She said she was going to tell the manager that she wanted to leave after her next set, and then we would spend the night at my pad. She asked if she could run backstage and show the ring to her stripper-friends before we left, so I handed it back to her.

Fifteen minutes passed, thirty minutes, forty-five minutes, and when I hadn't seen her for over an hour, I went to the manager, who knew me, and told him what I'd done. He said that she'd bailed about an hour ago, right after she told him she quit. He laughed like mad, and said that he'd be happy to call the cops so I could make a police report, but he really wouldn't recommend that I do it, seeing as how I was soliciting sex in exchange for a diamond ring, which would be illegal. I agreed, and left it at that. I spent that night alone, minus a fiancé, and minus a $3,500 diamond ring that I could have saved for my next wife.

———

At this point, I was almost forty years old, and for nearly two more years the cycle continued. I would violate my probation for one reason or another, a warrant would be issued for my arrest, I would go to jail for a few days until I could see the judge, and then the cycle would repeat. One time my PO got so pissed off when the judge reinstated my probation, he blew up and spoke directly to the judge in court. The judge reprimanded him, and just watching his face turn a brilliant pink was almost worth the violation. The judge was a fan of my dad's books, as most of the judges were, so that's probably why he reinstated my probation so many times.

My PO did his best to make my life as miserable as he possibly could. One time when the judge reinstated my probation, my PO ordered me into the harshest rehab in San Diego County. Only about fifteen percent of the guys who start the program, complete it, and those who fail either go to jail or prison. The completion rate was so low that a lot of the guys chose jail or prison time over doing the CRASH program.

I was one of the fifteen percent who completed the program, and on the day I got my completion papers from the program, my probation officer called me into his office and said that now he wanted me to go into sober living for a few months. Previously, he'd told me that if I completed the CRASH program I could rent an apartment, live on my own, and resume working. With that in mind, I'd already rented an apartment at the beach.

When I told him about the apartment, he said, "That's just tough shit! I want you in sober living by five p.m. tomorrow."

"Go fuck yourself," I said, right in front of his colleagues, and walked out the door. Twenty-four hours later, I had a no-bail felony warrant out for my arrest. Such was my life.

I lost the oceanfront apartment before I could even move in, since I knew the cops would find me there, so I was back to hotel hopping. I was accustomed to being on the run, so it wasn't that big of a deal, but I did hate having to constantly be looking over my shoulder. After I settled into my new hotel room, I started making calls and lining up some sign jobs. Living on the run was expensive. On my first day of soliciting, I got $7,500 in deposits for two jobs I was scheduled to do later that month.

The following morning I cashed the deposit checks, got a bottle, and then checked into a notorious crack motel in the 'hood. As soon as I got in the room, I scored some dope right away from a black guy called "D-Most". I holed up in the room, and D-Most would deliver crack to me every few hours. I was smoking like a forest fire! Between the crack and the two nasty, toothless crack whores he brought over, I blew over $2,500 in two days. The women were ladies of the night, with knee-slapping beanbag titties, and grills that left something to be desired--such as teeth.

I was getting bad vibes with D-Most coming in and out of my room, and the girls seemed to be getting antsy, so seeing as how I still had my two front pockets filled with Benjamin Franklins, I excused myself and told the ladies I'd be back in a few minutes. I went down to the lobby and asked the woman at the front desk if she had a safe, which she did, so I gave her the two envelopes I had containing $4,700. It never entered my mind to ask for a receipt since I was high, and becoming more paranoid about D-Most and the hookers by the second.

The first thing I noticed when I walked back into my room, was that my car keys were not on the table where I'd left them, and I looked out the window overlooking the parking lot and saw that my car was gone. As I sat there in shock, wondering what in the hell I was going to do, the San Diego Police busted the door down with their guns drawn. It was an embarrassing moment because there I was, half naked, with two black, toothless hookers, both with crack pipes hanging out of their mouths. One of the cops pulled out a booking picture of yours truly and asked if I recognized the guy in the picture. I told the cop I used to know that guy, but hadn't seen him in years. He cuffed me and took me to the station where I was booked into county jail on an outstanding felony warrant, and new drug charges.

My car was gone, my money was in the motel safe, and I was back in jail. I was totally freaked. That was definitely one of the biggest "dumb shit" moments of my life. That money was deposits on services not yet rendered, and if I didn't get it back, I was going to be in *deep* shit. While I was still in jail, I arranged for a friend to go get my money from the woman at the motel, and when he reported back to me, he said she told him there was only a thousand dollars in one envelope. I flipped out. I wasn't sure *who* stole my money at that point, the woman or my friend, but I knew if I didn't get it back, my clients would probably press charges on me for grand theft, and then I'd be doing prison time for sure!

When I appeared in court I was relieved when the judge reinstated my probation again and released me from custody the following day. All of my probation reinstatements were laughable. The bottom line was that my dad was very well known to law enforcement and to everyone in the judicial system. I'm sure the judges and DAs felt sorry for my parents on many occasions, and probably made their decisions based on what they thought my dad would want, which was to not lock me up.

I would make eye contact with the DA, the court clerk, the bailiff, and anyone else who could have any influence over the judge and give them my sheepish, humble, ashamed, guilty, never-do-it-again, please-let-me-go look. And I would stare at the judge and *will* him to look at me, so I could somehow pull his heartstrings and let him see that I was just a sick, innocent, pathetic victim of my own circumstance.

I would always get the DA to look at me and show him or her by the look in my eyes that I wasn't prison material, that I was just a screw-up son of a celebrity that couldn't get it together. I gave them looks that said, "Come on now, ma'am, you must've known a guy like me somewhere in your life: a cute, charming, articulate, engaging, seemingly intelligent LOSER. I'm just like *him* ma'am. Now you wouldn't want to put him away *would* you?"

By the time I would get my probation reinstated and be on my way back to the jail for release, I would imagine that on more than one occasion, both the judges and the DAs would be shaking their heads, saying, "What the hell just happened here? Did we just let that guy go again?"

Brian McDevitt, my attorney, said that I was the most charming felon he'd ever dealt with. He said I had boyish charm that was unparalleled, and it made him laugh at how I could so often get myself re-instated. However, there came a time after so many arrests, convictions, and violations, where I don't think my dad's name worked anymore, and my charm had worn off.

As soon as I was released from custody, I bolted over to the motel to confront the woman who had my money, and when I entered the lobby, she handed me the envelope and said that she would call the police if I didn't turn right around and leave. I opened the envelope and saw that $3,700 was missing, so I called her a thieving bitch, and she called the police. In what seemed to be seconds, the San Diego Police arrived and escorted me off the property. I was told not to come back to this place or I would find myself back in jail.

The young Asian cop who escorted me off the property asked what the hell was going on, so I told him the story. When I was done telling him about it, he grinned, shook his head slowly, and said, "Okay, let me get this straight. You came to this motel, bought crack from a guy named D-Most, had two black chicks keeping you company, and then you got taken for your car and thirty-seven hundred bucks?"

"At least!"

"Are you kidding me?" he said. "Dude, what were you thinking?"

Embarrassed, I said, "I don't know *what* the hell I was thinking."

He said, "The guy you call D-Most is really Dwayne, and he lives with his grandma on Thirty-Fifth Street. The two hookers you described are his sisters. Dwayne's a smalltime dealer and his sisters work the track here. Dwayne moonlights as their pimp because I guess they wanna keep it all in the family. And don't worry about your car. It's long gone. It was probably across the border within an hour after it was stolen, so some Mexican in Tijuana is enjoying your ride as we speak. The money's gone too, bro. I know that, because the chick behind the counter is Dwayne's on-again-off-again old lady. So, cut your losses and hope the old tweeker doesn't decide to take you to small claims court and sue you for her emotional pain and suffering.

I only walked as far as the nearest liquor store, bought a fifth of Bacardi, a couple of diet cokes, and headed back toward the motel. I was going to lie in wait until Dwayne made an appearance. I found a metal pipe next to a dumpster and I was planning to beat the shit out of him.

As I lay in wait, a white whore sauntered by, and said, "Hey, what are you doing here?"

I said, "I'm waiting for a guy named D-Most who ripped me off for a lot of money and stole my car. If I see him, I'm gonna kill him."

"Oh, I know that guy," she said. "He's ripped me off too. That's how this game goes."

"I guess so," I said.

"What's your name?"

"Dave," I said.

She said, "Why don't we just buy some rocks and go back to my apartment and party?"

I hesitated, and then said, "Oh, man, I shouldn't, because I'd be violating my probation again, but... fuck it. I'm down."

After we scored, we were walking to her apartment when she asked, "So do you still go to meetings?"

"What meetings?"

"AA meetings. I've seen you share at the Dawn Patrol meeting. You're really funny. You're the one who relapses all the time, right?"

"Yeah, but can we change the subject?" I said. "I really don't want to think about AA while I got a crack pipe locked and loaded."

I had way too much fun with the crack whore, so I didn't make it to the probation office within the seventy-two hours of my release from custody, therefore I knew that within another day or so I'd have another warrant out for my arrest.

At the end of the seventy-two hours I was still hanging with "AA-Sally", smoking crack and drinking vodka. We blew through all my money in no time at all, so I had to get another job.

The dealerships that had given me the deposits for sign promotions that I'd blown, both went out of business and didn't try to come after me, probably because I was too hard to find. That was another one of my problems that magically went away.

Very soon, I got a job lined up with another dealership where I'd done promotions several times over the past five or six years. When that job was over, it was time to party. I went by the car dealership to make sure my employees had cleaned up their messes and had put everything in order, and as I was walking around the lot, a cop car came out of nowhere, flew up onto the curb and damn near ran me over.

An old black cop jumped out of his cruiser and screamed, "Stop! Stay right there, or I'll taze you! I'll taze you, Goddamnit! Lay down right there! Lay down, and don't you fucking move!"

I slowly backed up, preparing to bolt because I'd been drinking, which was a violation of my probation, and I also knew there was already an outstanding warrant or two for my arrest, so I wanted to be outta there.

As I backed up I was explaining, "I work here. I do their advertising. I've done their advertising for the past ten years!"

He said, "I don't give a fuck what you did! I'm ordering you to lie face down and don't move, or I'll taze you right now!"

I turned to run, and he shot me in the back with the tazer at close range. The barbs knocked me to my knees. They were loaded with 50,000 volts of standstill, and once they get you, the small hooks sometimes have to be surgically removed. However, my adrenaline was pumping so fast, it didn't stop me. I got back up and he gave chase, and when I was just a few feet from my new girlfriend's car, the cunt bailed on me! There I was, with lifelong abandonment issues and racist tendencies, and I was ditched by the whore, and was being chased by a spook with a tazer gun!

As I was sprinting across the street, I tripped and fell, and when I got back up he shot me again, this time in the back of my leg. I ate shit on the pavement and decided to give up because I heard sirens coming from all around, so I knew I was busted. I stayed face down on the ground, and said, "Okay, okay, I'm done!"

As I was lying there, cuffed and shocked, three cops jumped on me and began beating the shit out of me, saying, "Quit resisting! Quit resisting, asshole!"

While I waited to see the judge the next morning, the public defender working my case told me the charges were being dropped. She explained that it was because National City had had several recent lawsuits filed against their Department for excessive use of force, so the D.A. didn't want to deal with my very brutal arrest. That was music to my ears! I was released -- just in time for happy hour!

I called my new girlfriend, and she picked me up from jail, but I'm sure the only reason she picked me up was because she knew I had another pocket full of money. She informed me that she liked to shoot heroin every now and then, and she even knew where to get it. Surprise, surprise!

After she scored, and we were back at her apartment, she pulled out a makeup bag that held syringes, spoon, lighter, and cotton balls. While going through the ritual, preparing to shoot dope, she tied off her arm with a beautiful crimson scarf from Neiman Marcus. I'm certain she slammed a lot more dope than she claimed, because her veins were few and far between. After watching her use her arms like a pin cushion for over thirty minutes, and still not finding a vein, I finally had had enough.

I said, "Jesus, what the hell's wrong with you? Can you *not* see that you have no veins left?"

She spun around and said, "Hey, at least I didn't give my car and four thousand bucks to some lowlife crack dealer!"

"Whatever," I said indignantly, "at least I don't have to suck dick for crack hits."

I could see her face turning red, and she seethed, "You're nothing but a drunk! Look at you! You're a limp-dick drunk!"

"Yeah?" I countered. "My dick was only limp because you're so nasty! How could I ever get wood for a filthy crack whore junkie who'll give up pussy for a couple of hits on a shit pipe. You can't get any lower than that!"

"Devoid of expression, she slowly got up, walked toward me, and when she was about two feet away from my face, she raised her fist over her head, and then brought it down, hitting my shoulder. It felt like a bee sting. I looked down at my shoulder and saw that she had plunged a syringe full of heroin right into my shoulder, and it was just dangling there, bobbing up and down.

I pulled the syringe out, and said, "You fucking bitch! What did you do to me?"

She said, "You shouldn't call people names."

"You bitch!" I shrieked.

That's the last thing I remembered. I woke up some time later in the intensive care unit of the hospital in Mission Hills, but I had no idea how long I'd been there. All I knew was that I had an oxygen mask on my face and was hooked up to a machine, and I was freezing cold.

When I'd been admitted to the ER I was in a coma, so someone called my dad in the middle of the night to tell him that I'd overdosed on heroin, and that he should come to the hospital because things weren't looking too hopeful for me. He came, and after seeing me, gave me a kiss on the forehead and said his last goodbye. He collected my urine-soaked pants and wallet and asked them to call if there was any change in my condition. That was the lowest of lows for my poor father. He was sure he was losing his second son.

The next morning, when I was finally able to clear the cobwebs, I had some recollection of what had happened so I knew I was in serious trouble. I had overdosed, which is a major problem if you're on felony probation, so I knew I had to get the hell out of there. I pulled myself free from all the medical devices, hopped off the gurney and frantically searched for my clothes. All my stuff was gone: my clothes, my wallet, my money, and my cell phone. Gone! I'd had $800 in the pocket of my pants, and I needed that money to stay on the run until I could get another job. I knew the law would be hot on my ass, so I had to keep moving.

There was a fat old man next to me in a coma of his own. He didn't look like he'd have any use for his clothes ever again, so I stole them. His soiled polyester pants had about a 48" waist and his white T-shirt was too gross to wear, so I ran out of the hospital shirtless, holding the big pants up with both hands. When I moved past the nursing station, no one confronted me so I picked up the pace and made a beeline straight to the house of the girl who'd almost killed me. She lived less than a mile from the hospital, so that was a good thing. I figured that since she got me into that mess, I was going to see that she got me out of it. When I showed up on her doorstep, clad only in the king-sized polyester pants, she looked like she was going to faint.

She slowly opened the door, and said, "Oh my God! I thought it was gonna be the police, here to arrest me for murder! Thank God! Thank God! Come in!"

I went inside, and said, "Listen, I have to get some clothes and some money. All my shit was taken from me at the hospital and I guarantee the cops aren't far behind me. I told you how much my PO hates me."

She said quietly, "Your dad has your stuff."

"What do you mean, my dad has my stuff?"

"I talked to him on the phone last night and he told me he had your stuff. He said you were in ICU and he didn't know if you were going to live or not."

I called my dad and when he answered, he seemed shocked to hear my voice. I was so desperate and groggy, I didn't even apologize for what I'd put him through, but demanded he give me back the money that was in my jeans. When I told him that I was on my way to his house to pick up the money, he said he didn't want me coming anywhere near his house, that he doesn't allow wanted felons in his home. He said he would FedEx my money to me and just needed the address of where to send it. Well, he didn't send my coin, but he sure as hell sent something else. And the joke was on me because he'd already given my money to Sarah and Jake, along with my pissy jeans that he'd laundered.

My girlfriend and I hadn't eaten for a while, so we decided to go to McDonald's and dine off the dollar menu. As I walked out her front door and started down the stairs, I noticed red dots all over the front of my shirt, and they seemed to be moving. I thought maybe I was still delirious from the overdose, but the dots were there, I was sure of it. At that very moment I realized that the red dots on my shirt were not figments of my imagination, but were actually coming from guns being pointed at me from all directions. The fugitive task force, which consisted of the San Diego PD, San Diego County Sheriffs, and U.S Marshalls, was there to apprehend me. I later found out from my dad that he'd called the police to let them know where they could find me and said that I may be armed. I never *had* a gun, but my dad believed that I might, seeing as how I was capable of doing anything at that point. Even I knew that.

They took me into custody, and drove me to see my probation officer before they took me downtown for booking. When we pulled up to the probation office, my PO was standing outside gloating. When they opened the back door of the Suburban so that he could see me, he giggled and said, "Hello, Mister Wambaugh. I'm very happy to say that you won't be on my caseload anymore. I've already spoken to the DA and you *will* be going to prison this time."

"Screw you," I said. "You've been saying that crap for the last year and a half, and it never happens. Watch me! I'll get my probation reinstated, dickhead." The cops laughed and closed the Suburban door.

I didn't go to state prison, but I did get a stiff jail sentence. It was just after my forty-first birthday in July, 2005, when I went in and I was released in October. I had been sentenced to a year, but only did 105 days because I'd already done 260 days in county jail over the past twenty years. You can only do so much county jail time before it's on to bigger and better things: state prison.

During those 105 days, I rose to the rank of the white rep for my tank. The sad and scary part was that I was beginning to fit in with those animals. I was getting comfortable in there, and this time I didn't even bother trying to fool myself into believing that I was going to stay sober after I got out.

Upon my release, I reported to my PO to give him an address and phone number where I could be reached until I could get a cell phone. He told me my new address was going to be another sober living home. He didn't think it was a good idea for me to be on my own at that time, so I told him to go fuck himself again, and walked out of his office. I assumed I would have another felony warrant out for my arrest within the next forty-eight hours, but I didn't even care anymore.

As the days turned into weeks, weeks into months, and months into years, I was fading away from the most precious gift that could ever be. My son was growing up without a father, and I felt totally powerless to change. I desperately and frantically wanted to be there for my boy, but the dream of capturing that moment was all too elusive for me.

Chapter Thirteen

A good friend of mine from AA had a job out in Palm Springs managing a mortgage company, and knowing I could be a good salesman, recruited me, paid my expenses, and gave me an allowance out of his own pocket. He put me up at a very nice hotel in downtown Palm Springs where I partied like a rock star, which was probably why I never closed any deals for him. I got to the desert at the perfect time because the cops were aggressively looking for me in San Diego.

I was forty-one years old and Jake was nine. I spoke to him on the phone quite often, but my trips to San Diego were rare since I knew the feds would be looking for me. I told him I had to stay in the desert to work, but I'm certain he knew something else was wrong.

I was drinking and drugging every night and wasn't producing any business for my friend, so I wound up doing what I always did. Back to the sign promotions, but being too afraid to go back to San Diego, I stayed in the Palm Springs area. I really began hating those sign jobs because they were getting old, and so was I. As soon as I did a couple of jobs and had some money in my pocket, I decided to look for some other type of work that didn't involve travel.

As time went on, I found a way not to be homeless. I had an ability to find women who would buy into my bullshit du jour, and within a few days I'd be shacked up with them, eating their food and drinking their booze.

I met Linda in 2005, at a friend of a friend's Christmas party in Palm Springs. I got completely blitzed, and was my same old vulgar self. The very first night we met, we went to her house after the party, and in trying to win her affection in my typically inappropriate way, I unzipped my pants and showed her my package. Instead of me shocking her, she shocked *me* by reaching over and slapping my dick as she laughed it off like a good sport. Within three days, I moved into her home. She happened to live next door to a close friend of my mom's, and said she'd met my mom a time or two, but that was about it. I stayed there for most of a year, and I think it would be safe to say that I was totally insane from the time I met her, so I thought she was either a saint, or really stupid--or both.

She rarely asked me questions about myself, but instead, asked all about my parents: their history in the desert, who they knew, how long they'd lived at the various desert country clubs over the years, and other questions regarding their position in life. Since she was so interested, I took her to meet my mom, and not long after that, Linda invited my mom to come to her house for dinner with us. They seemed to have more in common with each other than Linda and I had, and soon they became friends.

After all Linda's questioning about *my* family, I decided to ask her some questions of my own. Being the son of an ex-cop, and watching every cop show on TV, I'd say I'm pretty good at conducting an interrogation. I came to the conclusion that the reason she owned her home was because she'd married a lonely pathetic man, twenty-five years her senior, who was desperate for companionship. He was a business executive and had a lucrative contract with a company in Hong Kong. When her husband's contract was up, he and Linda bought a beautiful five-bedroom home in Palm Desert. And a few months later, she kicked him to the curb.

Linda told me that the final straw was when she came home one evening after enjoying happy hour at a nearby restaurant with girlfriends, and saw him in the back yard doing yoga in a Speedo. She said the sight of his enormous white belly spilling over his little Speedo was so disgusting, she turned around and went back to happy hour to have another drink. He suffered from depression, and his depression made *her* so depressed she canned him. However, she was kind enough to help him find a one-bedroom apartment, and she let him store his belongings at the house until he could find a bigger place.

Linda always had a good supply of Xanax, and high-grade weed and didn't mind sharing, but she certainly didn't appreciate it when I took the lion's share. She also had plenty of good vodka that I drank and then refilled with water, leaving only about 25% of the original booze. When she had her friends over for her special martinis, they probably left wondering why they never caught a buzz. Not only was I a dog, I was a pig too.

One night she found out I'd pilfered almost all of her pills and smoked most of her pot and gave me a tongue lashing about being a drunk and drug addict. I responded by telling her that at least I wouldn't take some poor old bastard's money and then leave him hanging like *she* did.

She said, "You're no better than me. *You'd* do it in a second."

"Maybe you're right," I said. "But we *know* I'm a scumbag."

After a few months our relationship became tumultuous and confrontational because of my drinking and womanizing. When I staggered home one night with female scent on my clothes, she was livid. She'd found a lust letter on top of my dresser that a woman had written to me. Then what made her *really* boil was when I told her my new drinking buddy wanted to swap partners.

She was appalled, and said, "What did you say to him?"

I said, "I told him that I'd love to take him up on it anytime."

That's when she threw an ankle weight from across the room and hit me square in the shin. We got into a huge yelling match and I called her every name I could think of that would insult a woman her age. During our screaming match, she said if I didn't calm down, she was going to call my mother.

I said, "What the fuck do you *mean*, you're going to call my mother? Don't you *dare* call her, you opportunistic whore! I've put my parents through enough shit, so leave them alone. I can't imagine how you would even think of such a thing. Call my mom? We're *not* little kids!"

Linda didn't say another word, however she took her cordless phone out on the patio and actually made the freaking call. I thought she was bullshitting me until twenty minutes later I saw my poor mom at the front door. She didn't know what to say about two adults, both in their forties, in a situation like that. She asked me to cool my jets and to quit being such an asshole, so I quit being an asshole up until she left to go home.

Less than a week later it happened again. I came home several hours after Linda was expecting me, and I hadn't answered my phone all day. She didn't confront me that night, but went off on me the next morning and stormed out of the house, saying we would finish the conversation when she returned from the gym. While she was gone I powered down six or eight screwdrivers to prep me for the confrontation that was sure to come.

When Linda returned, she found the O.J. and a 1.75 liter of Grey Goose on the kitchen table in front of me, like it was breakfast. Actually, it *was* my breakfast. She marched straight over to me, snatched my screwdriver off the table and poured it down the drain. Then she said she was calling my mom again to tell her I'd been drinking.

I didn't believe her and went outside to get a bottle of rum from of my car, and as I was walking back toward the front door, I could see her on the phone and could hear her tattling to my mom. As I passed by the new Mercedes she'd just leased, I pulled the spring-loaded emblem right off the hood.

A couple of weeks later she accused me of cheating on her again, which of course I was, so she ordered me out of her house for good. She threw all my clothes outside, locked the front door, and again got on her cordless phone. When I knew she wasn't going to let me in and when I could hear her talking to my mom again, I threw a rock and cracked the vintage window beside her front door. I thought that if someone was breaking all my shit, you can bet your sweet ass I'd be calling the cops, *not* someone's mother.

Linda did do me some good though. Through her connections, I got a job as the director of marketing for a cosmetic surgery center in Palm Desert on El Paseo Drive, the Rodeo Drive of the desert. I didn't know anything about marketing but I assured the old doctor who owned the business that whatever I didn't know, I'd learn immediately. I think he liked my spirit, and I figured I could just fake it until I made it. I was very good at fakery.

When the doctor discovered that I drank in my office every day, he fired me. In addition to drinking in my office, I'd go out to lunch and drink, then go to happy hour and drink, and then drink myself into a blackout every night, all alone.

I began seeing my psychiatrist again, hoping he could pull me out of my spiral because I had become totally non-functioning again. It wouldn't have been so bad if I could've held onto a job even for a short time, but I just couldn't put the plug in the jug.

My psychiatrist admitted me into a mental hospital in San Diego because the drug rehabs hadn't done me any good, and he came to the conclusion that I needed intensive daily psychiatric care. Initially, they placed me in the locked ward where I had to surrender my shoelaces, belt, razors and anything I might use to kill myself. I didn't object because I was so loaded on meds, I didn't even mind when they made me participate in finger painting, and puzzles designed for children.

After being discharged from the hospital, I went back to my mom's desert house, and she said she would help me formulate a plan of action about what I should do. We agreed that I should visit my psychiatrist first to ask his advice, so I went to see him. I didn't like what I heard, bought a bottle of vodka on the way home, and was immediately drinking every day. After my mom caught me drinking, she didn't have any choice but to kick me out of her house. Again!

One afternoon as I was driving aimlessly around Palm Desert, I found myself in the neighborhood of the cosmetic surgery center where I'd worked, and decided to drop in to say hello. I was hoping to make amends to the old doctor who'd fired me, but he wasn't in. However, one of the girls behind the desk who used to flirt with me asked how I was doing and said that it was so nice to see me again. That's all I needed to hear so I asked her to join me for lunch, and she accepted.

It's incredibly beautiful during the winter season in the desert and the weather was perfect, so I took her to a place down the street with outdoor seating so we could enjoy the beautiful day. The restaurant was located on a busy section of El Paseo Drive, which was a great place to people-watch and admire all the Bentleys and Rolls Royce Phantoms drive by.

She finished her sandwich and said she had to get back to work, but I planned to hang out there for a while and have a few more double vodka lemonades. While I was admiring her ass as she walked away, I noticed that beyond her were two guys in Kevlar Vests, holding what looked like assault rifles, running across the street in my direction. It became crystal clear that they were coming for me, so I looked to my right for an escape route, and saw three more coming from that direction. I was just about to stand up and run back through the restaurant's kitchen when I felt something hard and cold touch the back of my neck.

A voice said, "U.S. Marshalls. If you move one inch I'll blow your fucking brains all over this nice restaurant."

I was dumbfounded! I couldn't imagine how they'd found me all the way out in Palm Desert, especially on that upscale street full of fancy shops, and why in hell they came in such force. I wasn't Sammy The Bull Gravano or Whitey Bulger. I figured it must've been because of the episode in San Diego when they thought I was armed, and that had marked me as a dangerous fugitive.

I later learned that my mom had ratted me out. She admitted to me that when the Marshalls appeared at her door and asked if she knew my whereabouts, she gave them enough information where it wouldn't take them long to track me down. That was her way of trying to stop me before I killed myself, or worse yet, someone else.

I was booked into the Riverside County Jail, and then transported back to San Diego where I was facing three years in prison for the terrorist threat against the crazy bitch from Point Loma. I really lucked out because I was able to con my favorite judge once again, and he reinstated my probation one more time. However, he did it with the stipulation that I had to leave San Diego County and never come back. I thanked him, and got out of the county the next day.

My new Riverside County probation officer was great. He didn't even require that I report to him, and just told me not to break the law. Easy enough for a solid citizen like me. It was a good thing that I didn't have to report, because I was in and out of the mental hospital and Betty Ford center for the next few months. I was in such a fog, I still don't recall with any accuracy all the facilities I was admitted to during those months.

After my second discharge from the psych ward, I found a sober living home in downtown Palm Springs that had once been a nudist hotel. The place was owned by Chapman House, a well-known rehab center in Orange County, but it wasn't quite set up for occupancy yet. There was an onsite manager and only a couple of other guys living there when I moved in. My mom had gone to the Chapman House website and checked out their rehab center in Orange County. She was satisfied that the sober living place in Palm Springs was legitimate, so my parents paid for it.

I thought it was great! I had my own cabana and it was like having my own studio apartment with all the privacy I needed. And the nicest thing about the location was that the liquor store was less than fifty yards away. I could stumble there and stumble home without incident, and it was really cool, because I didn't have to be accountable to anyone. The so-called manager didn't give a shit what anyone did, so I was my own boss. But true to form, I went bug shit after a bender and ended up back in the psych ward.

———

For some reason the women in the psych wards were attracted to me, and on my first visit, I hooked up with a beautiful young, crazy girl who liked to cut herself, and pluck her eyebrows and eyelashes out. As luck would have it, the two of us were discharged the same day, so we left the hospital together and I spent the night at her house. When I tried to get intimate with her that night, it didn't happen. It couldn't happen. A truckload of Viagra couldn't have given me a woody because of all the anti-psychotics I was on, but unfortunately, she took it as if I wasn't attracted to her. She told me the reason she owned an iguana was because it never rejected her. I thought to myself, well, your iguana's got me beat. He's not taking an exorbitant amount of psych meds and his tongue is longer than mine.

During one of my other stints in the psych ward, I met a lady who resembled Farrah Fawcett, minus fifty pounds. She was about five-seven and weighed about eighty pounds. She'd been hospitalized there numerous times in the past for her alcoholism and for an eating disorder. She initially told me she was separated and in the process of a divorce from her abusive husband, but I grew a little suspicious when she called me after she'd left the hospital and said she wanted to meet me at a hotel in Carlsbad. That made me wonder just how separated she really was. When I asked why we had to meet at a hotel, she said it was because her son was going to be home that day and she wanted us to have some privacy. I didn't believe her, but that was okay. It's not like I hadn't slept with a married woman before.

I told her I was on my way, but of course I didn't go anywhere without my Big Gulp cup filled to the brim with my poison of the day, and that day my poison was Bacardi and Diet Coke. I was just over halfway there, and I had already polished off the bottle of Bacardi, so I pulled off the freeway to take a leak and open another bottle. Somehow, I wound up in the parking lot of Cal State, San Marcos and had no idea how I got in there, and no idea how to get out. The lot was almost vacant other than a woman sitting in her car, not too far from me. I drove up to her car and asked how to get out of the parking lot and back onto the freeway. She told me to follow her and she would lead me out of the parking lot, but instead, she led me to the campus police station.

Apparently, she'd phoned the cops while leading me right to them, and by the time I realized what was happening, two cruisers fell in behind me with their lights on. I pulled over right in front of the police station, got out of my car, put my hands over my head, and told the officer that it was unnecessary to give me a field sobriety test. I confessed that I was way over the legal limit and then turned around and put my hands behind my back. I knew the drill. As soon as the cuffs were secure and the cop started reading me my Miranda rights, I suddenly felt cold sober.

———

It was eerily quiet in the back of that police car, and time seemed to be standing still. I whispered, "What happened? What happened to me, God? What the fuck is *wrong* with me? I'm begging you, please help me. I can't live like this anymore. Please, help me live, or help me die."

God didn't answer me, but I really didn't expect Him to, seeing as how He'd never answered me before.

My mind drifted to my ten-year-old son and I wondered how he would feel when he found out that I wasn't going to be around for football season, and maybe many more seasons to come. I wondered what kind of stories he was going to tell his teammates about where his dad was. I tried to imagine what kind of stories and fantasies he made up about me throughout his life to lessen the pain. I thought about how grateful I should be, that for several years my parents provided housing and support for Jake when I simply wasn't there for him.

I wondered what kind of damage I'd done to the boy who I claimed to love more than life itself. When I didn't show up as promised, I wondered how long he peered out the front window of his house, looking up and down the street, waiting for my car to appear. Maybe he didn't allow himself too many close friends so he wouldn't have to answer the questions. I fully realized that I'd stolen a good portion of my son's childhood.

I thought about the fact that after my Jake was born, I wasn't around much. I'd fly in for a weekend here and there for a supervised visit, or a Chuck E. Cheese party, but overall I was an absentee dad. My justification for not being around was that I had to work to provide for my son, for him to have the best school, nice clothes, a decent home, blah, blah, blah. Of course I faltered on all of the above, so my parents picked up the slack, as always, and fulfilled my commitments. They even bought a perfect little three bedroom house for Jake and his mother to live in just a few blocks away from their Point Loma home.

Sometimes I'd be in town for months at a time, and I'd try to see him as much as I could, but I was drunk most of the time. Of course that meant I failed at that too, even though I was nearby. But I truly *wanted* to see him.

Jake went to a private school from Pre-K through eighth grade. It was an excellent school, but that's not the reason I liked it. I liked it because the playground was very small and right off the street, so I could sit in my car, drink large amounts of booze, watch my beautiful son laugh and play, and have moments sublime. Yeah, I'd go watch Jake at least a few days a week during P.E. or lunchtime, playing football, basketball or kickball. I'd sit in my car, stare at my boy, and fantasize about how he and I were going to be together some day. How we were going to go to sporting events, amusement parks, the beach and the mountains, and I even fantasized about him living with me parttime.

But Reality always came to visit and reminded me of the truth. After Reality spoke its peace, I'd sit there and cry because I couldn't drink away the truth that drove me into oblivion every day of every week. The truth was that I knew I'd never be able to quit drinking and breaking the law. I knew I'd never be able to function at a level where a court would see fit for me to have custody of my son even *part* of the time. I knew my chances of ever getting a valid driver's license and car insurance were slim to none. I also knew that I was going to die a violent death, either in a high-speed car chase, death by cop, or in some other manner I was capable of triggering. Jake was too young to hold, and to bear that cross. I prayed, saying, "Please God, don't let me do that to him. Please don't let him feel like I felt my whole life, abandoned and unlovable. Dear God, please take care of him, because we both know that I can't."

When the conversation in my head became deafening, I'd get out of my car, stumble across the street and summon Jake to the fence.

He'd run to the fence saying, "Daddy, Daddy, Daddy!"

He would stick his little fingers through the fence and we would hold hands. He was so happy to see me, and I was so happy to hold his fingers, I never wanted to let go. Jake's mom was a teacher at the school, and the teachers out on the playground knew me so they didn't object to my being there and left us alone.

While our fingers were intertwined, I'd tell Jake how much I loved him, and one time I told him I loved him so much I couldn't even explain it. A few days later, I went by the shcool to see him and when I told him how much I loved him, he finished my sentence and said, "I know, Daddy, you love me so much you can't even explain it."

He looked like he wanted to say, "Daddy, show me that you love me. I love you, but you're never there for me. I want a daddy like the other kids have!"

When I could see these questions wanting to surface, I'd tell my boy that I had to go because I didn't want to scare him by letting him see my cry. Sometimes I even failed at that.

Then I thought about my dad and how he must've felt when he received the phone call that I'd overdosed on heroin, and was in ICU. I wondered how he felt when he kissed me on the forehead and said his last goodbye. I wondered if the thought crossed his mind that maybe it would be better if I didn't come out of the coma. My parents knew it was only a matter of time before they got that final call saying that I was dead. *The Last Call.* How ironic.

I knew I wasn't going to get a response, but I said, "Lord, if you give me one more chance, I swear to you I won't let you down. I'll never let my family down again, and I'll never let you down again either. Please fix me Lord, I'm begging you."

God didn't answer me, but another mortal sounding voice in my head did. The voice that spoke said, *"You don't deserve another chance. I'm not going to bullshit you. Do you honestly think you should get another chance?"*

Amazingly, I wasn't scared of that voice! My despair overcame fear and all other emotions.

"No, probably not," I said, "But I'm praying for one."

"I'm telling you that you don't deserve another chance," the voice said.

"I know I don't, but it's different this time because I'm going to prison and I'll probably get killed in there," I said.

"You might be able to survive if you keep your mouth shut and listen," the voice said. *"You'll have to listen to me and trust me all the way. Your life's going to depend on it."*

"Okay," I said. "I understand, and I'll do it."

I realized that people who hear voices are either psychic or psychotic, so at that point I was willing to accept that I was psychotic and just listen to the damn voice. An auditory hallucination couldn't be worse than the voice I'd been listening to for the past thirty-five years.

Chapter Fourteen

In county jail I sought out other white guys who were either on their way to prison or had been there before. I needed to learn the ropes, to learn about prison politics, and about the rules and regulations I would need to follow.

The guy who helped me was a skinhead called "Irish". He was about my height, but spindly. He was all inked up, and had some very interesting tattoos. There was the number 88 on the side of his head and I assumed it had nothing to do with the number of Dale Earnhardt's race car.

When I asked him what it meant, he said, "Are you fucking serious, dog? It's eighty-eight! As in the eighth letter of the alphabet, the letter H. And two H's is HH, which means, Heil Hitler, and I hope you're fucking with me that you don't know what eighty-eight means, 'cause if you don't, your gonna have a world of problems inside, dog."

I told Irish, "I'm just playing, dog. Everyone knows what eighty-eight means. I know what eighty-eight means, of course. Heil Hitler, dog!"

When he blinked, I notice he had tatts on both eyelids. One said "WHAT" and the other said "EVER". The tatt that covered the back of his neck said, " FUCK BITCHES" and the one all the way across his back said, "STATE RAISED." He spent his teen years incarcerated for nearly beating his alcoholic stepfather to death with a ball peen hammer while the guy was sleeping. Irish said the dude used to beat the crap out of his mother and sister on a regular basis and even tried to rape his sister once when he was high on meth. The tattoo that was hardest to make out was the one inked on his chest because it was a sloppy prison tatt that read, "MOMMA TRIED."

Irish sounded serious when he said, "Oh, yeah, dog, if you get caught rubbing one out in the joint, you're fucked."

I said, "What's *rubbing one out* mean?"

He cackled, and said, "Whackin' off, chokin' your chicken, spankin' the monkey. Come on dog, don't play stupid."

I said, "I'm just messing with you, everyone knows what rubbing one out means. When in doubt, don't rub one out. Right, dog?"

He scowled, and said, "Yeah, right. You better hope you don't have *any* doubts when you get to where you're goin'."

In the morning when the nurse came around to dispense meds, she yelled out my last name, and when I returned to the table and sat down, Irish said, "So, your last name's Womboe?"

"Yes, but it's pronounced Wam-baah."

Irish said, "There's a writer like that. You heard of him?"

"Yes, I have," I said.

"You read his books?"

"Actually, he's my dad," I said.

He smiled, baring a grill that no dentist had ever seen. His teeth were like little bits of licorice. He said, "Check this out!"

He got up, went over to a cart of books that were there for the inmates to read, and shuffled through them. He found what he was looking for, and came back to the table with a copy of *The Onion Field*, the non-fiction book my dad had written thirty years earlier.

He handed it to me and said, "Your old man wrote this book?"

"Yeah, he did," I said.

His eyes got big as he looked around the room and then back to me, and said, "Dog, you're famous!"

I said, "No brother, I'm not famous at all. I'm pretty much just a fuckup who used up all his county jail time and now I'm on my way to prison."

I realized that I'd been given every opportunity to succeed in life while Irish had been given none. He never had a family to rely on, and I did. He had no support, and I had all the support in the world. It was understandable why he was here, but it didn't make any sense that I was here. Irish was destined to be in jail or prison, but that wasn't supposed to be my destiny. Or was it?

No sooner had this thought crossed my mind than the voice said, *"What in the hell makes you think you're not prison material? You belong there more than a lot of these guys."*

For most of my life all the judges and lawyers didn't seem to think I was prison material, but now I'd just found out from a hallucinatory voice that I fit the mold perfectly. More irony. How much of it could I take?

After Irish finished explaining the rules and politics of prison, he informed me that inevitably, someone was going to ask me if I was related to the author and I'd have to make the choice whether or not to tell the truth.

Irish said, "Dog, whether you think you're famous or not, the convicts are gonna think you are. Maybe not the skinheads, because most of them don't know how to read, but a lot of people read Womboe books in the joint. You're gonna be a target, homie."

"Why?" I asked.

He said, "Why do you think? Your old man's famous, so some convict who's doin' life can make a name for himself if he shanks you. *He'd* be a celebrity! Don't you get it, dog?"

"I guess so," I said. I did. I got it.

Irish filled me in on all the prison basics, like the whites stick with whites, blacks stick with blacks, and Mexicans stick with Mexicans. He said that we weren't supposed to engage with any of the other races. He explained that I was a "wood" and he was a "skinhead." Skinheads are white supremacists, and "peckerwoods" are just white guys who happen to be in prison. The blacks are called "toads" or "June bugs," or "*mayates*," meaning "niggers" in Spanish, and the Mexicans are "Southsiders," or "*paisas.*" Southsiders are born and raised in Southern California, and *paisas* are immigrants from Mexico, and almost all are gang members. The other races are just called *others.*

One evening while Irish was educating me on prison politics, a cocky lawyer came to the jail to offer his services to me and said he *only* wanted $25,000 as a retainer, like that was some kind of a bargain. I didn't say anything to him, but got up off my stool and waved for the deputy to take me back to my cell.

The following day a female lawyer from the same firm showed up. The deputy brought me out again and she told me she'd heard what had happened the day before when her boss came to see me.

Then she leaned closer and whispered, "He's a real asshole."

She said it was imperative that I have private counsel because a public defender probably wouldn't be right for me because of my lengthy record, and I could very well wind up with the maximum sentence. And then she came to the best part, that she was here to represent me *pro bono!* Bingo! That fit my budget perfectly.

I couldn't believe this woman had come to my rescue. She said the reason she took the case was because she felt I just wasn't prison material. Of course, it was most likely my dad's fame that impressed her. I sure as hell wasn't going to tell her what the voice in my head had to say about whether or not I was prison material.

After the judge at my hearing handed down the maximum sentence of three years in state prison, I turned to my attorney and saw that she was crying.

I winked at her, and said, "Hey, what are *you* crying for? I'm the one who should be crying!"

"I'm so sorry, David," she said. "I really tried!"

I said, "Ma'am, at this point, there's nothing that *anyone* can do for me. I deserve to be in prison." I hugged her and said goodbye.

Even though the sentence was for three years, I was credited with 365 days of accumulated county jail time that I'd served over the years and, being my first prison term, the three-year sentence was reduced to half.

When I got back to the jail that night I went to my cell and slept more soundly than I had in a very long time. I had dreams that put me far away from jail or prison walls. I had dreams about making a comeback, a *real* comeback, a comeback for my family as well as myself. When I woke the next morning I felt really strong, but the strength I felt was much more than just physical strength, it was an inner strength I'd never felt before. I finally felt at peace.

I stayed in county jail for a couple of months, but the day finally came when I was transported to state prison where I was to be incarcerated for the balance of my nine months and twenty days, which meant I was to become a *real* convict. Early one morning when it was still dark, a jailor called my name and punched my ticket. I was really on my way to prison. There were several inmates being transported to Donovan Prison with me, and I was shackled to a big-ass silverback, so I was shitting bricks!

Breaking through a shroud of coastal fog, we slowly approached the prison gates, and as we got closer, I prayed, "Please God, I need you to give me strength and guidance so I can get back to my family alive. Thank you, God. Amen."

When we got off the bus we were unshackled, strip searched, and then packed into small cages. The intake process took a long time and I could feel the evil in the air. There were killers, rapists, arsonists, and child molesters in this place. This was real!

After several hours, they called my name and a correctional officer escorted me into an office where a captain was sitting at his desk. The first thing he said was, "So what does your old man think about you being here?"

"I don't know," I said.

"He must be fuckin' pissed," the captain said.

"Probably, but as I said, I don't know."

"You don't belong in here, guy," he said.

I said, "That's not what *some* people think."

He chuckled and said, "There're some dangerous people in here."

I looked in the direction of the holding tanks, pointed, and said, "I'm sure of it. Those guys look pretty scary."

He said, "I wouldn't be pointing at people around here unless you're near and dear to them, dude."

"Thanks for telling me that," I said.

He said, "You'd better hope that no one finds out who your old man is. You'd be fucked."

"That's what I heard," I said.

"Do you have any kids?"

"Yes, sir, I have a ten year old boy," I said.

"What's your boy's name?"

"Jake. His name's Jake."

He said, "Jake Wambaugh, ten years old. And his father's in prison. What a fucking shame."

I said, "I know, sir."

He said, "Your dad's books are pretty popular in here, so I'm gonna recommend that you go into protective custody."

"Pardon me?" I said.

"I think it would be too dangerous for you in general population."

I was just about to thank the captain for looking out for me, when suddenly that voice came through loud and clear, and said, *"Tell him that you don't need to be in protective custody, that you can do your time just like everyone else."*

Holy shit! I couldn't believe what I was hearing. This inner voice is trying to get me killed. But I refocused on the captain, and said, "Sir, do I *have* to go into protective custody?"

"Well, no," he said, "but you could easily get sliced or shanked in general population. A lot of these guys have nothing to lose. You're dad's a famous ex-cop so that would give someone status."

"That's what Irish said."

"Who's Irish?"

"Some skinhead I met in jail."

He said, "Either way, make up your mind. I don't have time to fuck with you all day."

"Okay, sir, I'll go in general population, please," I blurted.

He shook his head, mumbled something under his breath, and yelled to another correctional officer, "Get this idiot outta here." He looked back at me and said, "Bud, I think you just made a very bad decision for yourself."

I said, "I sure hope not, but it wouldn't be the first time."

And I prayed that the voice in my head knew what he was talking about.

I was housed in building sixteen, a level-four maximum-security yard, for almost six months, and my building was notorious for being the most violent cellblock in Donovan State Prison. As I was walking in the lineup heading toward the building, I thought to myself, Oh my God, I can't believe I'm really here! I just can't believe it!"

I was placed in a six-by-ten-foot cell with a convict who was right out of a horror movie. He was about six-two, and weighed 230 pounds. He was about my age, and looked to be in really good shape. He had swastika tatts all over his body, including on his bald head. He was in prison this time for committing an ADW with GBI, which I learned was *assault with a deadly weapon with great bodily injury.* He told me that he nearly beat his wife to death with a hockey stick. He said he came home one afternoon while he was under the influence of alcohol and crystal meth, and when she confronted him about his whereabouts, he attacked her. He was very matter-of-fact about how he almost killed her. I kept wondering what a monster like him was doing with a hockey stick.

He read the Bible to me every night after dinner, and then he would want to discuss the readings and pray. I was just praying he wouldn't get horny after the readings. I thought, Jesus Christ, now this is *really* one day at a time, not that AA pussy version of the same!

We were on lockdown for most of my time at Donovan, but occasionally we got out to the yard. My first day on the yard was terrifying. It was like something out of *Lock Up Raw*, except worse. After I was checked for weapons, I walked out of cellblock sixteen and onto the prison yard. My cellmate told me he would show me the ropes so I wouldn't get into trouble. He said the first thing I had to do was to produce my paperwork for the white "shot-caller." The papers he referred to were the court papers that show what you're in prison for, and if you're in prison for child molesting, rape, arson, or elder abuse, there's a heavy price to pay, up to and including death.

I was totally fine because I only had seven DUI's, a couple of drug possession charges, several drunk in publics, an indecent exposure, and a terrorist threat against my goofy girlfriend. No big deal at all, except for the indecent exposure. I did have to explain that one to them.

That episode took place when I was with Ziggy on opening day of the races at Santa Anita. Twenty-four beers later I had to piss like a racehorse, and was trying to hold it until we could get out of the parking lot, but I was desperate. I was relieving myself on the fender of Ziggy's old beater when all of a sudden two old ladies saw me and both started screaming.

Soon enough, security was flying at us on foot and in golf carts. I was arrested, charged, and convicted of indecent exposure. The reason the indecent exposure stuck was because the two old ladies claimed that as soon as they screamed I turned around and wagged my piece at them. I don't *think* I did. The woods were all laughing while I told the story and they gave me a pass.

The prison yard was just like I'd seen in the movies. There must've been over a hundred skins and peckerwoods in a pack, like wolves, in one section of the yard, blacks in another, Mexicans in another, and all the other races in yet another.

Taz was the name of our shot-caller, and after he checked my paperwork, he smiled, stuck out his nasty little paw, and said, "Welcome home, wood."

Taz was about five-three, and just as wide, an ugly pit bull with lots of body ink and rotten teeth. I could smell his trench mouth from five feet away.

His smile vanished and he said, "So, wood, is this your first term?"

"Yes, sir," I said.

"Awright, we got rules here," he said. "My right-hand man will give you the rules. You read 'em, write 'em, remember 'em, and make sure you don't forget 'em. You down?

"Yes, sir," I said.

As I stood around listening to convict stories, I realized I was with very dangerous people who could very well be spending the rest of their lives here, and it didn't seem to bother them much. This was their world.

Taz, his right-hand man and his sergeant-at-arms wandered away from the pack, and as they did, Taz summoned me to follow. My heart sank as I walked over to them, and said, "What's up, Taz?"

He introduced me to his right-hand man and his sergeant at arms. The right-hand man carries out the orders for the shot-caller, and the sergeant at arms is the guy who leads the woods into battle. At least that was my take on it.

Taz looked at me with his vacant eyes, and said, "Awright, wood, I'll tell you the first two rules since you haven't read 'em yet. The first two are: Don't lie and don't steal. You with me so far?"

"Yes, sir," I said.

"Don't fucking call me 'sir'!" he snarled. "Are you trying to make me feel stupid?"

"No, dog," I said, shakily.

All three started to laugh, but Taz abruptly stopped, looked at me and said, "What are the first two rules, wood?"

I said, "Don't lie, and don't steal."

"Good," he said. "Now, remember those rules when you answer this question."

"Okay," I said, waiting for it.

He said, "If you lie to me, I'll kill you." Then he looked me dead in the eye, and said, "So, is your pop Joe Wambaugh?"

I thought about what Irish and the corrections officer had said about never telling anyone who my dad is. I was just about to say no, when the voice in my head said, *"Tell him the truth. Don't lie to this man! Tell him the truth, right now!"*

Now I was almost certain that this voice was trying to get me killed, but I said, "Yes, he is, Taz. He's my dad."

Taz looked at his posse and said, "No fuckin' way, dog! Is he really your pops?"

I said, "Taz, you told me not to lie to you. Yes, he's my dad."

His two henchmen were looking at me all gaga, like I was some kind of a movie star or something. Taz said, "I wouldn't be telling people that your pops is Joe Wambaugh. You might get into some serious wrecks around here." And he started laughing like a loon.

My first physical altercation took place on my second day in prison. As I walked out to the yard where the wolves gather, a fairly tall, overweight skinhead approached me, and said, "So, is your daddy rich?"

So the word was out. "I doubt it," I said. "I think he lost a bunch in the stock market."

He said, "Did the shot-caller check your paperwork when you got here?"

"Yeah," I said.

As he walked away, he grunted, and said, "Sure they did. Daddy probably had it altered for you."

My cellie came over to me immediately, and said, "Bro, that man just disrespected you. You gotta go smash him. I'm sorry, but it's part of prison."

"Jesus!" I said. "Are you serious? I don't *feel* disrespected. It's no big deal. Can't we let this go?"

"Sure," he said. "But then you'll get fucked up by ten woods instead of only one skinhead."

I turned from my cellmate, walked over to the fat skinhead and said, "Homie, you shouldn't have disrespected me like that." And then I took him to the ground and beat the crap out of him. My cellie looked proud of me when we went back to our cell.

Later I got into a worse fight with another skinhead who called me a punk because I didn't want a prison tattoo. My body was ink-free, and I wanted it to stay that way whether I survived prison or not. I lost that fight and broke my pinky finger. It hurt like hell, but I didn't go to the prison hospital because that would have been considered a lame thing to do for a little broken pinky.

I had yet another fight one night when I didn't want to drink "pruno" with the woods. It's prison booze made from the fruit leftover from meals. They add sugar and put it in a plastic bag to ferment for a few days. They have to keep removing the air from the bag to keep it from exploding, and they say the end product is like grain alcohol or white lightning. Because I chose not to drink that shit, one of the woods called me an AA cult member, and after trying to let that one pass, I finally had to fight him because too many other woods overheard him disrespect me.

A few riots nearly took place during my time at Donovan Prison but luckily, they were quelled. There was so much violence and evil in the air you could feel the electric buzz when something bad was about to happen.

After almost six months at Donovan I was transferred to another prison in Norco, California. I welcomed a change to California Rehabilitation Center, because at Donovan I was locked down twenty-three hours a day, but at CRC it was more like dorm living, but with a hundred men to a dorm. Unfortunately, I found there was a lot more violence because with more activity and movement, comes more drug dealing and drug debt.

By that time I wasn't so afraid of getting hurt, but fighting would get more time added to my sentence, and I sure as hell didn't want that to happen, so I tried to stay low-key. I didn't get any decent sleep the whole time I was locked up and would only get catnaps during the day, but always there were sleepless nights. I'd think about my family during those hours, wishing I could take back some of the damage I'd done, and I'd fantasize about a comeback. My fantasies would always be interrupted by the screams of men who'd been in a cage of one kind or another for a lifetime. It was bone chilling. To keep the violence to a minimum, there were no two bunks with men of the same race next to each other. They went in a certain order: black, white, Mexican, and on down the line.

On the bunk next to me was a huge black man about seventy years old, called Dickie. He was a lifelong heroin addict and smalltime criminal who'd been in and out of prison most of his life for stealing, to support his drug habit. Dickie was about six-five, and weighed over 350 pounds. He was the shot-caller for the blacks, so it was permissible for him to talk to me, but I wasn't supposed to talk to him. So on a few occasions when I was confronted by the woods for talking to Dickie, he would tell them it was his fault, that he was asking me a question. Dickie was actually a big black teddy bear and he came to be my best friend in prison.

He told me outlandish stories that I'm not sure I believed, like claiming he'd slept with a midget, made love to a quadriplegic, and even had wild sex with a ninety-two-year-old woman who paid him fifty bucks for his company. And he said he'd fathered over one hundred children, which was his only story that *might've* been true.

Dickie and I talked about all sorts of things. I'd tell him all about the comeback I was going to make and how things were going to be different this time, and he'd ask me questions about what it was like to have grown up so privileged. He was full of questions. He'd read some of my dad's books, so sometimes we would talk about them.

He told me that he'd been in prison with Jimmy Smith, one of the killers from *The Onion Field*, the true story that my dad had written back in the seventies. Dickie said he knew Jimmy Smith well, and said that Jimmy had been paroled several times but couldn't manage living out in the real world, so he would commit petty crimes to get himself back to his home in prison. The last time Jimmy Smith was out on parole, he finally overdosed on heroin and died.

When my prison term was coming to an end, I had a final altercation that almost got me ninety more days. There was a violent young skinhead in my dorm who was always looking for trouble, and less than a week before I was to be paroled, he came over to my bunk, and in front of several other inmates, said, "Hey, dog, give me a shot of coffee."

I said, "Sorry, bro, I only have a little bit left."

"What a punk!" he said as he walked away,

I knew what I had to do. I went over to the white shot-caller, told him what had happened, and he said, "Take it to the shitter."

We walked into the bathroom, and all I could think about was that the bastard wanted to screw things up for me. He wanted to take away my chance to get out and be decent father, a decent son, a decent person. I was enraged!

As soon as we got into the bathroom area I bull-rushed the ginger-headed prick and drove him straight back into the tiled wall. When his skull made contact, it sounded like an egg cracked and he crumbled to the floor. After that, I jumped on top of him and gave him a beating and left him wedged between two shitters. Everyone dispersed before the guards got there, and there was no further investigation.

When I got back to my bunk, Dickie and a few of the blacks were there waiting. Dickie said, "Hey, man, me and the brothers here are gonna call you *Raw-D* from now on."

I wasn't sure what he meant, but I got the general idea. I said, "I'm not proud about smashing that loser, Dickie. I don't feel good about hurting anybody anymore. I just want to get out of this place without any more trouble."

"I feel ya, Raw-D," Dickie said. "I feel ya."

During my last month in prison, I began corresponding with my dad. We hadn't talked since I overdosed, and I honestly didn't think he would talk to me for a long time, if ever. He sent me a letter that further helped change the direction of my life, not because of what he wrote, but how I *perceived* what he wrote.

When I read the letter I was really pissed off because I thought some of the things he said were completely out of line. He said I should give my car away so I wouldn't be tempted to drive, and that I should get a bus pass to get around. He said that my job, flying from city to city doing the sign promos, was deadly for me, and that I should get an entry level job at any place that would hire me. He also said that I should find two or three other AA guys to share an apartment with, and that if I didn't do all these things, my son would probably grow up without a dad, and how dare I do that to Jake who had done nothing to deserve a father like me.

My plan was to get out of prison and resume my old job. I'd made really good money with the outdoor sign promotions, and I thought it was the only way I *knew* how to make money. I felt like tearing up the letter.

Dickie could see that I was fuming, and said, "Damn, Raw-D, what's up with you? Did your wife send you divorce papers or somethin'?"

I said, "All my divorces are final, bro. No, this letter's from my old man. He wants me to do a bunch of bullshit when I get outta here that I'm afraid I just can't do."

"What kinda bullshit, Raw-D?" Dickie asked.

"Here, read this thing and tell me what you think about it. It's ridiculous!" I handed him the letter, and he must've read it three or four times.

When he finished, he said, "Raw-D, this really ain't a bunch of bullshit. He thinks you might have a chance if you listen to him and do what he says. Listen to him, Raw-D. He wants to help you."

I snatched the letter from his hand, and said, "Did you read the same letter I read?"

"Raw-D, it's all in there. Can't you see?"

I said, "No I can't! I *can't* see, Dickie!"

My dad said in his letter that I could call him collect if I wanted to, so I decided to call him the following day. When a collect call is made an automated voice announces that the call is coming from a state prison, and it interrupts your conversation every couple of minutes to repeat the information. That was the first call I'd made since being incarcerated so when my dad answered the phone and the automated voice came on, I thought, Great! Another reminder about what a loser his son is.

But he answered the phone, accepted the call, and sounded really upbeat. He asked me how I was doing, and if I knew when I was getting out. He also asked if I had read his letter, and if I was going to do the things he'd suggested.

He said, "Dave, will you get rid of your car? It's too tempting, and you're sure to drive if you keep it."

I knew what my inner voice would want me to say, so I said, "Sure dad, I'll get rid of it."

"You will?" he said.

"Yes, I will."

Then he said, "What about never doing those goddamn signs again. It takes you away from having to be accountable to anyone and you just wind up getting drunk. That job will land you back in prison."

The voice said to me, *"He's right! Tell him you'll give up the signs."*

"Sure, Dad, I'll give up the signs," I said.

"You will?"

"Yes, I will."

"Are you okay, Dave?" He sounded like he wanted to ask me if I was drunk, maybe on jailhouse hooch.

"Yeah, I'm fine," I said.

"You should get a job where you can go every day, one that's not so stressful. Something where you can just punch a clock and get some consistency going in your life."

"I think that's a good idea, Dad," I said. "In fact, I think that would be really good for me."

"After your release, I'll pay for your bus pass," he said.

A second went by and then he said, "David, are you just blowing smoke? Will you really do these things?"

"Yes, I will," I said.

Then he asked, "Are you on medication or something?"

"No, Dad, I'm not on anything," I said. "I'm going to do everything you want me to do. But I gotta go. An inmate's missing, so we're going on lockdown right now. I love you, Dad."

"I love you too, son," he said.

I admit that I gave my dad all those answers against my will, but I'd told the voice I would follow his direction for the rest of my life and I was planning on doing exactly that.

F87244

WAMBAUGH, D

DOB   7/15/64

Wht

This is the photo taken when I was being moved from Donavan State Prison to California Rehabilitation Center in Norco, CA. on Dec. 17, 2007.

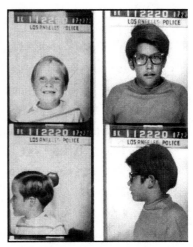

Little did my dad know when he took these mug shots at the police station as a joke in 1971, it would be the first of many to come for me.

1978
Ziggy and I are with our "dates"
Junior High Graduation Dinner

Chapter Fifteen

The day finally came when I was paroled from prison, and I honestly couldn't believe I had survived those nine months. I said goodbye to Dickie, and told him how grateful I was for everything he'd done for me. I didn't have time to explain *why* I was grateful, and I wasn't so sure he would've understood anyway, but nonetheless, he helped me see the flaws in my perception of reality. He was my only friend in prison, and was the second teacher I'd learned anything from, the first being Connie Henderson from COBAR House, and they were both black. More irony, because all my life I'd been such a racist.

I walked through the prison gates expecting to see a friend from AA who was supposed to pick me up, but he was nowhere in sight. I was surprised because he was usually reliable. As I was surveying the parking lot, I was shocked to see one of my old flames from the mental hospital sitting on the trunk of her beat-up Chrysler LeBaron convertible, smoking a cigarette, and wearing a revealing sundress several sizes too small. She'd written to me a few times while I was inside, and sent me a couple of books, but that was the extent of my connection to her, except for the time we swapped spit in the linen closet, only because I was still detoxing and looped on Valium. She must've thought our relationship went much deeper, seeing as how she found out my release date and took it upon herself to show up.

As I got closer I could see that she wasn't wearing panties, and her come-fuck-me pumps didn't come close to containing her gnarly bunions.

She was about five-one, and weighed about two bills, give or take, but it was hard to tell her age, because of layers of makeup she'd caked on her face. She must've been pretty old though because four or five wiry whiskers were popping out of her chin, and there was one at the corner of her mouth.

Alarmed, I said, "What's up? What're you doing here?"

When she hopped off the car, one of her mammoth tits bounced out of her sundress and came to rest just above her swollen belly. She wrestled it back inside, smiled, and said, "I just wanted to surprise you so we could spend a little time together. I know it's been a long time for you."

"A long time for what?"

She winked at me and said, "*You* know."

I said, "No, I *don't* know, and a friend is picking me up here anyway, but I appreciate the thought."

"Oh, does your friend drive a BMW?" she asked.

"I think so. Why?"

She looked me up and down like I was a lamb chop, and said, "Well, I dismissed your friend and told him that me and you had some business to take care of."

I explained that I couldn't have sex because I was too traumatized from my prison experience for hanky-panky, and I was useless without the help of a Viagra anyway, so it wasn't going to happen. At least not on *that* day. She didn't believe me and I didn't care, but I persuaded her to drop me at my friend Mike's house.

I'd been placed on high-control parole status because I'd had a violent crime, so that meant I had to have an address where my PO could check up on me at any time, and Mike's place was a landing spot for me.

The day after I was released from prison, I re-enrolled in the DUI class that I'd been in and out of for almost two decades and had yet to complete. Every time I got close to finishing the program I would either get another DUI or wind up in jail for some reason or another, and then I'd have to start the class all over again. It took me over eighteen years to complete the program. That means that I had no valid driver's license for well over *half* of my adult life. I started the program that day and completed it without a hiccup.

Because of my terrorist threat charge, I was required to enroll in a fifty-two-week Domestic Violence class that I also completed with flying colors. Actually, I didn't mind that class at all because it made me feel better about myself, knowing that I wasn't the only scumbag in town.

After making it through prison in one piece, I thought everything would be downhill, but that wasn't the case. I quickly became aware that I was emotionally and mentally crippled, and had a whole lot to learn. I knew I had no room for error.

As I was walking to my first Domestic Violence class, I came to an intersection that had a green light, but the "don't walk" sign was blinking. I was just about to start jogging across the street before the light turned yellow, and the voice in my head stopped me in my tracks, and said, *"What are you doing, you dumb shit? I thought you weren't going to break the law anymore.*

"Okay, okay, I'll *think* next time," I said under my breath.

The voice said, *"Trust me, your thinker is busted. Your mind is like a bad neighborhood and you should never go there alone."*

From day one, I made all my commitments on time and did everything I was supposed to do. I'd never filed a tax return in my life because I once knew a guy who told me there was no such thing as a debtor's prison, and if that was the case, I couldn't imagine why anyone would *bother* paying. I'd made a lot of money during the fifteen years before going to prison, so I was shocked when I learned what my back taxes were estimated to be.

A couple of months out of the joint, I was lonely for female companionship, but the only girl I still knew was the Farrah Fawcett look-alike I'd met in the psych ward. She was the one I was on my way to see on the day I'd gotten arrested. I called and asked how she was doing and told her what had happened to me. She said that she couldn't believe I'd been in prison, because in her mind, I just wasn't prison material! I didn't respond to *that* statement.

She was really excited to hear from me and wanted to see me

immediately. She must've been excited, because when she picked me up that day we went shopping at Nordstrom's where she spent several hundred dollars on clothes for me.

We drove up the coast highway toward Santa Barbara in her husband's new Mercedes, stopped at a quaint little cafe along the way, and then on to a seaside motel. The sex was frightening because, unlike our previous encounters, I was sober. She was so frail, I thought she might blow out a hip. Her oversized fake tits looked like they'd been attached with Velcro, and in her ultrathin face, her veneers were enormous.

She said she was still in the process of divorce, and that it was a real uphill battle because her husband was a psychiatrist who had a lot of money and power. She told me he was the head shrink at Donovan State Prison where I'd spent almost six months. I later found out that it was *his* credit card that she'd used to pay for our drive up the coast and to purchase my new wardrobe.

After one of our shopping sprees, she went on a bender, and her husband got his hands on her cell phone and checked all her texts and call logs. She had plenty of racy stuff on that phone between the two of us, and he saw it all. He called me, and said he knew who I was, knew where I lived, knew I was on parole, and was going to call my parole officer and have me violated and returned to prison. He said he knew all about Nordstrom's, the Cheesecake Factory, Footlocker, and Victoria's Secret. I told him I'd take the blame for everything except Victoria's Secret because there was nothing in that store I would even consider wearing.

I went directly to my parole officer and told him what had happened. When I was done, he laughed, and said, "Let me get this straight. You banged Farrah Fawcett's anorexic twin, who just so happens to be married to the head psychiatrist at Donovan, and he wants to violate you?"

"Yes, sir," I said.

He said, "Mister Wambaugh, I really don't think he would want to do that. I mean it would be a little embarrassing for him to have to explain to his colleagues how his wife hooked up with an ex-con she'd met in a mental hospital. And I don't think he'd want it known that he paid for your wardrobe from Nordy's. I think you're safe on this one, even though some guys get pissed off when you bang their wife and buy expensive clothes on their tab."

My P.O. was right. The prison shrink and his wife went away and I never heard from either of them again.

My roomy, Mike, had a girlfriend who was heavily involved in a local animal shelter where she volunteered regularly. I was only three months out of prison when she showed up at our house one day with a nine-month-old black cat that had the skittish personality of an abused animal. She said that if someone didn't adopt him by five p.m. that day, they were going to put him to sleep. She was crying, and Mike was consoling her, when she suddenly looked up at me and said, "Dave, can you take him?"

"No," I said. "I'm sorry but I can't take him. I don't have a home of my own, and I wouldn't even know how the hell to take care of him!"

Mike tried to make me feel guilty and muttered, "That poor little cat. You really should take him, Dave. You can keep him here until you get your own place."

I said, "Dude, please, I can't even take care of myself, let alone some frickin' cat!"

His girlfriend, still crying, said, "David, I think he'd be good for you."

I was thinking, How in the hell does she know what's good for me? I looked at the black cat, the cat looked at me, and I wasn't feeling any kind of emotion at all, when suddenly the voice came through so loud and clear I was afraid *they* could hear it.

The voice said, *"Your life was spared, so why don't you spare his? It's not just about you anymore, remember? That cat has contributed more to this world than you have."*

I looked at the girl and said, "Alright, I'll take him. I don't know what I'm gonna do with him, but I'll take him."

I finally named him "B" because "B" is for "*bug*" as in "*June bug*," as we'd referred to the black convicts. I'd called him J.B. at first, but when my one black friend asked me what the J.B. stood for, I changed his name to just plain old "B".

Mr. B turned out to be one of the best things that ever happened to me. I gave him my word that we would never be homeless again, and I promised to take good care of him until he dies. Unless I die first.

Right around that same time I met an incredible woman who was about my age, very attractive, kind, and smart. We dated off and on for a while, but I proved to be an unfit boyfriend and not ready for a reciprocal intimate relationship. For the time being, I was quite content with having Mr. B as my significant other.

————

I made good on my word to my dad that I wouldn't do the sign jobs anymore, so I had to re-invent myself. It was time to get a new job, but I had no idea where I'd find employment because not too many people want to hire ex-cons on parole.

On February 1, 2009, I decided to call on my friend, the same doctor, who owned the rehab in San Diego where I'd stayed as a patient on several occasions over the years. We'd first met when we were in rehab together nearly twenty years earlier. A couple of years after he got out of treatment, he started his own facility in San Diego.

I told him I needed a job and asked if he had anything available. He said he needed a director of marketing, and although I didn't know much about marketing, I walked out of that meeting with the job and a base salary of five thousand a month. I also negotiated a handsome commission for myself on each patient I brought into treatment. Not bad for an ex-con fresh out of the joint. I was very grateful to get work in a field where I had so much experience. I knew *plenty* about rehabs and recovery homes.

The day I scored that job, I called my roommate, Mike, to tell him the good news. He had known me for almost twenty years, and was always amazed how quickly I came up after being down and out. Somehow I'd always made money.

After I told him the good news, he said, "Are you sure you're not Irish? You seem to have the *luck* of the Irish. But even so, you just have to stay away from the pink and green, and you'll be fine."

I knew what he meant: pussy and money."

My pro bono lawyer contacted me to see how I was doing and said she'd like to have lunch or dinner with me sometime. I thought that would be cool because I wanted her to see how well I was doing and give her a positive report about my progress.

She was about ten years my senior, had dark auburn hair with noticeable silver roots, usually worn pulled back off her collar, perhaps a style left over from her Marine Corps days. She was about five-two, a little on the chubby side, but had very pretty eyes.

She showed up at my apartment, coming straight from court, and was wearing a tailored navy blue suit, and matching pumps. Even though I wasn't attracted to her, I thought it was a sexy looking outfit, and her designer glasses completed the businesswoman-lawyer look I'd fantasized about. We went out for dinner, and afterward, came back to my apartment where we wound up in bed. That was a mistake, because she went from being a helping hand to an open hand, hoping for money to come her way. I'm sure she pursued me for the same reason every other chick in my life did, all having their eyes on the prize that didn't exist.

When we took our clothes off, things went south quickly. Her breasts were small, but one of them was noticeably larger and misshapen. She had a smooth round belly and her ass was nothing but a vertical surface. And, maybe because she was a former Marine bomb explosive expert, she forgot which of us was the dude. I wasn't about to go hand-to-hand with a Marine so I just pulled a two-pump chump, rolled over, and played dead. She got the clue, got dressed and bailed. I was just hoping that Mr. B wasn't traumatized by the ordeal.

We soon stopped seeing each other, but after several months she sent me an email to see how I was doing. I told her I'd been working on a book but hadn't been able to complete it yet. She told me that she and her law partner would love to help me shape up my manuscript and get it ready for a publisher to look at it. She said that her law partner's husband had a master's degree in English, was also a published author, and would be a very good editor. The two women came to my office on two occasions and we sat for at least an hour both times, talking about how we were going to execute our plan and what roll each person would have in the book project.

During our two meetings we also discussed the prospect of doing an alternative sentencing campaign in downtown San Diego Superior Court. What we were planning to do was to talk to the Superior Court Judges into sending the guilty parties to the rehab that I was working with, as opposed to doing jail time, and I would give them a commission on every client they got for me. We were also going to approach other criminal lawyers who everyone knew had big caseloads of DUI's, and clients with first or second time drug offenses.

The attorney had a copy of my manuscript for a few months but did nothing with it, so I told her I wanted it back, and I would be writing and editing the book on my own. When she returned it, she burst into my office, and in front of my assistant, yelled, "I don't fucking care if you don't want us to edit your book, but Jennifer told me that you also wanted to talk to the judges and lawyers on your own, without us! You're not an attorney and there's no way that you'd be able to get into chambers because you're a convicted felon. The criminal lawyers won't want to talk to you because you have no credibility and no rapport with them."

"Get out of my office!" I said.

As soon as I said that, I saw fire in her eyes, and remembered that she'd been a bomb explosive expert in the Marine Corps for many years. She was the person who wore the bomb suits and detonated bombs. She also carried a .357 Desert Eagle in her purse.

She stood her ground and said, "No one down there will listen to you. For you to get any clients, we'll have to tell everybody that you're with us and that you're okay."

I said, "You have no idea what I can do down there. I talked my way out of doing time on countless occasions, so I'll be able to get into chambers and talk them into sending me clients. Watch me."

She said, "Fuck you, David," and she stormed out the door, mumbling something I didn't understand.

The only thing that scared me worse than her .357 Desert Eagle was her paisley print granny panties. When I cooled off and thought about it, I realized that she was probably still hurt because I'd jilted her. What did she expect? She was there when they sentenced me to prison and she saw my whole rap sheet. And she wanted to be my *girlfriend?*

What would she have said to her friends who live in Newport Beach if they invited us to dinner some evening? "Oh, I'm sorry, we can't make it. My boyfriend just got out of prison, and he's on high control because he was convicted of a terrorist threat and can't go outside of a fifty-mile radius from his parole office. But maybe next year when, or if, he's off parole.

———

Finally, at age forty-five, my life was great. I was out of prison for a year and had a great job, and hadn't missed one appointment. I'd become responsible and accountable. Jake was thirteen, and lived and breathed sports. I went to every one of his football, baseball and basketball games. He regularly had sleepovers with me and Mr. B. We'd hang out and watch sports on TV. The woman who'd supervised our visits years earlier, said in her report to the court back then that Jake and I had a very close bond and she was right.

Mr. B and I rented a small apartment in Oceanside with a great view of the ocean. It was hard for me to imagine that only one year earlier I was owned by the state of California. My name had been F87244, and I lived in cell 222, building sixteen, on the level-four maximum-security yard. Now I had an ocean view. Amazing!

On the second morning in my new apartment, I got out of bed and started walking toward the kitchen to feed Mr. B, and to make coffee. I was stopped in my tracks when the voice said, *"Is there a reason that you'd leave your bed unmade?"*

"I just woke up, and I was going to make coffee first," I thought.

The voice said, *"You need to do things in order. It's discipline, structure, consistency. If you start out the day doing the right thing, it will be easier for you to keep doing the right thing throughout the day. And you'd better hope Mister B doesn't escape.*

"Why?"

The voice said, *"Because then, you won't have anyone to talk to, except for me."*

After a couple of months working at my new job, I became the director of admissions and interventions, taking the inbound calls from people inquiring about treatment, and flying nationwide to do interventions. The doctor and I worked closely together, traveling to conferences on chronic pain and chemical dependency. I would sit for hours, listening intently to pain specialists from all over the world. I listened and I learned.

My first intervention was very interesting. The husband of a middle-aged, professional woman called and told me about his wife's chronic pain, drug addiction, and crazy behavior. He explained at length how she hardly slept at night and just wandered aimlessly around the house, hooked on pain pills. He told me about her isolation, and how she'd slowly withdrawn from him. He said she seemed to be dying a slow death, and after I saw her, I agreed.

When he picked me up at the San Francisco International airport, I felt I had all the information I needed to do a successful intervention. While we were driving to his home, he said that in recent days, she'd become verbally abusive and physically violent. He told me he was afraid to go near her, and that's why he'd hired me. He also said that he didn't tell me these things before, because he was afraid I wouldn't come.

When we walked through the front door of his beautiful Victorian home, he motioned toward the stairs, and when we got to the top of the staircase, he pointed at a bedroom door and quietly said, "She's in there."

I pushed the door open, and saw a woman who appeared to be in her fifties, down on her hands and knees, scrambling around on the floor as if she were looking for something. I quickly knelt down next to her and said, "Ma'am, are you okay?"

She looked up at me with a grimace on her face, and said, "Are you just gonna stand there, or are you gonna help me find my fucking pills?"

I said, "Ma'am, I know you're suffering, and your husband, who loves you very much, is suffering too. I know that most people don't know what it's like to really suffer, but I do. And I can help you."

Then she said, "If you wanna help me, you'll shut your fucking mouth and help me find my pills!"

"Ma'am, please, come with me," I said. "I can help you, I promise."

She looked at me with an empty stare, not saying anything. As I started to walk out of the room to make a plan B, she said in a soft and pleading voice. She said, "Do you *really* think you can help me?"

I said, "Yes, ma'am, I do."

We talked for a long time. I learned about her, and she learned something about me.

When were finished talking, her husband packed her suitcase. We got her out to his car and he drove us to the airport. When we were taking her out of the car, I glanced at him and noticed he had tears in his eyes.

He said, "I never thought this day would happen. God bless you, David."

It had been a long time since anyone said that to me.

―――――

Another memorable intervention took place in New York a few weeks later. A young woman called and said she was concerned about her boyfriend's alcohol and crack addiction. She told me that he was a successful business owner and also owned a lot of property in Brooklyn.

"It's kind of complicated," she said, "but I'm Greg's mistress, and actually his wife and I *both* want him to get into rehab. We both want him in rehab so he can be in his right mind when he chooses who he wants to be with. Me, or her."

"Okay," I said, "so are you and his wife both going to be involved in the intervention?"

"Oh, no," she said. "I hate that cunt. I'd never be in the same room with her."

"So who's going to participate in the intervention?" I asked.

"Oh, it would be just you. He hates people, to begin with. Actually I hope he doesn't get too upset with *you* being there."

"Yeah, me too," I said. "Okay, I'll do it, but I'm flying from San Diego, so I'll need to get a cashier's check for my fee as soon as I step off the plane, regardless of whether or not he comes with me. This is a little sketchy."

"Sure," she said. "No problem."

She picked me up at JFK, handed me the cashier's check, and we drove to her boyfriend's place of business. It was on a huge lot with at least twenty-five trash trucks on the property. Standing outside a large trailer was a group of what looked to me like a bunch of thugs from *The Sopranos*.

She pointed to them and said, "There he is, the tall one talking to all those guys."

"Okay," I said. "I'll call you when I get him to San Diego." I got out of her car and cautiously approached them.

As I got close they all checked me out, and the tall man broke the silence. He said, "Can I help you?"

"Yes, sir, I hope so," I said. "I'm looking for a gentleman named Greg. I believe he's the owner of the business here."

He said, "Who wants to know?"

"Well, sir, my name's Dave Wambaugh," I said, "and I came here from San Diego to speak to Greg, if he can give me a few minutes of his time."

"Do you know where you are now?" he asked.

I didn't know how to respond, and I didn't want to make him mad. Those guys looked like they wouldn't hesitate to give me a pair of cement boots and put me in the harbor. I took a chance and said, "Yes, sir. I'm in New York City."

He said, "No, you're on my property and you're trespassing. Now get the fuck outta here before I feel the need to protect what I own."

"Yes, sir," I said, and as I turned and started walking away, he yelled, "Hey, San Diego, come here."

I felt like running, but instead I turned back around, and said, "Yes, sir?"

He dismissed his mob and waved me into his trailer. He closed the door behind me, offered me a seat, sat down behind his desk, and said, "I'm Greg, so what's up? What're you doing here?"

"I came here from a drug and alcohol treatment facility in San Diego," I said, uneasy about being alone with him.

He looked surprised and said, "California?"

"Yes. San Diego, California," I said.

"Why're you here?"

"Your girlfriend called me," I said. "She hired me to come here, do an intervention, and get you into treatment."

Greg said, "An intervention? What the hell does that mean?"

I said, "Well, I guess it's where I convince you to come to rehab with me so you can get your shit together, before you lose it all."

He started laughing, and said, "That douche bag paid you money to come across country to get me to go to a rehab with you? In San Diego?"

"Yes, sir, she did," I said.

He said, "Well, did she give you any idea about what the fuck I was supposed to tell my wife about going away to rehab?"

"Actually, your wife wants you to go too," I said.

"Get the fuck outta here," Greg said. "She wants me to go too?"

"They both want you to get clean and sober," I said, "so you can make the right decision about which one of them you want to be with."

He gaped at me for a moment and said, "What's your name again?"

"Dave. Dave Wambaugh."

"Listen, Dave," he said, "if I got sober, I wouldn't be with either one of those cunts. Trust me on that."

On his desk was a framed photo of a small girl hugging a stuffed animal. I pointed toward it, and asked, "Who's the little girl?"

He said, "That's my daughter, Vicki."

"How old is she?" I asked.

"She just turned five."

"So, what do you think?" I asked. "Do you have a drinking or drug problem?"

Yeah, I guess I do," he admitted. "No, I'm *sure* I do."

I said, "Okay, if that's the case, you've got to get stabilized to get back on track. I don't care if you go to AA or NA, or any of that, but you need to get it together for your daughter. I have a twelve-year-old son who suffered for a long time as a result of my addiction. God only knows how much damage I did to my boy."

"I hear ya," he said.

"You seem to be smart," I said. "I can help you get it together. For your daughter's sake, come with me. Vicki needs you at full strength. Don't steal her childhood. I did that to my son and I'll never forgive myself. Come on, Greg, let's do it for Vicki."

He shook his head, and said, "I can't, Dave. Honestly, I want to go, but I've got too much shit going on here. I'm sorry."

"Okay," I said, "but can I please tell you something without you getting violent or anything?"

"Sure."

"If your daughter grows up suffering from alcohol, drug, or emotional problems of her own, please don't try to fool yourself into thinking that it's not your fault, because it *will* be your fault. I'm sorry to tell you that, Greg, but it's the truth."

He sat silently for a moment, and then said, "Well, you can give me that brochure and if I ever decide to go to rehab, you'll be the first guy I call."

"Okay, sounds good to me. Good luck, man," I said.

As I was leaving the trailer, he leaned down and hugged me, and then walked me off the lot.

When I turned my cell phone back on after landing in San Diego, there was a text message from Greg, saying he was on his way to San Diego, and that his girlfriend or his wife would be calling me with his flight number because he'd already forgotten it. He arrived later that day, and told me the reason he came was because of all the things I'd made him think about. He said everything I said made sense to him, and that he'd never thought about how his behavior might damage his daughter's life, and everyone else's who loved him. I found it interesting that he thought I'd said so many profound things when all I really offered him was basic honesty and common sense.

Greg came to San Diego, but left·rehab after only two days. He said he hated it there because of the doctor and his staff, and he wanted to go home to be with his wife and daughter. The real truth was, Greg wanted a drink.

Less than a month after that, I took some drinks of my own. Yes, I was trying to never let that happen again, but I found out that I'm still far from perfect, and I did make a mistake. Like all alcoholics, the urge to drink eventually came to me at a time when I wasn't wearing my spiritual armor. Alcohol is cunning, baffling and powerful. And patient. One day, not unlike any of the rest, I drew a mental blank spot, got a bottle and drank, in spite of all the damage that booze had caused in my life. I had a hundred excuses why I drank, but no honest answer. To this day, the most honest and accurate answer to that question is, "I don't know."

Thank God I remembered what some old-timer from AA told me some years before. He said, "My man, I've seen you come in and out of these rooms for almost twenty years, and I've seen you get enough 30 day chips to tile my master bath. I don't think you'll ever get sober, and I think something is much more wrong with you than just addiction, but it's about the elevator ride you take every time you leave these rooms. You know what they say about some being sicker than others, well I'd say you're sicker than most. Maybe you're constitutionally incapable of being honest with yourself. Maybe you're just a crazy bastard with a death wish. Who knows?"

I was detoxing at the time so my patience was thin. When I told the old guy to get to the point, he said, "There's no doubt in my mind that you'll drink again, so I want you to remember the next time you get on that one way elevator going down, you can make the choice to get off on any floor. You don't have to take it to the bottom. I know that goes against some of our beliefs, but I'm convinced that we *do* have some control over our actions, disease or not. So, you don't have to go down, no matter what. It's now a question of how far down are you going to let yourself go. Are you going to be a punk-ass bitch and continue to ride that thing to the bottom or are you going get off early and realize that elevators are really dangerous for you."

Thank God I remembered what the old man said when I chose to take another ride. I'm certain that the cable on my elevator has been badly frayed, so now I take the stairs and don't have to *worry* about where I'm getting off.

———

A few weeks after I did the intervention with Greg in New York, the father of a nineteen-year-old boy called me from Seattle to set up an intervention with his son who'd been shooting speed and heroin. He told me that the boy had behavioral problems and drug issues from the time he was fourteen. They said that they'd tried everything they could think of to fix him, just as my parents had done with me, but to no avail. The kid had stolen everything he could get his hands on to score dope, including his brother's top-of-the-line Fender guitar that he sold for an eight-ball of meth.

When I landed in Seattle I rented a car and met the boy's parents at a coffee shop near the proposed location of the intervention. They were in their late forties, but looked much older, and when either of them spoke it was with desperation and sadness. There they were, two successful people, crying out to a complete stranger in a coffee shop about their drug-addicted, slowly dying son.

I try not to get emotional during interventions, but I couldn't help thinking about what I'd put my own parents through. This kid was G-rated compared to me. He'd been possessed by his demon for only five years, as opposed to my *thirty*-five.

We decided to do the intervention at his sister's apartment, so when I phoned her before we arrived, I told her to keep him occupied until we got there. I suggested she get him some smokes or some brew, anything that would stall him for as long as possible.

When we walked through the front door the kid was sitting on the sofa, smoking a cig and drinking a coke. The dude was a stick figure. He looked like Woody from *Toy Story*. He was close to six feet tall but weighed no more than a hundred and fifteen pounds. His beady eyes darted around the room assessing the situation, and zeroed in on his mom.

He said, "You fucking bitch! I knew you'd screw me over like this!"

His dad said, "Steven, please, don't talk to your mother like that."

"Fuck you, you queer!" he said.

I said to him, "Hey, Steven, please just hear me out for five minutes! Your parents paid me a lot of money to come and talk to you. I wanna help you get your life back together."

He said, "Who the fuck're you? And why the fuck're you wearing a suit? What's the occasion?"

I said, "Well, my name's Dave, and I'm from a drug treatment facility in San Diego. Your parents asked me to come and help you."

"I don't need any help," he said. "What the fuck's going on around here?"

"Steven, just hear me out," I said.

"Okay," he said. "Let me go take a piss, and then I'll listen to your pitch."

After he was fifteen minutes in the bathroom, I told his sister to go check on him, and a few seconds later she came back down the hall, and yelled, "He's gone! He jumped out the window."

I said, "Oh shit!"

The mom looked over at me, and said, "Dave, you guaranteed you'd stay here until you got him to treatment. Is that right?"

"Yes, ma'am, that's right," I said. "I'll stay until my mission's completed."

"Well, Dave," the father said, "I'm afraid this is gonna be a very long mission!"

"I won't leave without him," I said.

It took two and a half days to corral the wily little bastard. When we got to the airport and were boarding the plane to San Diego, I turned to wave goodbye to his parents. I could see they were both crying.

It made me think about all the times I must have made my parents cry. I accomplished my mission, but somehow I didn't feel rewarded.

———

Doing interventions, and seeing nineteen-year-old Steven so screwed up, made me think of Ziggy and all the shit we both went through together for so many years. Ziggy was still messed up, and I was hoping he might let me help him. He'd lost everything during the same year I was arrested for my seventh DUI. He became homeless almost immediately, and wound up on the street, in and out of Las Vegas shelters for years, panhandling, shoplifting, and committing other petty crimes for crack and booze. He'd disassociated himself from reality. That was how he was able to exist. Otherwise, he might have committed suicide.

He'd wound up back in Los Angeles, living on Skid Row with other mentally ill addicts. I'm sure they talk about the same shit every day, about the pie-in-the-sky comebacks they're all going to make someday--a day that never comes. He eats welfare food and lives in government housing for people who are incapable of functioning in society.

While I was working on this book, I got in touch with Ziggy in an attempt to try to help him. I picked him up on skid row in Los Angeles and arranged to get him into a sober living home, away from the skids. He said he hadn't smoked crack in almost five years, but I saw burn marks on his thumb and index finger, which are indicative of crack pipe burns.

Ziggy didn't look too bad, other than his teeth were worn down, and turning yellow and brown where pricey veneers used to be. When I asked him what had happened to his $25,000 veneers, he said that a black guy pistol-whipped him over a five-dollar rock, and knocked them out. When Ziggy took off his dirty pungent shirt to put on the new one I brought for him, he was soft, fleshy, bruised and scarred, with what looked like cigarette burns. Those kind of scars come from being a drug addicted street person. At one time, Ziggy had a great physique, but now he looked and behaved just like a skid row bum that he'd become.

I drove him to his mom's house before we went to his new sober living home. I wanted her to see him and I wanted him to say in front of her that he's the only one to blame for his condition. I said I would help him if he was willing to man up and take the blame for everything that's gone wrong in his life. I made it a requirement that he call each of his family members once a week just to ask how *they're* doing. I told him that he needed to get a job doing something where he had to be accountable.

I said that I could be his guide until he got his shit together. I sold Ziggy's whole family on the fact that some kind of an angel's voice saved my life, and his mom asked a Catholic priest to come to her house so I could tell him about it. Ziggy's brother, who also is a Catholic priest, said he was not inclined to give much credence to guardian angel claims, but in my case, he believed something miraculous had happened to me.

When I hugged Ziggy and said goodbye, a very sad feeling came over me because I realized that he hadn't changed and didn't seem to *want* to change. I think he set me up just to get some money from his family. Ziggy had been a crazy street person for at least a decade so maybe he'd been there too long. He still had resentment against everyone and still talked about how he was screwed by the world. He had three children that he hadn't seen for almost ten years, and he hadn't even made an attempt to see them. I tried to make him understand that his comeback is not just for him, but for his family, and that's the secret. I told him that several times, but he doesn't quite grasp my point.

When he starts hearing voices, I hope he finds a benign one.

———————

One of the zaniest interventions I got involved in took place in Laguna Beach, not too far from our facility. I was called by the husband of a young woman who suffered from chronic pain, alcoholism and opiate addiction. Chase told me that Lauren popped Vicodin like Jelly Bellys, and powered 100 proof vodka like a Russian sailor.

When I pulled up outside their beautiful home, there were two Range Rovers, three Beemers, and a Benz parked out in front. Each of the vehicles had either "USC Gould School of Law" license plate placards or just plain "USC alumni." I was greeted at the door by Chase, and ushered into the expansive living room where at least a dozen people were anticipating my arrival.

It was a good feeling for me to know that these people were counting on me to save this young woman's life. They'd been trying for years to get Lauren into treatment, but no one was ever able to make it happen.

Chase pointed toward the master bedroom upstairs, and said quietly, "Lauren's up there. So, should I go in with you when you talk to her?"

I said. "No, just tell her that she needs to get out of bed and come downstairs for a minute, that there's someone here who wants to talk to her."

He said, "Oh, no. I can't go in there alone."

I said, "Listen, she doesn't know me. I can't walk into her bedroom like that. If you can't get her to come downstairs, we'll have to go in together."

"Okay, let's go," he said, and we walked upstairs and slowly opened the bedroom door.

She popped up from her pillow like the girl from The Exorcist, and said, "What the fuck're you doing in here, Chase? And who the hell is he?"

He said, "Lauren, this is Dave, and he's here to help you."

"Oh, yeah?" she said. "Well, if you and Dave don't get the fuck out of my room by the time I count to three, I'm calling the cops and telling them that he's trying to rape me and that you aren't doing anything to stop him because you're a pussy!"

"Lauren, honey, please!" Chase pleaded.

She said, "One, two, three, you're out!" And she dialed nine-one-one.

When the dispatcher answered, Lauren said, "There's a man in my room, and I have no idea who he is. And he's touching me inappropriately."

Chase stayed there pleading with her, and I ran! When I hit the bottom of the stairs and was heading out the front door, Lauren's father grabbed my shoulder, stopping me in my tracks, and said, "What the hell happened up there, David?"

I said, "Sir, she's on the phone with nine-one-one, and she told them that there's a stranger in her room who's molesting her! We're in the Orange County Sheriffs jurisdiction, and those guys're dicks!"

He said, "We have four attorneys in the house, one of whom works for the D.A. You'll be fine. We'll meet the deputies at the front door. Just get my daughter into treatment, please!"

I reluctantly said, "Okay, I'll try."

I talked to her from outside her bedroom door for at least an hour, and was finally able to convince her to come downstairs. I said that I was on her side, that I wouldn't let her suffer, that there was hope, and I would try to help her get her life back. I explained that I'd been much worse off than she was and that if I was able to come back from hell, so could she.

We walked down the stairs and entered the living room together. She surveyed the room, focusing on one individual at a time, and finally pointed to her sister-in-law who was absolutely beautiful. Lauren said, "Dave, first of all, if you don't get that tramp out of my house, this meeting is off."

Then she looked at her brother, and said, "Jeff, did you know that when your lovely wife and I were sorority sisters, she fucked half the football team? She's spread her legs for every frat rat desperate enough to pork her."

Lauren's sister-in-law got up off the couch, walked out of the room, and never returned.

Then she shifted her focus onto her mother and said, "And what are you doing here, you slut? I can't believe Dad was spineless enough to take you back after you were screwing his best friend."

At that point, I just wanted to slink out of the room and refund the $3,500 fee that Chase had paid me for my services.

Lauren eyeballed her attractive sister, and said, "And you, you bitch, have had everyone fooled all these years. You were the biggest coke whore in Laguna. You'd fuck *anyone* with a bag of coke, and doesn't your stupid-ass husband realize by now that you're banging what's-his-name, the guy he plays golf with? I'm amazed you'd have the nerve to come into my house and talk your holier-than-thou shit!"

All of this excitement was exhausting me, so I interrupted her, saying, "Please, Lauren, can I talk to you alone? Please?"

"Sure," she said, "I need a smoke anyway." We went outside together and eventually I won her over by convincing her that coming with me would be better than being subjected to all the two-faced bastards in that room. I became her protector and her pal.

Suffering addicts are like injured animals. They can be vicious until they know you're not going to hurt them, and then they'll drop their defenses and come to you. Most of the time.

Chapter Sixteen

About a year and a half later I was living the dream. I had a beautiful oceanfront, one bedroom apartment with Mr. B. I had a driver's license, car insurance, bank account, and no warrants out for my arrest. And I was saving to pay IRS and the State Franchise Tax Board what I owed.

When I wasn't out capturing drug addicts, I was in the office trying to figure out ways to generate more income. Every Wednesday morning I would take my boss, Dr. Irving, out to breakfast where we would discuss marketing strategies, personnel, patients, and other business related issues. One morning, as we were discussing a very difficult patient who'd been threatening to sue for the poor treatment she felt she was receiving at our facility, the doctor blurted, "Oh, by the way, you know I'm dating Linda now."

"Who's Linda?" I asked.

He said, "Your old girlfriend, Linda, who I met at your mom's house."

I was shocked, and the words tumbled out of me. I said, "What the fuck? What do you mean, you're dating Linda? I told you what scheming bitch she is. She hooped her ex-old man, and I *mean* old man, for everything he had. I guarantee that Linda will make it so that I can't work for you anymore, one way or another. Before you know it, Linda and her daughter will be running your place, and you'll wind up being the bitch around there. Trust me!"

Irving looked stunned and slowly responded, "Ohhh-kaaay, but remember, I'm an old man. You should be happy I'm getting laid."

"Oh, my God, I can't believe it!" I said. "I don't want to hear another word about it. Screw breakfast, let's go."

I went home to cool off for a while, and when I got back to the office later that morning, my assistant ran up to me and asked, "Who the hell is Linda?"

"What?" I said. "What's wrong?"

She said, "You know the project I've been working on for over a month now?"

"What?" I said. "About getting me on NBC, channel ten, about the Oxy epidemic?"

"Well, Linda took it over!" she said. "She told the doctor she wanted to take over the project, and he *let* her!"

"You're kidding me!" I said. "The project is already done!"

"You know I wouldn't kid you about this, David," she said.

I called the doctor on his cell, and said, "What's wrong with you? Linda's taking credit for the month of hard work that Sherry did!"

He said, "Linda's a professional, and she has a degree in marketing. You should always want for the success of the company, not just your own personal success. She'll take us to the next level. That's what she promised me."

I said, "You're an idiot!"

I hung up on him, told Sherry how sorry I was about Linda, and walked out of the office.

The following week, when Linda brought her daughter to the facility, the doctor called a meeting with his corporate staff and introduced Linda's daughter as the new head of marketing.

I didn't attend the meeting, but called my dad to tell him the story, and when I was done, he said, "You'd better start looking for another job today, Dave. I'm afraid that one's over. She won't relent and he'll eventually fire you. I'm sorry about that, son."

I called Linda, outraged about what she'd done to Sherry, and told her to go back to where she came from, to get out of my world. Then she did what she always did. *She phoned my mom.* When my mom called me to see what had happened, I was too angry to carry on a mature conversation, so I just told her that I'd have to talk to her later.

Linda was making a five-hour, round trip commute from Palm Desert to San Diego about three times a week to pursue a fantasy that somehow, someday, she would become a Wambaugh. She wasn't coming around our facility because she wanted the doctor or the work. Not only was the doctor almost broke, he was unattractive, and had absolutely no social skills. In fact he made Woody Allen look like Fabio. It was obvious that Linda was after me, with my family's money as still the main attraction.

About two weeks after Linda came onboard at the rehab, my assistant, Sherry, said she overheard the doctor saying something about Linda going to a San Francisco convention with us. It sounded so absurd I thought she must be pulling my leg. I thought the last thing Linda would have the nerve to do would be to show up at my gig in San Francisco, so I laughed it off and made my convention plans.

———

After arriving in San Francisco, I was standing in the checkout line at a Target store with some of the things I needed to set up our display booth when I got a text from Linda.

The text said, "Hi, I'm here."

I was shocked. I could *not* believe what was happening. I texted her back, "You're where?"

Within seconds she texted back, "At the hotel. I'm gonna call u."

And I'll be goddamned, a moment later, she called me!

She said in an upbeat, over-the-top, ditzy voice, "Hi, David."

I said, "You're not really here, are you?"

She said, "Well, Irving thought it would be a good idea to have a girl here, to attract the guys to the booth. You know how conventions are."

"What does he want you to do?"

"Oh, just hook 'em," she said. "I'll hook 'em, and you cook 'em. Sound good?"

I said, "I don't cook, I don't hook, and I don't need your help. Do whatever you're gonna do, but please stay away from me."

After I left the Target store and was on my way back to the convention center to set up the booth, Dr. Irving called to say he wanted me to come by the hotel for a few minutes to discuss something having to do with the convention. They were in the same hotel as I was, about four doors down the hall from my room. After some small talk, he insisted that Linda go with me to the convention center to give our booth "a woman's touch."

I had no choice but to interact with her over the next couple of days. She inappropriately would bump her breasts and ass against me every chance she got, and right in front of the doctor. I was totally humiliated, and I figured Irving was too.

I made it through the first night without being with them for dinner by feigning illness, but the next night they insisted, or should I say, Linda insisted, that I go to dinner with them. she wouldn't accept my excuses so I decided I'd go just to spare myself more grief. Linda wouldn't take no for an answer. She was as relentless as a pit bull from the day I'd first met her.

The three of us walked to a restaurant at Fisherman's Wharf, and when we were looking at the menus, Linda insisted that we all order seafood because we were at the Wharf, it's tradition. I told her it's not *my* tradition and ordered a steak, medium rare, but Irving let her order for him.

She ordered crab legs for the both of them, and the doctor, having no table manners, made a huge mess out of his king crab legs. He couldn't manage the utensil to extract the crab, so he used his sausage-like fingers to bust the shell. When he was covered with debris she told him to go to the restroom and wash himself off, which he obediently did.

As he got up and walked away, Linda said, "Eeeww, he's disgusting! He's too *muchy!* Did you see him eat?"

I didn't answer, but got up and waited for them at the front door of the restaurant.

When I got back to my room I was lying on the bed, exhausted by all the bullshit I'd been dealing with, when the room phone rang. It was Linda.

When I answered, she yelled, "Dawa, let's go out and do something! You can't come to San Francisco and not go out. I know the area pretty well, so let's go. Come on, Dawa."

God, how I hated that name. I said, "Where's Irving? Is he going out?"

"Oh, he's sitting right here," she said. "He's too tired to do anything. He's had a long week. So let's go see what's happening. I know you don't drink anymore, but we can have coffee and dessert, and check out the touristy shops. Come on, Dawa, let's go explore Fisherman's Wharf!"

I said, "Linda, I'm not an explorer and I'm not going out with you. I'm not going *anywhere* with you. Do you understand me?"

She said, "*GOODBYE!*" and hung up the phone.

I usually don't call my dad at night, because we both turn in early, but I was so beside myself I had to talk to somebody who would understand.

He listened to the whole story without saying anything, and when I was finished, all he said was, "Well, your job was already gone as soon as she hooked up with Irving, but now it's just going to be gone sooner than we thought. Again, I'm real sorry, Dave."

"I've gotta get outta here, Dad," I said. "I can't stay another day in San Francisco with her here."

"Yeah, you may as well leave," he said. "She's doing your job anyway, isn't she?"

———————

Several weeks later, when Linda finally realized that I wasn't going to have anything to do with her, she bailed on the good doctor, and Irving took it out on me, just like my dad said he would. My dad predicted that I would be forced out of there within six months, and he was only one month off.

The doctor began making it impossible for me to earn the kind of money I'd been making before Linda came along. The incoming calls, which had been the main source of my income, were taken from me and diverted to a flamboyant gay guy in the office, making it impossible for me to continue. I finally quit, and took them to small claims court for the money they owed me, but as always, I hadn't kept good records, and won only a small judgment.

I can only look at it one way: Linda cost me a friend *and* a ninety-thousand-plus-dollar-a-year job.

As I walked out of court, pissed off at myself for not keeping better records, I suddenly realized something. I'd been given a gift that neither Linda nor the doctor could ever take away from me, the talent to save lives and to make money doing it. I knew then, that it was what I was meant to do with my life.

I realized it was dangerous for me to dwell on Linda's conniving so I forced myself to let it go. When I had some time to reflect, I thought it was *especially* low of both of them because they only knew about the *old* me who would've self-destructed. Out of all the women I've been with in my life, all the dopers and dysfunctional dummies, Linda was the worst. At least the straight-up junkie bitch that tried to kill me with a syringe was forthright in her intentions.

Some time after Linda was gone from his life, I called the doctor to ask him what in the hell he was thinking when he started up with Linda.

All he said was, "Dave, you made her go away. She didn't want to, but you forced her to leave me."

I said, "Linda didn't want *you*. Can't you can't *see* that now?"

"You just think she wanted you," he said. "That's just your grandiosity. It's part of your addictive personality disorder," the doctor said.

I said, "No, my friend, it's part of *your* personality disorder now.

Chapter Seventeen

Not long after I parted company with Dr. Irving I got word that my grandmother's health was declining due to her emphysema, and wasn't expected to live much longer. I gave my landlord notice and moved to the desert to be near my mom even though she's very strong in every way. I don't know if she really needed me, but I felt I should be there for her.

I spent the last few days of my grandmother's life with her. It was the first time I'd ever been there for either of my parents when it mattered. I stayed right beside her until she passed away, and my inner voice told me not to get overly emotional, just to be strong for my mom. Just be there.

As I was sitting beside my grandmother's body just after she passed, I felt a hand on my shoulder. It was Linda. I hadn't seen her come in.

With her hand on my shoulder, she said, "Come on Dawa, why don't you come outside and have a cup of coffee with the girls?"

I said, "*Please* don't call me Dawa, and can't you see I'm sitting here with my grandma? Jesus Christ!" I was waiting for some fallout from my mom for hurting Linda's feelings, but guess what? She didn't tattle to my mom this time.

About a month after I relocated to the desert, I got a job offer in Orange County as the director of admissions and interventions at Chapman House in Newport Beach. So, Mister B and I packed up our belongings and made another move. I found a really cool little oceanfront apartment overlooking the pier in San Clemente, and it was a perfect location for us because it was halfway between my job and my family in San Diego.

The first intervention I was called to do for Chapman House came up right after I'd made my move from the desert. It was a nerve-racking intervention, in that it had the most potential for some violence. A woman named Breda O'Malley called me, saying that her thirty-five year old son who had been sober for six years, had recently relapsed and was on a rampage. Breda was one of the top dogs for the L.A. Unified School District, and as such, had been given some training in substance abuse, so she had some idea of what we were dealing with.

She told me that during his sobriety, her son had gotten his contractor's license, had a thriving construction company, had gotten married, had two kids, and had even dropped out of his gang. He was doing so well, she even bought a house for him and his family that he'd remodeled into a very nice home.

Breda found out about her son's relapse when he didn't show up to the family picnic they had on the last Sunday of each month, but his wife showed up with a fat lip and a bruise under her left eye. Breda said that when he smoked PCP he could turn violent.

"So, what's his name?" I asked.

"Rudy Oriiz," she said. "His dad's Mexican. I took back my maiden name when I got a divorce. I think his macho Mexican dad is the main reason Rudy went down the path he did."

"How's that?" I asked.

Breda said, "Well, when I met him, the teacher in me, the nurturer, wanted to think I could change some thug and rescue him from his street ways. Rudy's dad had been in a gang called "White Fence," back in the day when they used bats and knives to settle scores, not AK-47s. I got him to give up drugs and his gang, for a family life with me. I also have two daughters with him who turned out beautifully. He doted on the girls, but he was hard on Rudy. I think he forced Rudy into the gang life without even realizing he did it. He's a real piece of shit, that man."

"What's the name of the gang Rudy joined?" I asked.

"The Little Diablos, part of Eighteenth Street gang," she said.

I said, "So he's dropped out now?"

She said, "That's what he says, but I've heard you can't just *quit* from a gang like that. So I'm not really sure."

"Has he ever done time?"

She said, "Oh yeah, he's done time. He was in youth authority for six months on an assault charge, and he went to state prison for another assault charge, grand theft auto, and drug possession. You know how it is, right?"

"Unfortunately, I do," I said. "How much time did he do?"

"Almost four years."

"So what does his wife think about all this? Is she willing to follow through with an intervention and keep the integrity of her boundaries intact no matter what Rudy does or does not do?"

She said, "Absolutely, she will. I think she fears *me* more than she does Rudy. She was there the time Rudy had one too many Coronas, and thought he could run his filthy mouth to me like his dad used to do. I hit him with everything in my house that wasn't too big to pick up. Yeah, Cindy will do *exactly* what I tell her to do."

"Okay," I said. "You tell me where we can meet to discuss the intervention and then we'll take it from there. I need to know the players, and what part they play."

"Okay," she said. "Shatto Park would be a good place. Is that okay with you?"

"That's fine," I said, "I'll meet you there at six p.m."

When I pulled up to Shatto Park on West 4th street in Los Angeles, I got a little nervous. I was out of place there in my fifty thousand dollar Lexus and wearing an eight hundred dollar suit. The family was waiting in the parking lot as we'd agreed, and as I drove toward them I could see them first smiling, and then laughing.

I got out of my car, introduced myself to everyone, and then asked, "What was so funny?"

Rudy's mom chuckled, and said, "Oh, Robert here, had to be a wise ass, as always. He said, you look more like a lawyer than a drug counselor."

I smiled and said, "Okay, so here's the deal. We're going to make a very specific plan of action that we'll execute together, with me as the leader. At the end of this day, Rudy will either be going to rehab with me, or he will be on the streets, or he will go to jail. If any one of you caves, we all lose. Understood?"

Everyone nodded in agreement except for Robert. He said, "Hey, bro, I'm on parole so I can't have any negative police contact if there's violence. And if I were you, I wouldn't put Rudy on Front Street with his family present. Seeing the shape he's in now, I wouldn't diss him. No disrespect to *you*, bro, but I wouldn't mess with Rudy right now with a big surprise meeting. I think he's been smokin'."

Cindy said, "Fuck you, Robert! You're the one who's been giving it to him!"

Robert said, "Giving him *what?*"

"The meth and the sherm sticks!" she said.

Rudy's mom said, "What the hell're sherm sticks?"

Robert got up and made a beeline for the front door, leaving me to answer the question.

I said, "It's a cigarette dipped in PCP, which is basically an elephant tranquilizer. It has different effects on different people, but police report that PCP can give one man the strength of ten.

Rudy's mom said, "Jesus, I hope he's not smoking that crap today!"

"Yeah, me too," I said.

When we caravanned to Rudy's house, he was passed out on his bed. Everyone got seated in the living room to wait. Cindy said that for three days he'd been vacillating between crying jags to outbursts of rage. She thought it was mostly directed toward his father, a heroin addict, who was not only losing construction customers for Rudy but was also stealing money.

When Rudy appeared in the living room, he had surprise written all over him. I stood up and introduced myself with an outstretched hand, but he waved me off.

He may have told his mom he'd given up the gang, but from the looks of him, I didn't think so. He had a shaved head, a goatee, and was tatted all over. He had tats like I'd not seen before. One was all the way across his stomach that read, "9+9=18." I wondered if it was something he'd gotten in juvie, maybe because he couldn't add or something, but I later learned it was an Eighteenth Street thing. Another was on his neck that said "666," as in three times six equals eighteen. And he had still another one on his hand, the number "99," as in nine plus nine is eighteen.

He looked around at everyone in the room and then finally to his mom, he said, "What is this? Why're you all here?"

She said, "Rudy, I want you to listen to this man. Sit down on that chair, and don't move until he's done. I paid him thirty-five hundred cash to speak to you for five minutes, so don't you dare run your mouth on my dime."

Looking at the scowl on Rudy's face, I had a sinking feeling that after forty-one successful interventions so far, this one, number forty-two, might be a bust.

"What the hell's happening here?" Rudy said, looking at me, and then at his mother.

I said, "Hey, brother, my name's Dave and I'm from a drug rehab in Orange County. Your mom called me because your family's concerned about you."

He said, "Whoa, bro. First of all, I didn't invite you into my house, and second of all, you don't know me, to talk to me like that."

I said, "I understand that. But please, as your mom asked, hear me out for just five minutes and then I'll leave." I looked around the room, pretending to be admiring the excellent work he'd done on his home, and said, "So, Rudy, did you do the remodeling here? It's really beautiful."

He said, "Come on, dude, don't act stupid, blowing smoke up my ass. Just tell me what you gotta tell me, and then let me go back to sleep."

"Okay, brother. You got it," I said. "So anyway, I understand from your mom that you used to be a juvenile delinquent, then you became an adult delinquent, and then you got sober. You became phenomenally successfully in a very short period of time, but then you started drinking on the weekends, hanging with the homies, and missing family functions. I guess you hired your dad about a year ago and he's messing up for you, even stealing from you, but you feel guilty to put him out because he's your family. Am I good so far?"

"Pretty much," he said.

"Here's the problem, Rudy," I said. "You've been to prison before, so even if you only get popped for being under the influence of sherm or meth, you're gonna to do prison time. Off the top, you're gonna get a year for having a prior, and you're gonna do eighty percent of your time. So no matter what, you'll be doing some real time."

He said, "How do *you* know about time? You a lawyer?"

I said, "I'm definitely not a lawyer, but I do know about prison time because I had to do a little of my own."

He said, "Yeah? Where'd you do time?"

I said, "Donovan, and then CRC."

"What building in Donovan?" he asked, as though I'd have no idea.

"Building sixteen," I said. "Mister White was the C.O. when I was there in '07."

Rudy said, "No way! I *know* that dude!"

I said, "He was a cool guy, wasn't he? He never messed with the woods or southsiders, just the *mayates*."

Rudy giggled and said, "Yeah, homie, Mister White was funny. He didn't like the niggers at all."

I said, "Listen, bro, you have a beautiful life that you've created with your own hard work and the help and commitment of your family. You've got it going on. Look at you, how you rose above all the homies. Don't take yourself out now. You're just beginning, brother. Do it for your mom."

He said, "What about my wife?"

"Well, your wife told me you'd never do it for her," I said. "And I figured your mom probably has a little influence over you, so I say do it for *her*. Let's just get your head clear and figure out what you're gonna do to continue to build your success, and then you're back on track. Cool?"

"How long I gotta go for?"

I said, "A month."

He said, "Damn, homes, that's messed up!"

He sat quietly for a minute or so, leaning forward with his head in his hands, thinking, and then said, "This shit sounds stupid to me, but I guess I'll do it. Not for my mom, but I'll do it for myself."

I said, "Right on, brother. Whatever works."

His family members were obviously stunned that he actually caved like that. They followed us to the rehab facility in their car, and as we were driving, I asked, "Rudy, what were you thinking when you started smoking PCP again, knowing you'd go back to prison and lose everything if you got busted?"

He said, "I thought you said, *you* been to prison."

"Yeah, I *did* go to prison," I said.

He said, "Well, before you were locked up, you knew that if you kept fucking up, *you* would go to prison, right?"

"That's right," I said.

"So, what the hell were *you* thinking when you were fucking up, knowing that if you got busted, you were going to prison?"

I smiled, shook my head slowly, and said, "Honestly, Rudy I haven't a clue as to what I was thinking."

He said, "Then why would you ask me such a stupid question, homes? My therapist told me the reason I went to prison was because I didn't *think*, and I didn't *listen*."

I said, "That's why I went to prison too, because I didn't think and I didn't listen. My therapist didn't tell me that, but somebody else certainly did."

I don't know if Rudy stayed clean after he left rehab, but apparently *his* thinker wasn't too busted, the way he turned the tables on me like that!

———

I went home to feed Mr. B, and to change into my workout clothes. And as I was asking my cat how his day had been going, I kept thinking of Rudy, hoping he would make it after his rehab. And that made me think of family and friends who had affected my own life.

Sarah and I had developed a good working relationship for the sake of our son, and she had become engaged to a very nice man that Jake liked and respected. Jake was big, smart, good looking, and a fine athlete who'd made his varsity football team as a freshman. He was at the age where he didn't really want to hang around his old man a lot, but we did spend some quality time together. I always made sure to tell him how much I loved him, just in case it was the last time I got to say it.

I thought of Ziggy back out on the streets, and recalling our crazy times together. It made me think about how strong my mom and dad had to have been to withstand parenthood. They'd survived the loss of a son, the abandonment by a daughter, and many years of my alcoholic and drug madness. They still had two houses, and I sincerely *loved h*anging around with them. They were sort of like that voice in my head, in the sense that they constantly busted my balls, but I liked it. When I was with them at the desert house, which was often, my mom and I played golf, enjoyed the great dinners she makes, and watched TV together. I went out to a restaurant with my dad every week when he was at the San Diego house and was able to fit me into his novel-writing schedule, which is about all he did anymore. But no matter what, we talked almost daily.

Throughout my life, I had numerous people ask me if I had any siblings, and if so, where did they live, what did they do, and what was their deal. I always claimed Mark because he usually had my back, and I think in a strange way, we really loved each other. We were an unorthodox pair, but nonetheless, I always claimed him as my bro.

As far as Jeannette was concerned, I stopped claiming her as my sister after Mark died. From that point on, I pretty much just told people that I was an only child. I didn't want to have to explain that I had an adopted sister who lived somewhere in the L.A. area, but I hadn't talked to her for years. I never saw much of her, never really got to know her, and never cared to. Our lives crossed paths at various times, and that's about it. It was just a feeling of indifference on both our parts, and that's how it's remained. We had nothing in common, and were related only by the letters in our last name. When she was young, she wanted me to like her, but I just didn't have it in me. Jeannette is married, and has a daughter who is going to a Catholic high school for girls in the Los Angeles area.

All of the random memories, triggered by my intervention of Rudy made me understand that a miracle can happen whether it comes about with the help of AA, a guardian angel, or a hallucinatory voice, or all three. I will always have remorse for all the pain I've caused my family. I knew I must remain vigilant and work very hard to ensure that I never hurt them again. If that's all I achieve during the rest of my life, I will die a successful man.

Sarah's phone call interrupted the blizzard of memories.

"Hey, what's up, Dave?" she said. "I haven't talked to you for a while. How *are* you?"

"Oh, pretty good," I said. "I just got home from doing an edgy intervention in East L.A. I thought he might be my first failure, but I finally convinced him to come to rehab. I just dropped him off at Chapman House an hour ago."

"That's great," she said. "I'm so happy for you. That must feel good, helping people like that."

I said, "Yeah, it does. It really does." Then I said, "Hey, I'll call you back. I have a really important phone call I need to make right this minute."

I hung up, and then picked up the phone again and dialed the man's number, the man who'd made all those memories come flooding back.

He picked up on the third ring. "Ted Hoffman speaking."

I said, "Hello, Mr. Hoffman, it's Dave Wambaugh. I spoke to you earlier today regarding your son."

"Oh, yes. Hi, Dave," he said.

I said, "Mister Hoffman, I felt compelled to call you back and tell you some of my story because I was so much worse off than your boy is. Maybe by hearing my story you might better understand your son, and it could possibly give you some hope."

He said with guarded enthusiasm, "Bless you, Dave, but you have no idea what this boy's put his mother and me through."

With sadness in my voice, I said, "Sir, I think I do. I think I have a *very* good idea of what he's put you through."

Afterword

Since my release from prison on March 3rd, 2008, I've been working in the drug rehab industry, and have successfully executed over 40 interventions around the United States.

I'm currently the Director of Interventions at Chapman House and Teensavers, a dual diagnosis residential inpatient treatment facility in Orange County.

CPSIA information can be obtained at www.ICGtesting.com
Printed in the USA
LVOW13*1452050813

346363LV00002B/51/P

9 781477 262733